**St. Louis Community
College**

Forest Park
Florissant Valley
Meramec

Instructional Resources
St. Louis, Missouri

The Heart as a Drum

The Heart as a Drum

Continuance and Resistance in American Indian Poetry

Robin Riley Fast

Ann Arbor

THE UNIVERSITY OF MICHIGAN PRESS

2002   2001   2000   1999   4   3   2   1

*A CIP catalog record for this book is available
from the British Library.*

Library of Congress Cataloging-in-Publication Data

Fast, Robin Riley, 1948–
     The heart as a drum : continuance and resistance in American
Indian poetry / Robin Riley Fast.
        p.   cm.
     Includes bibliographical references and index.
     ISBN 0-472-11077-2 (cloth : alk. paper)
        1. American poetry—Indian authors—History and criticism.
     2. Indians in literature.   I. Title.
     PS310.I52F37   2000
     811.009′897—dc21   99-40577
                                                                        CIP

**A portion of the author's income from the sales of this book
is being donated to the Native American Rights Fund.**

In memory of
Maria B. Gildersleve

CONTENTS

ACKNOWLEDGMENTS

I have taken the title of this book from Joy Harjo's "Autobiography." In the context of that prose poem "the heart as a drum" serves as an analogy for memory and continuity. When, searching for the right title, I came anew upon this line, I saw how powerfully it suggests many of the concerns and commitments that unite the poets whose work I discuss: it evokes memory and life itself; the rhythms of nature and spirit, and of the songs and stories that voice and connect them; the world of communal relationships in which the drum sounds and which is the ground of Native people's resistance and their continuance, their survival. Other poets, too, evoke the drum's rhythms to remind us of the power of spirit and the hope for continuity. In Gail Tremblay's words, "Song and story / filled the room and beat as steady as the heart / of the people" ("Reflections on a Visit to the Burke Museum, University of Washington, Seattle"). I am grateful to all of the poets for their words, which continue to enlighten and challenge me. I particularly wish to acknowledge the generosity of Robert Davis, who in Juneau several years ago gave me a wonderful morning of conversation about his poetry.

Many others have helped me along the way toward completion of this book. My first and oldest debt is to Doris Ann Bartlett, who gave me the love of poetry. Thank you, D. A. Numerous colleagues and friends have encouraged and advised me. I am especially grateful to Deborah Bluestein, Joan Dalla, and Douglas Clayton, and to Flora González, who has been not only a good friend and colleague but also, from the start of this project, an invaluable mentor. Anne Hoppe, Ingrid Knapp, and Rebecca Lavine provided bibliographical and editorial assistance; Roseanne Hoefel gave excellent advice on short notice. Brian Wogenson helped enormously with research and by sharing his insights on some difficult material. Readers for *Contemporary Literature* and the University of Illinois Press gave valuable suggestions regarding early versions of chapters 1 and 2. I was fortunate to have the assistance of Marilyn Pryle in the final stages of preparing the manuscript. I am grateful to the staff of the Emerson College Library, most especially to Jennifer Hoff, Kerry O'Brien, and Joanne Schmidt, and to the staff of the Malden Public Library. Special thanks are due to LeAnn Fields, of the University of Michigan Press, for her faith in this project.

Emerson College provided me with a course release and research support and granted the year's sabbatical leave that enabled me to complete the manuscript. I am grateful to Mrs. Helen C. Rose for her generosity both to the college and to me.

Finally, thanks to Paul, for your patience, good sense, and love.

Grateful acknowledgment is made to the following authors, publishers, and journals for permission to reprint previously published material:

Sherman Alexie, "The First and Last Ghost Dance of Lester FallsApart" and excerpts from "That Place Where Ghosts of Salmon Jump" and "Defending Walt Whitman." Reprinted from *The Summer of Black Widows*. Copyright © 1996 by Sherman Alexie, with permission of Hanging Loose Press.

Paula Gunn Allen, excerpts from "Pocahontas to Her English Husband, John Rolfe" and "The One Who Skins Cats." Reprinted from *Skins and Bones, Poems 1979–87*. Copyright © 1988 by Paula Gunn Allen. Used by permission of West End Press.

M. M. Bakhtin, excerpts from *The Dialogic Imagination: Four Essays*, by M. M. Bakhtin, ed. Michael Holquist, trans. Caryl Emerson and Michael Holquist. Copyright © 1981. Used by permission of the University of Texas Press.

Jim Barnes, "Forche Maline Bottoms" and excerpts from "After the Great Plains" and "Castle Keep." Reprinted from *The Sawdust War*. Copyright © 1992 by Jim Barnes. Used by permission of the author and the University of Illinois Press. Excerpts from "A Season of Loss," "Call It Going with the Sun," "The Long Lone Nevada Night Highway," and "Autobiography, Chapter X: Circus in the Blood." Reprinted from *A Season of Loss*. Copyright © 1989 by the Purdue Research Foundation. Used by permission of Purdue University Press.

Joseph Bruchac, excerpts from *Survival This Way*. Copyright © 1987 the Arizona Board of Regents. Reprinted by permission of the University of Arizona Press.

Gladys Cardiff, excerpts from "Where Fire Burns." Reprinted from *That's What She Said: Contemporary Poetry and Fiction by Native American Women*, ed. Rayna Green (Bloomington and Indianapolis: Indiana University Press, 1984), 61–63. Reprinted by permission of Indiana University Press.

Chrystos, excerpts from "I Like to Think" and "Just Like You." Reprinted from *Dream On*. Copyright © 1991 by Chrystos. Published by Press Gang Publishers. Used by permission of Chrystos. "Ya Don Wanna Eat Pussy" and excerpts from "I Am Not Your Princess." Reprinted from *Not Vanishing*. Copyright © 1988 by Chrystos. Published by Press Gang Publishers. Used by permission of Chrystos.

Robert H. Davis, excerpts from "At the Door of the Native Studies Director," "What the Crying Woman Saw," "Saginaw Bay: I Keep Going Back," and "Raven Dances." Reprinted from *Soulcatcher*. Copyright © 1986 by Robert H. Davis. Published by Raven's Bones Press. Used by permission of Robert H. Davis.

Louise Erdrich, excerpts from "Captivity" and "Family Reunion," from *Jacklight*. Copyright © 1984 by Louise Erdrich. Published by Henry Holt and Company.

Joy Harjo, excerpts from "Deer Dancer" and "We Encounter Nat King Cole as We Invent the Future," in *In Mad Love and War*. Copyright © 1990 by Joy Harjo, Wesleyan University Press. Used by permission of the University Press of New England. Excerpts from "She Had Some Horses" and "The Woman Hanging from the Thirteenth Floor Window," from *She Had Some Horses*, by Joy Harjo. Copyright © 1983 by Thunder's Mouth Press. Used by permission of the publisher, Thunder's Mouth Press. Excerpts from "The Woman Who Fell from the Sky" and "The Place the Musician Became a Bear." From *The Woman Who Fell from the Sky*, by Joy Harjo. Copyright © 1994 by Joy Harjo. Reprinted by permission of W. W. Norton and Company, Inc.

Lance Henson, excerpts from "we are a people." Reprinted from *A Cheyenne Sketchbook: Selected Poems, 1970–83*. Copyright © 1985 by Lance Henson. Used by permission of the Greenfield Review Press.

Linda Hogan, excerpts from "It Must Be," "The New Apartment: Minneapolis," and "Those Who Thunder." Reprinted from *Savings*. Copyright © 1988 by Linda Hogan. Used by permission of Coffee House Press. Excerpts from "Mountain Lion," "Drum," and "Map." Reprinted from *The Book of Medicines*. Copyright © 1993 by Linda Hogan. Used by permission of Coffee House Press. Excerpts from "Morning: The World in the Lake" and "The Truth Is." Reprinted from *Seeing through the Sun*, by Linda Hogan, by permission of the University of Massachusetts Press. Copyright © 1983 by Linda Hogan.

Maurice Kenny, excerpts from "Rokwaho," "First Meeting with Kiotsaeton," "Approaching the Mohawk Village," "Bear" (25), and "Bear" (43–45). Reprinted from *Blackrobe: Isaac Jogues*. Copyright © 1982 by Maurice Kenny. Published by North Country Community College Press. Used by permission of Maurice Kenny.

N. Scott Momaday, excerpts from "The Man Made of Words." Published 1970 by Indian Historian Press. Copyright © 1970 N. Scott Momaday. Used by permission of N. Scott Momaday.

Simon J. Ortiz, "I've forgotten," and excerpts from "Later on, I will remember" and "This or This," from *After and Before the Lightning*, by Simon J. Ortiz. Copyright © 1994 Simon J. Ortiz. Reprinted by permission of the University of Arizona Press. Excerpts from "What I Mean," "A New Mexico Place Name," "The State's claim that it seeks in no way to deprive Indians of their rightful share of water, but only to define that share, falls on deaf ears," "That's the Place Indians Talk About," "Back into the Womb, the Center," "Two Coyote Ones," "Telling About Coyote," "It Was That Indian," "To Change in a Good Way," and "Final Solution: Jobs, Leaving." Reprinted from *Woven Stone*, by Simon J. Ortiz. Published by the University of Arizona Press. Copyright © 1992 by Simon J. Ortiz. Used by permission of Simon J. Ortiz.

Carter Revard, excerpts from "How the Songs Came Down." Reprinted from *Ponca War Dancers*, by Carter Revard (Norman, OK: Point Riders Press, 1980). Copyright © 1980 by Carter Revard. Used by permission of Carter Revard.

Wendy Rose, excerpts from "Margaret Neumann," "Excavation at Santa Barbara Mission," "For the Campus Committee on the Quality of Life," "For the Complacent College Students Who Don't Think People Should 'Live in the Past,' " and "To Make History." Reprinted from *Going to War with All My Relations.* Copyright © 1993 by Wendy Rose. Published by Northland Publishing. Used by permission of Wendy Rose. Excerpts from "Trickster," "Builder Kachina: Home-going," "The Endangered Roots of a Person," and "Matriculation." Reprinted from *Lost Copper.* Copyright © 1985 by Malki Museum, Inc. Used by permission of the Malki Museum Press.

Brian Swann and Arnold Krupat, eds., *I Tell You Now: Autobiographical Essays by Native American Writers.* Copyright © 1987 by the University of Nebraska Press. Excerpts used by permission of the University of Nebraska Press.

Mary TallMountain, excerpts from "Crazy Dogholkoda." Reprinted from *The Light on the Tent Wall,* by permission of the American Indian Studies Center, UCLA. Copyright © 1990 by the Regents of the University of California.

Gail Tremblay, excerpts from "Indian Singing in 20th Century America," "Urban Indians, Pioneer Square, Seattle," and "Relocation." Reprinted from *Indian Singing in 20th Century America.* Copyright © 1990 by Gail Tremblay. Used by permission of Calyx Books.

Roberta Hill Whiteman, excerpts from "Reaching Yellow River" and "Steps." Reprinted from *Star Quilt.* Copyright © 1984 by Roberta Hill Whiteman. Used by permission of Holy Cow! Press.

Elizabeth Woody, "Translation of Blood Quantum" and excerpts from "Waterways Endeavor to Translate Silence from Currents." From *Luminaries of the Humble,* by Elizabeth Woody. Copyright © 1994 Elizabeth Woody. Reprinted by permission of the University of Arizona Press.

Ray A. Young Bear, excerpts from "Emily Dickinson, Bismarck, and the Roadrunner's Inquiry," "The Handcuff Symbol," "Always Is He Criticized," and "The Black Antelope Tine." Reprinted from *The Invisible Musician.* Copyright © 1990 by Ray A. Young Bear. Used by permission of Holy Cow! Press.

An early version of chapter 1 was published as "Borderland Voices in Contemporary Native American Poetry," *Contemporary Literature* 36.3 (Fall 1995). Copyright © 1995. Reprinted by permission of the University of Wisconsin Press. A shorter version of chapter 2 was published as "Who Speaks, Who Listens? Questions of Community, Audience, and Language in Poems by Chrystos and Wendy Rose," *Other Sisterhoods: Literary Theory and U.S. Women of Color,* ed. Sandra Kumamoto Stanley (Champaign: University of Illinois Press). Copyright © 1998 by the Board of Trustees of the University of Illinois. Used with the permission of the University of Illinois Press. A shorter version of chapter 7 was published as "Resistant History: Revising the Captivities of Mary Rowlandson and Isaac Jogues in 'Captivity' and *Blackrobe: Isaac Jogues,*" *American Indian Culture and Research Journal,* 23.1 (1999), by permission of the American Indian Studies Center, UCLA. © 1999 Regents of the University of California.

Every effort has been made to trace the ownership of all copyrighted material in this book and to obtain permission for its use.

CHAPTER 1

Contested Spaces, Contending Voices

Girl, I say,
it is dangerous to be a woman of two countries
    —Linda Hogan, *Seeing through the Sun*

This morning,
I have to buy a permit to get back home.
. . . .
SEE MUSEUM FOR MORE INFORMATION
    —Simon J. Ortiz, *Woven Stone*

We have learned
to barricade
the village
and have our weapons
closer at hand
    —Wendy Rose,
      Going to War with
      All My Relations

Chickasaw writer Linda Hogan's lines, from "The Truth Is," allude most directly to dangers known by a person of mixed blood, for whom questions of identity, affiliation, and responsibility can be starkly aggravated in a world shaped by theft and denial. Equally painful is the experience of dispossession evoked by Simon Ortiz's "A Designated National Park." Ortiz (Acoma Pueblo) voices what might be the ultimate dread of the colonized. The park and museum, where the remains of an ancient people and their culture are preserved, are exposed as contested sites. They symbolize the lines drawn by the dominant society around contemporary Indians, too, who are cut off from home literally, as they are excluded from ancestral lands, and spiritually, as they bear the cultural costs of such exclusion.

Hopi/Miwok Wendy Rose's "December" recognizes both danger and the necessity, in murderous circumstances, of protective barriers. This poem's epigraph alludes to the Wounded Knee Massacre; we can read it as a response to that particular event in the history of the American Indian holocaust and a defiant appropriation, perhaps, of the practice of drawing boundaries—a practice integral to the displacements of Native peoples and the enclosure of their lands. Because Rose is imagining the voice of a survivor, we can read these lines as speaking, too, for contemporary survivors—responding to the conditions of extremity in which many Native Americans today find themselves.

> The two worlds often clashed in me . . . The rez is another
> nation, another worldview that functions in a space relevant only
> to the elements strung together with language that also relies on
> the elements. The space is so specific that translation is
> impossible . . .
>   We are city cousins. The ones who didn't know how to ride.
> Or jump arroyos. Sometimes it didn't matter if you were full-
> blooded because they knew you weren't from the rez.
>   —Esther G. Belin, "In the Cycle of the Whirl"

> I grew up in a household where Indian was spoken all around
> me but never to me. I would sit on the periphery, unable to
> comprehend, though I did manage to learn a few words. This
> experience precipitated my love of language.
>   —Gloria Bird, "Breaking the Silence"

Esther G. Belin's memories of a childhood divided between the city and her Navajo parents' reservation home demonstrate how a geographic border can also mark a cultural one and how such divisions, which may be simultaneously imposed by external pressures and internalized, can be painful regardless of one's blood quantum. As Gloria Bird (Spokane) recalls a particular experience of impossible translation, she, too, testifies to the divisions produced within Indian families and communities by colonization. Yet Bird also tells us that the experience of being linguistically marginalized became the source of her love for language, a love that in turn has empowered her as a witness and an activist for resistant survival.

> Sometimes, we whispered, it was the missionaries who needed
> to be saved. We lived in a world of comedies, thunderstorms,
> chances like a flight of passenger pigeons over the lake, and
> surprises, dreams about whales in a fish barrel . . . The biblical
> stories were fun to tell, the old men turned them over in the oral
> tradition . . . these missionaries were never loons, never bears,

their wives and mothers were never killdeers on the shoreline.
We were animals and birds, even when we were converted, and
that was the difference between culture and civilization.
　　—Gerald Vizenor, *The People Named the Chippewa*

What Oklahoma becomes, in a sense, is a dream, an alive and
real dream that takes place inside and outside of the writer . . .
Our words begin inside of the dream . . . Living voices surround
us and speak from the diverse and many histories that we have
been . . . The stories and poems are in motion within the red
earth—which has the boundaries that dreams have.
　　—Joy Harjo, "Oklahoma"

In Anishinaabe Gerald Vizenor's "Shadows at LaPointe" tribal people
elude the divisions and distinctions imposed by outsiders, by creatively
adapting, transgressing, or blurring those imposed categories, by continu-
ing ancient and empowering habits of mind, vision, and story. In "Okla-
homa: The Prairie of Words" Joy Harjo (Creek) shows how what was once
primarily known as a place of exile for displaced peoples of many tribes, a
place of confinement within imposed boundaries, is transformed. As Okla-
homa becomes one with dream and language, it becomes a source of
power, conceptual boundaries become fluid, and visionary creativity, as in
Vizenor's story, offers the possibility of continuity.

These passages by Vizenor and Harjo offer ways out of the impris-
oning definitions and the despair of "two worlds"—out of the assump-
tions and story endings imposed on Indian people by the concept, and
the history, of "two worlds," one of them superior in physical power
and, by self-proclamation, in civilization. Making their worlds multiple
and changeable through story, dream, and vision, they suggest ways
of resisting dualistic constructs (and politics) and thus the dominance of
one "world" over the other. They claim spirited imagination as a way of
healing, a way of changing the terms by which their people live—a way
of reclaiming, adapting, transforming a still-vital inheritance.

It is crucial to recognize that Vizenor and Harjo are not denying the
material, political realities of the past or the present. Both of these pieces
bear witness to those realities, as do the previously quoted passages.
Rather, they are suggesting how, through language, dream, and vision,
Indian people can know that incarceration in museums, alienation from
home and culture, utter defeat, are not the only possible outcomes of
their stories. This is one implication of Gloria Bird's paradox, the empow-
ering love for language growing out of exclusion from language. It is a

healing and resistant recognition that moves much contemporary Native American writing (including the other works quoted above) and that, even in its remarkably varied manifestations, unites many contemporary Indian poets as they write for survival and continuance.

The passages I have quoted in the preceding pages suggest some of the ways in which Native American writers—mixed- and full-blooded; men and women; urban and reservation identified—have responded to circumstances they all recognize. These circumstances, consequences of colonialism and its aftermaths, may all be said to have originated in contests for land, and thus often involve relationships to geographic places, but they are equally likely to affect any aspect of experience—historical, cultural, spiritual, linguistic, emotional. How contemporary American Indian poets deal with such circumstances and their effects was the originating question for this book.

"THE FIRST AND LAST GHOST DANCE OF LESTER FALLSAPART"

It rained buffalo
in a wheat field
just off the reservation.

Confused and homeless
but otherwise free
of injury, the buffalo were rounded up and shipped
to Spokane's Walk in the Wild Zoo.

From behind a symbolic chain link fence
the buffalo stared
           intelligently

at white visitors
who soon became very nervous.

Everything beautiful
begins somewhere.

           (Sherman Alexie 18)

American history, past and present, conspires to make the whole continent a contested space for Native Americans and to make virtually inevitable, for contemporary Indians, an acute awareness of boundaries

and divisions—between Native and non-Native, the reservation or ances-
tral lands and the city, and also, for example, within tribal communities,
between traditional and modern ways, full-blood and mixed blood, Na-
tive languages and others, Native spirituality and Christianity.[1] We have
seen Ortiz's "National Park," Hogan's "two countries," Belin's "two
worlds," Bird's "periphery." Spokane/Coeur d'Alene Sherman Alexie's
poem gives us the wheat field, the reservation, and the zoo as contested
spaces. The chain-link fence is a startlingly vivid image of the boundaries
dividing Natives and whites; symbolically, the buffalo and the fence to-
gether suggest European-Americans' history of taking over or redefining
not only land but political, cultural, emotional, and spiritual "spaces,"
while the buffaloes' intelligent gaze suggests the potential of resistant
consciousness to break through those fences. As all of the passages
quoted here imply, contested spaces may be internal as well as external,
and their implications can be as varied as the writers themselves are
diverse. A rich spectrum of possibilities is evident in contemporary Na-
tive American poetry, which often reflects both an awareness of division
and conflict and a commitment to traditional beliefs regarding the whole-
ness of the universe and the relatedness of all beings. Both Harjo and
Vizenor, in the passages I've just quoted, evince that awareness and
variations on that commitment. So, in yet another way, does Alexie's
poem. Such a double perception implies, in many instances, the mutabil-
ity of boundaries, literal and other, and the fluidity of experience in the
fields of tension and possibility that surround them.

Contemporary Indian poetry itself suggests that, with important
modifications, the terms *border, borderland,* and *border writing,* used most
frequently in discussions of Chicano/a culture, can help to elucidate these
diverse and variously contested spaces and the responses they incite.
Revised to acknowledge the differing realities of Native American experi-
ence, some elements of border theory are well suited to serve a poetry
often defined by its commitment to political struggle.

Gloria Anzaldúa, with reference to Chicano/a experience, defines
borders as being "set up to . . . distinguish *us* from *them.* A border is a
dividing line, a narrow strip along a steep edge. A borderland is a vague
and undetermined place created by the emotional residue of an unnatural
boundary" (3). This statement implies major differences between Native
and Chicano/a borderlands: while for Anzaldúa there is one border, that
between Mexico and the United States, and the geography of the border-
lands is subject to shifting, for American Indians there are many such

political borders. Further, a reservation (whether or not the concept is contested) is not such a "vague and undetermined place," and the reservation, literally or otherwise, is a major site, source, and image of much Native American border experience. (Yet it bears recalling that reservations have been subject to encroachment and forcible redefinition, and thus "vague and undetermined" might not be wholly inappropriate in relation to such Native borderlands.)[2]

The borderland, Anzaldúa continues, in terms applicable both to reservation lands and to other contested spaces, cultural, spiritual, and emotional, "is in a constant state of transition . . . Tension grips the inhabitants of the borderlands like a virus. Ambivalence and unrest reside there and death is no stranger" (3–4). Oppression clearly is also no stranger: borders are often imposed by the powerful to contain and control the disempowered (as in the history of Indian removal, reservations, and relocation in the United States). Yet the ambivalence Anzaldúa notes is implied, too, in Renato Rosaldo's observation, also applicable to many Native writers, that, "for Chicanos, the border is as much a homeland as an alien environment" (67). For American Indians borderlands can be considered "alien environments" with certain important qualifications. People uprooted from ancestral lands, especially if they have been relocated to cities or to institutions like boarding schools, may find themselves in "alien" borderland environments that are both geographical and emotional locations. Gail Tremblay's "Relocation" (16–17) and Robert Davis's "At the Door of the Native Studies Director" (27–28) evoke such experiences. Harjo's "Oklahoma: The Prairie of Words," on the other hand, shows how a developing relationship between land and people can make an alien place a home. As for those who remain on or near ancestral lands, while the physical environment is hardly alien, the land and people have often been subjected to alienating pressures that create cultural, political, and emotional borderland effects. Simon Ortiz's "A New Mexico Place Name" (*Woven Stone* 207–9) and Davis's "Saginaw Bay: I Keep Going Back" (14–21) are representative. In such conditions ambivalence like that which Rosaldo implies seems especially likely to surface.[3]

Inevitably, borders and borderlands, geographical and other, harbor conflict; thus, border writing enacts and reflects conflict in its voices and languages: D. Emily Hicks notes that "border writing emphasizes the differences in reference codes between two or more cultures" (xxv), and José David Saldívar refers to border culture in the Southwest as "a serious contest of codes and representations" (259). Such a contest characterizes much contemporary Native poetry, too.

For writers like Anzaldúa and Rosaldo and, I argue, for contemporary American Indians, *border* and *borderland* connote more than a political-geographic reality. The depth and the multivalenced changeability of border experience derive from the fact that it is internal as well as external. "The two worlds often clashed in me," Belin tells us. Anzaldúa identifies the interior self as the central site of border conflict: "The struggle has always been inner and is played out in the outer terrains" (87). Here another important difference must be noted: historically, for Native Americans border conflict began with the external assaults of colonization; the ongoing, related pressures of land loss and aggression against traditional cultures eventually made the conflict an internal one for many. For contemporary Indians, and in contemporary Native poetry, inner and outer struggles have often been simultaneous, with different aspects coming into sharper focus, depending on the context.

Rosaldo signals the relation between struggle and creativity when he suggests that "the creative space of resistance for Chicanos be called the *border*, a site of bilingual speech" (67); for Native Americans analogies might include bilingual speech, foregrounded dialogism in one language, or some combination of these. Anzaldúa manifests a creativity born of struggle when she imagines "a new culture—*una cultura mestiza*," the product of knowledge, growth, and the courage to cross borders and to challenge "all three" of her cultures: "white, Mexican, Indian" (22).[4] Contemporary Native poets express and assess mixed cultural influences variously. While they may associate the tensions and fluidity of borderland experience with creativity, they are often engaged in reclaiming or affirming aspects of traditional culture—even as they acknowledge and participate in the change that is inevitably part of all living cultures. Among the Native writers I've quoted so far, none makes that clearer than Vizenor, in "Shadows at LaPointe." Thus, I would argue that Hicks's claim that "border writers ultimately undermine the distinction between original and alien culture" (xxiii), while consistent with Anzaldúa's intent, is contrary to the practice of most contemporary Native writers. Further, an important concern for some, as for Wendy Rose in "December," and one that sets them apart from Anzaldúa's project (and Hicks's claim), is the maintenance of protective boundaries, as a way of asserting and defending cultural integrity. (This position may parallel Indian communities' actions

to defend tribal sovereignty and reservation lands, and may also be evi-
dent in other contexts—for example, in ongoing debates about sharing
Native spiritual traditions with non-Indians.)

While the experience implied by Anzaldúa differs in some important
respects, then, from those of contemporary Native Americans, the border
theory that she, Rosaldo, and others elaborate offers insights into Ameri-
can Indian experience and poetry, as it illuminates some of the implications
of tensions that engage many contemporary Native writers. Especially
relevant to contemporary Indian poetry are Anzaldúa's location of such
conflicts within the individual as well as between the self and others, an
insight that allows for the recognition that the self (or the community) may
be experienced as a borderland; Rosaldo's identification of the borderland
as not only alien but home, and as a site of creativity; and the fore-
grounding of culturally centered political struggle. Border conditions and
contexts, of course, will be differently meaningful for differently situated
writers. Thus, though I have chosen mainly to discuss work by poets who
address fairly directly the experience of borderland contests, each re-
sponds distinctively, their responses colored by such factors as their cul-
tural and geographic locations, and family and tribal histories.

The usefulness of border theory is at once confirmed and enhanced
as it is modified by Native American critics who are both attuned to the
potential utility of theories originating outside Native communities, and
wary of language and approaches that in effect would recolonize the
literature. Cherokee/Choctaw novelist and critic Louis Owens illuminates
the conflicts and creative potential of the borderlands even as he defines
his preferred term *frontier.* Despite this term's highly charged implications
"within the language of the colonizer," he suggests that, seen "from the
other direction," it may be particularly apt for "transcultural zone[s] of
contact": "because . . . 'frontier' carries with it the burden of colonial
discourse it can only be conceived of as a space of extreme contestation."
A "trickster-like, shimmering zone of multifaceted contact . . . frontier is
always unstable, multidirectional, hybridized, characterized by hetero-
glossia, and indeterminate—a liminal space existing as a matrix for com-
munication, including, of course, unequal political struggles."[5] He distin-
guishes between *frontier* and *territory,* which he defines as "that space
which is mapped fully imagined as a place of containment, invented to
control and subdue the wild imaginations of imagined Native peoples"
(" 'The Song Is Very Short' " 58–59). Owens in a sense draws finer distinc-
tions than do Anzaldúa and Rosaldo, distinctions that I will sometimes

invoke to differentiate among varied "borderland" practices. Largely because I think contemporary Native poets demonstrate that "frontier" energies and intentions *can* disrupt "territorial" containment plans, I will continue to use the broader terms *border* and *borderland*. This will, I hope, help to keep open a space in which an ongoing and potentially creative dialogic contest between *frontier* and *borderland* is visible.

Anishinaabe writer and critic Kimberly M. Blaeser employs these terms virtually interchangeably. Her practice keeps both, with their complementary and competing potentials, in the foreground as terms that may be usable in part because the contest is ongoing. Blaeser addresses the complications inherent in "theorizing American Indian literature," complications multiplied by the fact that "the literary works themselves are always at least bi-cultural," and "generally proceed from an awareness of the 'frontier' or border existence where cultures meet." Like Owens, she points out the inadequacy of criticism based on binary, oppositional, distinctions that "reinforce . . . the Euro-American literary aesthetic" at the expense of the Native American. As alternatives, she recommends approaches that "proceed from an awareness of the border quality of native speech, writing and criticism" and use "dialogue or mediation" to "explore the wavering and delicate balance in the frontier text" ("Native Literature" 54–58).[6]

Reading Native American literature critically requires openness to the ways in which it does not comply with the expectations of the dominant culture—and recognition of the ways in which theory invented to illuminate the literature of the dominant culture may be inapplicable, intrusive, or inclined to appropriate other literatures. (Thus, while another virtue of border theory, for this project, is its grounding in the history and effects of "new world" colonialism, the theory's very specificity of origin implies the need for flexibility when we use it to read literature developed in different American contexts.) M. M. Bakhtin in essence denied that his theory of language would apply to poetry, and he evidently had no knowledge of Native American cultures or literatures. Yet his ideas about language are highly adaptable to contemporary Native poetry. Like the border theorists and like Owens's definition of *frontier,* he emphasizes the inherent conflicts and creative potential of living language. His belief in language's social, hence political, grounding is in accord with Indian writers' commitments to the struggle for survival. By drawing on insights from Owens and the border theorists, we can locate Bakhtin's theory in the particular realities from which much contemporary Native poetry springs and modify his theory accordingly. Further,

Bakhtin's style—heavily reliant on repetition with variations—invites interpretation, modification, and struggle. As Arnold Krupat observes, his work is marked by "an openness or ambiguity of a particularly pronounced kind" (*Voice in the Margin* 135). In what follows I aim to acknowledge the range (not the totality) of meanings found in Bakhtin's theory by various readers, in order to make room for such variety as I approach the poetry and to open my readings to the rich diversity of the poets' culturally and politically committed language. Such an intention also requires recognizing when the theory appears unsuitable and attempting to identify terms that are more germane to the works in question. It is to delineate such a flexible appropriation of Bakhtin's terms to Native poetry that I now turn to his theory and some of its interpretations.

Bakhtin's theory, especially as developed in "Discourse in the Novel," affords concepts and a terminology useful for analyzing the poetry of contested spaces, even as his terms are contested by diverse interpreters. Border conditions and experience foreground heteroglossia and render the discourse of the borderlands, as of the frontier, acutely dialogic.[7] In turn, the contemporary Native writer's unavoidable awareness of the complex tensions of borderland spaces can make for an art—including, Bakhtin's negative notwithstanding, a poetry—that foregrounds heteroglossia, hybridization, and the dialogic (all of which, again in turn, may draw attention to the conditions that incite and nurture them).[8] "Language is not a neutral medium," Bakhtin insists (294), and border conditions explode any illusions of neutrality, as Owens's definition of *frontier* makes abundantly clear. Borders would force one to be on one side or the other, and even those who resist, as they work to breach boundaries or redefine contested spaces, do so from the knowledge of borders' divisive purposes. And in the American borderlands, what Bakhtin calls "the authoritative word . . . the word of the fathers," can clearly be heard as the voice of the (great) white father(s), sounding against "the other internally persuasive word that is denied all privilege, backed up by no authority at all, and is frequently not even acknowledged in society . . . not even in the legal code" (342). But the contrast between "the authoritative word" and the "internally persuasive word" can be complicated and enriched, in Native contexts, by the voices (sometimes strong, sometimes faint or conflicted) of indigenous social and cultural authority. Such voices are audible in the excerpt from "Shadows at LaPointe" and in "The First and Last Ghost Dance of Lester FallsApart."

Not only does "authoritative discourse" sound loudly in the borderlands; it often creates and enforces the borders (343) that divide "two worlds," "two countries," and that we infer, too, from Ortiz's "Designated National Park" and Bird's essay. Yet heteroglossia and dialogism, despite being grounded in "socio-ideological contradictions" of all kinds, and while the oppositional mode is often salient, may also work to counter the binary, oppositional thinking that border conditions can invite. For the " 'languages' of heteroglossia . . . do not *exclude* each other, but rather intersect with each other in many different ways." Or, as Harjo says, "Living voices surround us and speak from the diverse and many histories that we have been." And even what Bakhtin insists one *cannot* do— "play with the context framing [authoritative discourse] . . . play with its borders . . . [make] gradual and flexible transitions . . . [create] spontaneous . . . stylizing variants on it . . . divide it up" ("Discourse in the Novel" 291, 343)—Native speakers and writers continually *do*, with humor, determination, and sometimes great risk.

Blaeser illuminates some of the ways in which Bakhtin's theory may be helpful for readers of American Indian literature when she identifies affinities between Native (oral and written) literary practice and dialogism. For example, she shows how Gerald Vizenor uses silence as "a dialogic device to engage the reader"; more generally, she identifies "the energy of orality" as dialogic, and explains that the "dialogic quality of oral tradition . . . bears responsibility for the formation and the sustenance of community" (*Gerald Vizenor* 22, 27). At least to the degree that a contemporary Native writer is engaged, in whatever way, with oral tradition or with issues of community, she implies, we can expect to find dialogic energy in the writing. Blaeser shows how the dialogism of the oral can translate into the realm of the written, when she elucidates the "dialogic relationship" between text and reader created in Vizenor's *Dead Voices* (193).[9] Throughout her discussion she demonstrates how Vizenor's dialogic techniques enable him to subvert the expectations of binary thinking and "structured oppositions" (65).

Peter Hitchcock's reading of dialogism is grounded in the necessity of opposition; as such, it might seem inimical to an approach like Blaeser's (and Vizenor's). Yet it too offers the possibility of illuminating important aspects of some Native poets' works. Hitchcock aims "to offer a dialogism at or beyond the limits of Bakhtin's formulations" (2). He privileges "the dialogics of the oppressed" as the heterogeneous assertions of "subaltern agency" engaged in subverting hegemonic power.[10] Heteroglossia is merely "the objective state of language's plurality of accentuation" (6);

struggle is the essence of true dialogism: "If dialogics become the celebration of the many-voicedness of language without showing the constraints on intersubjective exchange, then they quite clearly fail as a paradigm of social formation. Without struggle dialogic discourse is heteroglossia without limits: one has only to utter to become part of the great democratic dialogue" (7). Thus the "point in analyzing the dialogics of the oppressed is to examine subversive signs as signs of subversion, language use as signs of struggle, of disruption, of transformational possibilities" (8). In such passages, I think, we can detect both the limits and the usefulness of Hitchcock's dialogics for reading Native literature. On the one hand, his language betrays a sense of the purposes of dialogism that is, potentially at least, quite restrictive (this may be related to the fact that he evinces no particular interest in the oral). On the other hand, his emphasis on the language of subversion, disruption, and transformation suggests a potentially important commonality with many contemporary Indian writers (and may also make a poet's or critic's disruption of his strictures not entirely untoward).

David Moore's dialogics, like Hitchcock's, are grounded in social specificity, but Moore aims to identify models of intercultural relations not based on conquest and submission, models, particularly, that will be applicable to relations between American Indian and non-Native cultures.[11] He finds ways of "eluding" dualistic and dialectic systems, by focusing on the "open-ended"-ness of the dialogic, its capacity for "blurring . . . categories," for "suggesting further that categories of nature and culture," for example, "if they are useful at all, are porous and quite flexible." The dialogic, then, "continues to 'dialogue' . . . by opening up more than binary possibilities" (10–12).[12]

Moore's reading of the Maria Chona / Ruth Underhill text, *Papago Woman*, illustrates the possibilities opened by his approach. He finds in it three kinds of dialogical exchange: that of the Tohono O'odham culture with the natural world; that between the Tohono O'odham and the Apaches, which also involves relations between the living and the dead; and that between the Tohono O'odham and white European-American Christians. While the second and third implicate dialogics in struggle, Moore argues that in the third the Native subjects may be engaged in a positive process of conceptualizing themselves not as an oppressed people but as people "acting in a nexus of exchange rather than being limited . . . to either absorption by or resistance to Christianity" (12). And, importantly, Moore's first instance of dialogic exchange, that between the

Tohono O'odham and nature, does not involve struggle at all but, rather, an active reciprocity with the land. Such a concept of reciprocity is rooted in oral culture and is suggestive of the ways in which, as Blaeser maintains, the dialogic energy of the oral contributes to community.

Greg Sarris (Coast Miwok / Pomo) shows how the critic's own stance in relation to the literature is crucial to dialogical practice; the model he offers strongly suggests a similar sense of reciprocity. Sarris proposes a critical practice based on dialogue within the self and with speakers and texts. "Understanding and not control is the goal . . . and this understanding is dynamic, dialogical in nature" (153). "How," he asks, "do scholars see beyond the norms they use to frame the experiences of others unless those norms are interrupted and exposed so that scholars are vulnerable, seeing what they think as possibly wrong, or at least limited?" (29). His discussion of Erdrich's *Love Medicine* demonstrates how a critic's recognition of his own historicity and limits can make the "reading and criticism of American Indian literatures . . . the occasion for a continuous opening of culturally diverse worlds in contact with each other" (131).

Moore argues that Native cultures "often conceive of" (and I would add, effect) "their own survival" via dialogical exchanges (8); Sarris shows as much when he describes his conversations with Pomo dreamer and basket maker Mabel McKay (for example, see 17–34). Their readings of dialogue and dialogics as creating possibilities for survival—the necessity Blaeser implies when she emphasizes dialogism's role in "the sustenance of community"—make all of these approaches useful for studying contemporary Native poetry. In my discussions of the poetry I will use *dialogics* and *dialogism* without, generally, specifying a particular reading of these terms. I hope thus to invite readers to participate in the interpretive process by testing, amending, or elaborating on the nuances of the dialogism apparent in particular poems.

Contemporary Native poetry is generically and distinctively dialogic, grounded as it is in a complex of specific historical, geographical, and cultural contexts within which its multiple voices resonate. This poetry has antecedents in traditional song, chant, and story, forms that are generally anonymous, tribal or communal, rather than authored by one person. As Owens explains, "for the Indian author, writing within consciousness of the contextual background of a nonliterate culture, every word written in English represents a collaboration of sorts as well as a reorientation (conscious or unconscious) from the . . . world of oral tradition to the . . . reality of written language."[13] A contemporary poet, then, who writes in relation to a Native oral tradition, even tenuously, inevitably participates in a dialogic project from the moment that a "speaking" voice identifies itself in any way. Wendy Rose articulates another source of dialogism when she comments on her poetry's relationship to both European and Indian traditions: "I use . . . [my poems] the way that many Indian people traditionally use songs. They, in a sense, mark the boundaries of my life." Yet, she continues,

> my . . . work probably leans more toward European-derived ideas of what poetry is . . . in spite of the subjective feeling I have about the way that the poems are used in my life . . . The need to express the self, the need to make one's own emotions special and to explain it to other people, I don't think that really exists in most Native American cultures. And I think that is an important component in my work.[14]

Further, Native writers use numerous means to create dialogic poetry. Evoking traditional stories or modes, drawing on traditional convictions (for example, beliefs about the efficacy of language), and cultivating the stylistic traits most common to traditional songs—brevity, repetition, allusiveness, minimally elaborated images—make heteroglossia and dialogism implicit subjects of many poems. Other devices that foreground dialogism include puns, mixing of English and Native languages or multiple levels of discourse, using traditional figures in contemporary contexts or colloquial expressions in contexts that undermine their intents, using multiple speakers or a single voice that employs both direct and indirect discourse, and historical or cultural allusions in contexts that foreground contrasting interpretations.

Simon Ortiz reclaims the strata of heteroglossia and implies the dialogic quality of English (and of allusions to European culture) for Native peoples, when he refers to "the creative ability of Indian people to gather in many forms of the socio-political colonizing force which beset them and to make these forms meaningful in their own terms" as part of

> the Indian struggle for liberation . . . this was the primary element of a nationalistic impulse to make use of foreign ritual, ideas, and material in their own—Indian—terms. Today's writing by Indian authors is a continuation of that elemental impulse.

Ortiz continues,

Some would argue that this means that Indian people . . . have forgotten or been forced to forsake their native selves. This is simply not true. Along with their native languages, Indian women and men have carried on their lives and their expression through the use of the newer languages . . . There is not a question of authenticity here; rather it is the way that Indian people have creatively responded to forced colonization. And this response has been one of resistance. ("Towards a National Indian Literature" 8, 10)

(If Wendy Rose's commentary on the double orientation of her poems might recall David Moore's exchange-oriented dialogics, Hitchcock's reading of dialogism strikes a responsive chord with Ortiz's affirmation that Indian writers made the colonizers' "forms meaningful in their own . . . struggle for liberation.")

The dialogism of contemporary American Indian poetry can reflect both internal and external borderland experiences. Emotional, political, economic, and cultural conditions imposed on Native peoples from without may be internalized by individuals and communities. The appropriate response, the poets often suggest, is first to recognize these conditions for what they are. Depending upon context, recognition may then imply different kinds of responsibility. It may lead to a redefinition and reinforcing of some borders (recall Rose's "December"), as a way of reclaiming and reasserting the power of cultural, communal self-definition. Borders, then, may sometimes be understood as functional, even desirable. In other contexts (and more commonly, in the poetry I discuss) border consciousness is consciousness of imposed definitions or distinctions that have contributed to the distortion of Native lives and voices—that is, awareness of the effects of what Owens would call territorial intentions. Seen in this light, borders are impediments to be exposed, opened, crossed, or blurred by the poets' "wild imaginations" (Owens, " 'The Song Is Very Short' " 59).

Clearly, awareness of borderland circumstances can complicate the relationship of the poem or the poet to the audience, and this complication, too, may resonate dialogically with the oral traditions to which many contemporary Native writers link themselves. Borders may be invisible, to a given audience: "The reader of border writing will not always be able to perceive the 'logic' of the text at first. *Nor will she be able to hear the multiplicity of discourses within a single language*" (Hicks xxvi; emphasis added). Such nonperception might result from factors other than a reader's failure to recognize a given allusion or context. The English language itself might render borders invisible. For some poets the use of English may constitute a border crossing (as Ortiz's remarks indicate) or an inability to cross a border, and some of the interplay of dialogized language may be muted or lost, especially to a non-Native whose first language is English. Conversely, use of a Native American language, with or without notes or translations, draws attention to a border and requires readers to define themselves in relation to it.

Speaking in diverse, dialogically inflected voices, Native American poets address issues of language and contested space in diverse ways. (Of course, not all Native poets make borderland issues a major focus of their work.) This book explores how some contemporary writers use the fluid and multilayered possibilities of dialogic language to reflect and negotiate the experience and implications of life in the borderlands in colonized North America. As Anzaldúa observed, borderlands can be dangerous; Owens reminds us that "political inequality is an unavoidable fact within colonized space" (" 'The Song Is Very Short' " 51). As depicted by Native writers, the dangers and inequalities range from starkly simple to complex and deceptive. Drawing attention to them also foregrounds the necessity of an ongoing effort for survival—a need and an effort that infuse contemporary American Indian poetry and, in their great variety, most of the poems discussed in the following chapters. Brian Swann, while cautious about generalizing, finds that "what is striking about Native American poetry . . . [w]hat is impressive is the courage to continue," which includes "an *insistence* . . . on rich survival" (intro. xxxi).

The poems to which I now turn make acute awareness of heteroglossia and of borderland vulnerabilities mutually illuminating; in some the dialogic power of language offers a means of circumventing or overcoming the dangers. These issues may also heighten our awareness of the poems' relations to audience, relationships that are always important, both because of the contemporary poets' dialogues with oral traditions dependent upon communal audiences and because borders tend to imply a "you" or "them" as well as an "us," while heteroglossia implies different possibilities for access to a borderland text's languages. Thus, although chapter 3 treats audience as a major topic, I will draw attention to it, in a preliminary way, here.

Osage poet Carter Revard's "Discovery of the New World" (43–44) draws us in with its science fiction opening: "The creatures that we met this morning / marveled at our green skins and scarlet eyes. / They lack antennae"—and then shocks us with the familiarity of the speaker's mission, language, and assumptions. The border here is that defined by the colonizer's greedy assumption of racial/cultural superiority, and the language of Revard's space age conquistador-pilgrim is that of the victors of American history:

> it is our destiny to asterize this planet,
> and they WILL not be asterized,
> so they must be wiped out.
> WE NEED their space and nitrogen
> which they do not know how to *use.*

In this poem's vision the border where cultures meet is simply lethal, and the raw clarity of the situation offers the audience no respite. Revard has drained the poem of any of the complex and appealing personal element that infuses much of his work, in order to force us face to face with the unreal reality and whatever it means to each of us.

The bitter anger of "Discovery" and Revard's interweaving of the discourses of science fiction and Manifest Destiny, with echoes of anthropology and "scientific" colonialism, are representative of the tones and practices of many Native contemporaries. Wendy Rose, for example, juxtaposes auction-catalog descriptions of Indian relics with the imagined voices of the dead, in "Three thousand dollar death song":

> . . . . Invoiced now,
> it's official how our bones are valued
> . . . .
> As we were formed to the white soldier's voice,
> so we explode under white students' hands.
> > (*Lost Copper* 26)

and in "I expected my skin and my blood to ripen":

> . . . . My leggings were taken
> like in a rape and shriveled
> to the size of stick figures
> like they had never felt the push
> of my strong woman's body
> walking in the hills.
> > (*Lost Copper* 14–15)

These and similarly focused poems tend to create us-versus-them situations (or to draw attention to preexisting polarization) in which, the more attentive one is to the poem's language, the more one is involved in questions of complicity and of one's own relationship to the poem's story.[15] (I'm referring first to my own reading experience and assuming that other non-Natives might respond similarly. I expect that, with all of the poems I'm discussing, the personal ramifications will be somewhat different for readers of different origins, especially Native readers, but that we will all be moved, even if to different effects, by many of the same elements—contrasting discourses, as in these poems, allusions, repetitions, and so on.)

In "Wazhazhe Grandmother" (Hobson 141–42) Revard subtly demonstrates the dangers that a border mentality (here evident in the prerogative presumed by the descendants of conquerors) creates for those who are trapped within the borders—or, in Owens's sense, within territorial boundaries. Here his long lines and intricate sentences convey a pleasure in language and story that plays against the speaker's and reader's growing recognition of the loss resulting from colonization and material progress and the ongoing historical meanings of his story. For the speaker this recognition comes with adulthood; it is signaled, in part, by the difference between his early, unquestioning reference to his grandparents' "allotted land / out west of the Agency" and his later angry statement that "Bird Creek, / blessed with a dam, / is all psyched out," while the "politicians promise" the loss of the land will provide water in "municipal pools" and "asphalt gutters." For readers the recognition may only come when these later passages send us back to the first lines and make us realize that the dam was implicit in the allotment policy and reservation system that defined the grandparents' choice of land. This recognition not only embitters, while it dialogizes, the implications of "allotted" and "Agency," but also turns the lovely and engaging memory of the old homestead— "where Bird Creek meanders in / from the rolling grassy plains with their prairie chicken dancing in spring, / . . . where deer came down / at dusk with the stars"—into an elegy without resolution or reconciliation.

A highly charged dialogism is discernible in words like "a happy future" and "blessed with a dam"; heteroglossia is further foregrounded by the presence of Osage words and by the epigraph, which gives a sense of the layered meanings of place and the magnitude of loss. The epigraph is preceded by an untranslated line of Osage: "*-i-ko-eh, tha-gthi a tho*"; the body of the epigraph is from Francis LaFlesche's *Dictionary of the Osage*

Language. I quote it in full, from Revard's text, to make available the possibilities for allusiveness that differently located readers may recognize.

> (*HO-e-ga,* literally "bare spot": the center of the forehead of the mythical elk . . . a term for an enclosure in which all life takes on bodily form, never to depart therefrom except by death . . . the earth which the mythical elk made to be habitable by separating it from the water . . . the camp of the tribe when ceremonially pitched . . . life as proceeding from the combined influences of the cosmic forces.

For many readers such an epigraph must highlight our limited access (for example, by referring to an elk not mentioned in the poem itself), yet its reference to mythic transformation allows us at least a hint of the poem's deeper resonances, and the whole reinforces our awareness of borders and of the vulnerability of the old people, language, and land to those who define the borders.

Linda Hogan's "It Must Be" (*Savings* 14–16) shows that the dangers of living in a territorial world are not only external; the perceptions of those whose power is validated by borderland inequalities can invade and undermine the convictions of the disempowered, taking away one's ability to define herself. Hogan's protagonist begins,

> I am an old woman
> whose skin looks young
> though I ache
> and have heard the gravediggers call me
> by name.

Pathologists and doctors, "with their white coats and masks," diagnose her "disease": "It must be / her heart, let us cut her open with knives." The poem's discourses include not only the old woman's direct address to the reader, the reported speech of the medical experts, and her responses (spoken or thought). She tells us, too, that one of the "old women inside" her sometimes "lashes out at the nurses / and all who remain girls, / and at bankers and scholars" and that "there are days / the old women gossip and sing." The old woman must struggle against the experts who would define her, but the struggle is also internal, for she admits that sometimes she watches "the wrong face / in the mirror"; sometimes her hands become the banker's or the scholar's and want to strangle "the old woman

inside / who tells the truth / and how it must be." The poem ends by
affirming her love of "the ancestors / in and around me," yet the ending
may be as open as it is conclusive: "And . . . On those days I love the
ancestors" might suggest an unfinished, perhaps unfinishable, story, as
might the final image of "the oldest one . . . taking stock / in all her
shining / and with open hands"—hands that might be asking, giving,
questioning, blessing. The possible ambiguity, however, does not dimin-
ish the fact that Hogan's old woman actively resists the presumptions
of those who would contain her. (This ending suggests the openness
Bakhtin considers an important element of dialogized, "novelistic" dis-
course.[16]) Hogan foregrounds heteroglossia and dialogized discourse in
the repetitions of "it must be," in lines like "they make me carry on . . .
about the sad / state of the nation," "they have big teeth," and "that crazy
one . . . baring herself to the world," and in her use of contrast and
repetition, which enhance the poem's colloquial, storytelling effect to
counter the clinical discourse of the doctors.

Some of these poems, and others, suggest that the dangers of life in
the borderlands actually make protective barriers necessary. While the
borders that perpetuate or justify oppression have been imposed on Na-
tive people from without, as Owens's definition of *territory* makes clear,
the poets sometimes indicate that protective barriers need to be estab-
lished and maintained by Indians themselves. Revard's "Discovery of the
New World" indicates the need for such protection in the method by
which the Natives are killed: they are "snuffed out / by an *absorber*
swelling / into their space" (43; emphasis added), destroying the body's
own borders. Hogan's poem also conveys the threat of bodily invasion,
while it implies the need for protective internal boundaries if the old
woman is to hold off, rather than adopt, the doctors' prescriptive defini-
tions. And in a pragmatic political move, Menominee poet Chrystos
("Those Tears") insists on the right of "Women of Color / only" "to de-
fine our terms our turf," for "no matter how sensitive you are / if you are
white / you are" (*Dream On* 130–31). Within this protective border she
works to break down the boundaries dividing women of color. Such
poetic moves may have analogues in some Indian communities' policies
of excluding visitors from religious events and controlling tourists' pic-
ture taking and other culturally protective border maintenance.

Many poets explore the meanings of crossing geographic, linguistic,
cultural, or other kinds of borders. Border crossing may be compelled by
external or internal forces (economic necessity, for example, which forced

many Indians into compliance with the relocation policy of the post–World War II years, or the mixed-blood person's need to negotiate an identity in relation to different worlds). Whatever the impetus, the effort is likely to entail danger and to require daring and an ability to create and maintain balance in shifting conditions. Gail Tremblay (Onondaga/Micmac), in "Indian Singing in 20th Century America," speaks of urban Indians' border crossings:

> We stumble out into streets;
> patterns of wires invented by strangers
> are strung between eye and sky,
> and we dance in two worlds,
> inevitable as seasons in one,
> exotic curiosities in the other
> which rushes headlong down highways.
>   (14)

As these lines suggest, Tremblay keeps her balance with a recurring pattern of contrasts, while the subtly hinted, underlying circular movement and cyclic repetitions help affirm the continuing presence of Indians *as* Indians in a world of change, a world in which survival requires dealing with "the boss" who "tries to shut / out magic and hopes we'll make / mistakes or disappear" (15).

The poets often use humor to enact, enable, or comment on border crossing and the risks it entails. In Ortiz's "The Creation, According to Coyote" (*Woven Stone* 41–42) humor and a grounding in tradition combine to make for a safe crossing. The story Coyote tells is part of the Acoma emergence myth, which recounts the people's movement from world to world until they emerged into this world. As Ortiz retells it, through Coyote's, his own, and, indirectly, his uncle's voices, he crosses borders of time and culture; he both evokes contemporary skepticism and transcends it, treating the story with both the humor Coyote often deserves and the respect, and finally commitment, the story merits. The complex mix of intentions that makes this rendition of a traditional story truly dialogic is represented by Ortiz's repetitions of the hybridized "you know": "But, you know, Coyote, / he was mainly bragging"; "Coyote told me too, but you know / how he is"; and finally the poem's last line, which affirms that one can cross borders and retain cultural integrity: "And you know, I believe him." Non-Acoma readers especially may find themselves mystified by some elements of the poem, and, without undermining his story's integrity, Ortiz reaches out by acknowledging that "They looked strange. / Everything was strange." The certainty afforded by syntactical repetition and a chronological sequence also provides us with a partial entrance to the tale. Again, a grounding in tradition—and a sense of tradition and one's response to it as evolving—may allow for both cultural integrity and two-way communication in the borderland.[17]

Wendy Rose's "Trickster" (*Lost Copper* 70) celebrates the mix of creativity, foolishness, and verbal power that Coyote shares with Raven, Blue Jay, and other tricksters in Native cultures, and suggests that the trickster is the perfect border dweller—constantly crossing, remaking, transcending the lines and rules that would constrict him:

> Trickster dashes under cars
>   on the highway and leaves
>   the crushed coyote,
> Trickster bounces off whistling
>   with his borrowed coat of patches
>   and upside-down kachina mask.

The "upside-down" mask might make Trickster a Hopi sacred clown.[18] It might also imply borderland issues important for many of these poets, for it seems to suggest both the tension between the mixed-blood person and the traditional community that Rose's autobiographical poems sometimes reflect, and her efforts to use the traditional flexibility of Hopi Kachina lore to make a place for herself in relation to Hopi culture. Her emphasis on Trickster's verbal power suggests further that he might be a model for the poet who lives in contested frontier or borderland spaces: "He lives in his own mess of words," "sees / when the singers are . . . trapped by their songs," "steals all the words / we ever thought / we knew." At the same time, his takeover of language animates the concept of heteroglossia, of language "populated . . . with the intentions of others," and its capacity for dialogic creativity ("Discourse in the Novel" 294).

The people's movement from world to world in the Acoma emergence story, like the ability of Vizenor's tribal people, in "Shadows at LaPointe," to be animals and birds, manifests the continuity, in traditional contexts, of the mythic and the mundane. (So do similar transitions in poems I discuss in later chapters, e.g., Davis's "Raven Dances" and

Harjo's "The Woman Who Fell from the Sky.") They demonstrate that, as Harjo says, "myth is present in the everyday" (*Spiral of Memory* 130). Though from a non-Native or nontraditional perspective such transitions may be seen as border crossings, they don't involve the kinds of conflict or "extreme contestations" (Owens, " 'The Song . . .' " 58) identified by Anzaldúa and Owens as characteristic of borderland or frontier conditions. On the other hand, when Rose locates Trickster on a busy highway—the scene Tremblay's poem also associates with the non-Indian world—he is definitely a participant in the dynamics of dangerous borders and contested spaces.[19]

Ortiz's "What I Mean" (*Woven Stone* 326–29) blends humor with a story of borderland oppressions that inspires another kind of border crossing, into a prophecy of solidarity that transcends racial and cultural barriers. The poem tells the story of Agee, who was "just one of us, but a hero," and moves, first, from the dialogism of that line to a fuller rendition of linguistic oppression and the creative border crossings it inspired: at school, where the teachers were "always on him," he resisted the imposition of English and denigration of "Indian":

> Agee was always laughing and fooling around
> and talking Indian
> (you couldn't do that)
> and making English sound like Indian
> (you couldn't do that either.)
>
>   (326)

Agee crosses more borders when, as a young mine worker, he goes to Grandma's Café and, enacting Saldívar's "serious contest of codes and representations" (259), argues "with white miners who made jokes / about squaws and called you chief" (327). Not "shy or reserved," having broken free of those stereotypes imposed on Indians by the terrors of the borderland, he has joined the union and is arguing for a strike. Agee's border crossing is stopped when he is killed, "maybe" accidentally, but Ortiz makes his story the promise and means of a transformative transition. In the final verse paragraph he moves from the past tense, in which he has told the story, to the present, and from "what I mean," a phrase he's repeated throughout the story with subtle modulations of effect, to "what we mean." These changes explicitly open the poem's embrace to include an audience made up at least of all of the cultural groups it finally names and may implicitly invite the self-inclusion of any readers who recognize Agee's heroism:

> But what I mean is:
> Although Agee never made it beyond young,
> the mines were still there
> and the workers were still fighting
> and old people still needed help
> and the language of our struggle
> just sounds and reads like an Indian,
> Okie, Cajun, Black, Mexican hero story—
> that's what we mean.
> That's what we mean.
>
>   (328–29)

Ortiz's poem implies internal border crossings as vital and necessary as the externally evident ones that make up the surface of his story. In her beautiful "If I Am Too Brown or Too White for You" (*Going to War* 63–64) Wendy Rose evokes the difficult internal self-transformations of a mixed-blood person the grounds of whose identity might be thought of as a borderland and who thus is always crossing, yet can never fully cross, the borders. Though humor is hardly unthinkable in such a context, Rose's tone is seriously cautionary and, finally, celebratory. The poem may suggest an impulse toward something like Anzaldúa's vision of a new mestiza person (though it must be said that Rose's tendency is always to align herself with the Indians in red-white conflict). It echoes both Anzaldúa ("con imágenes domo mi miedo, cruzo los abismos que tengo por dentro" ["with images I overcome my fear, and cross the abysses within me"] 71) and Linda Hogan, who has said in response to a question about being of mixed blood, "It's a very difficult position to be in, but, on the other hand, it allows for a great deal of freedom. If you live on the boundaries between cultures, you are both of those cultures and neither of those cultures, and you can move with great mobility in any direction you want."[20] Hogan's statement, especially, indicates the way this poem lyrically evokes some of what was suggested obliquely and humorously, in Rose's "Trickster": the tensions of being mixed-blood in a world ("brown or . . . white") that prefers simpler definitions of identity. Here the danger is in the inclination of others, "you," to impose a static, thus limiting, definition of the speaker, a "territorial" definition, perhaps, in

Owens's sense, and the poem's struggle is not to make a place for the mixed self, but to imagine a mode of being in process, in motion.

The poem is daring in its fluidity, its openness to question and to ambiguity. Its clearest acknowledgment of heteroglossia is in its continuous invitation to interpretation and equally continuous disruption of hard-and-fast definitions of its images' meanings. It also exemplifies the implicit dialogism Rose defined in talking about her work's affinities with both Indian and European traditions—used, like Indian songs, to "in a sense, mark the boundaries of . . . [her] life," it also enacts "the need to make one's emotions special and to explain it to other people."[21] The poem is in constant motion, thanks to the imagery of stones, light, and water; to the rhythmic syntax that runs, virtually free of punctuation, from one stanza to the next; and to its appeal to (and thus partial dependence on) the audience. In these ways, I think, it also exemplifies the capacity for equanimity in the midst of often dangerous flux that living in the borderlands requires. Emphasizing its speaker's identity as organic process, the poem insists on her multifaceted, living reality, and rejects anyone's preconceptions and impositions: "I am a garnet woman / whirling . . . giving birth / over and over, a single motion."

Rose's title (which also serves as the poem's first line) invites—or chides—all readers into her intended audience. None of us is excluded; all are challenged. We are both included and put on notice. We may want the speaker's garnet self to be "perfect . . . less clouded, / less mixed," but she reminds us that it is rather that self's fluid undefinability that is the source of its purity and its voice. And, in a move that makes this one of her more hopeful poems, she affirms our ability to recognize this:

> but you always see
> just in time
>
> . . . .
> there is a small light
> in the smoke, a tiny sun
> in the blood, so deep
> it is there and not there,
>
> so pure
> it is
> singing.

Ending the poem with the simple certainty of her own "singing," Rose reaffirms the creativity necessary for, and potential in, negotiating contested spaces.

For Tlingit poet and carver Robert Davis, as for others, the dangerous realities of Native life in the borderlands make the affirmation and protection of integrity essential. In "At the Door of the Native Studies Director" (27–28) we again see Saldívar's "serious contest of codes and representations." The poem evokes two places, the school, which as in Ortiz's "What I Mean" is a scene of border conflicts, and "that other place, / that country hidden within a country"—the past, the remembered traditional life of the Tlingit people. The poem directly addresses the Native Studies director, who as a boy was ripped from the old village life and sent to boarding school, where

> they educated old language out of you,
> put you in line, in uniform, on your own two feet.
> They pointed you in the right direction but
> still you squint to that other place.

These lines bitterly foreground heteroglossia and enact dialogic struggle in their complacent clichés, while the shift into the present tense demonstrates the boarding school teachers' failure. There is a terrible ambiguity in the lines that follow: in that hidden country,

> You chase bear, deer. You hunt seal. You fish.
> This is what you know. This is how you move,
> Leaving only a trace of yourself.
> Each time you come back
> You have no way to tell about this.

These lines seem to refer both to literal realities and to imagination, the coming "back" being both to the Native village and to the boarding school. The ambiguity of *back* and *this* involves the speaker, too, in both worlds and thus exposes an evidently painful dialogic awareness in *his* discourse (which ironically parallels the older man's devastating loss of effective language in both worlds).[22] Years later, having met the "qualifications" and been designated a "native scholar," the man is "instructed to remember / old language, bring back faded legend, / anything that's left," and his internal divisions break out in sickness and the smell of "cheap wine" on his breath.

Through the first two verse paragraphs Davis uses contrast to sharpen the borderlines and emphasize the dangers of a forced crossing. But, as the second paragraph ends and the poem becomes more intimate, contrast becomes a means for the speaker to reach out to the older man across the division between youth and age that has so often been deepened by the undermining of the old ways: "Tonight, father, I wrap you in a different blanket, / The dances come easier, I carve them for you. / This way you move through me." The "different blanket" has a dialogic quality, for it suggests not simply a piece of bedding but, more importantly, the blankets worn by some Tlingit dancers and by people of high status on ceremonial occasions. He continues, "Everyone thought I would take your place / but as I turn in your dark chair / I recall . . . I remember." We see that, while the speaker won't take his elder's tenuous place in the academy, he may, with the other's help, grow into his own place within their culture: "Your sleep-speech grows guttural"—a trait of Tlingit speech—"and I feel something pull / that when you wake I want to ask you about." With this recognition and the anticipated, though unvoiced, question, Davis leaves his poem's end open for renewed speech and growth and perhaps renegotiations of the borders.

But what he offers seems only a tentative, un(der)stated possibility for limited recovery, in circumstances that will continue to be painful. Any more hopeful border crossing that the poem might anticipate will inevitably be difficult and dangerous. Thus "At the Door of the Native Studies Director" offers contrasts, and the possibility of dialogue, with "If I Am Too Brown or Too White for You" and, in different ways, with "What I Mean." Juxtaposing these poems prompts me to ask why Rose is able to end hers with a celebratory affirmation, while Davis must, it seems, confirm a bleakness that promises little. The differences between these poems illuminate, I think, some of the possible effects of audience and place in borderland texts. Rose's poem is absolutely personal, lyrical, its imagery subjective, as befits its emphasis on internal experience. The figurative dominates:

> . . . I am a garnet woman
> whirling into precision
> as a crystal arithmetic
> or a cluster and so

> why the dream
> in my mouth,
> the flutter of blackbirds
> at my wrists?
>
> (63)

The poem is far from being abstract, but, except for the words "too brown or too white" and "red or white," it is abstracted from cultural particulars, historicity, or a sense of place. It is not locatable except in the dynamics of the speaker's voice and emotions and her relationship with "you." Further, "you," the audience, is universalized and thus also removed from time, place, or any other historically or culturally defining particulars. Having so abstracted the audience, Rose frees her poem from that audience's possible history and the poem might be said to transcend borders.

Davis's poem, in contrast, is located in a specific geography, culture, personal and communal history, and relationship. It, too, addresses a "you," but a very particular, historically and culturally identified "you." What Davis is creating, then, is not simply a personal, "you-and-me" matter but also a communal experience. This distances the reader, whoever she or he might be, to some degree. We are eavesdroppers and must consider our right to listen in and the meaning(s) of our listening in, according to our own locations. (As a non-Native Alaskan who went to elementary school with similarly displaced Native classmates, I inevitably hear the voice of Davis's poem differently than will readers from other backgrounds.) Locating the primary audience so concretely makes the lyrical affirmation and celebration of Rose's poem (and the kind of challenge Rose issues to "you") impossible and *any* contemplation or crossing of borders painful. A difference in stylistic emphasis is involved, too: like "If I Am Too Brown or Too White for You," "At the Door of the Native Studies Director" is highly figurative, but Davis derives his figures directly from literal, concrete experience and/or from culturally located emotional experience.

I bring Ortiz's "What I Mean" into the dialogue because this poem accomplishes its particular effects in part by a combination of traits that, looking only at the other two, we might consider contradictory. Unlike the others, Ortiz's poem is virtually free of figurative language; the emotional intensity of its response to borderland realities is conveyed in relatively simple, straightforward language, through episode and repetition, and through subtle variations on these. Ortiz locates both his speaker and his protagonist, Agee, in the same cultural and historical particulars, and, while the audience is never directly addressed, it seems to be characterized as both present (this is a very *oral* poem) and in need of explanations— probably not Indian but not specifically identified. By the poem's end Ortiz has, in a sense, transcended some borders by the inclusiveness of his solidarity, but he's done so by the solidity, the specificity, of his story.

None of what I have said should necessarily imply valuing one of these poems over the others. But juxtaposing the poems and allowing them to question each other can enable us to consider some of the effects, opportunities, gains, or losses that may accompany or result from the border conscious writer's perceptions of audience and of place in a given poem. Rose's poem, for example, might be understood as calling attention to the liberation potential in seeing race as a construction, a complex of figures and responses, while Davis's warns of the consequences of ignoring or minimizing concrete contexts, and Ortiz's invites his listener-readers to revise the meanings of the real conditions in which they live.

The poems I have discussed in this chapter demonstrate their writers' shared sensitivity to the implications of living in multiply contested spaces, acute awareness of heteroglossia and the dialogism such experience engenders, and recognition of the potential of these factors, with all of their rich variousness, to clarify and complicate each other and thus to foster more complex and empowered understanding(s). Each poem responds, at least implicitly, to some of the dangers of the borderlands, and in each the imperative of survival—personal, cultural, communal—is an informing motive. Ortiz's definition of his own work as oriented toward survival in fact applies directly to much contemporary Native American writing.[23] Further, these poems suggest that recognizing and exploiting the dialogic potential offered by heteroglossia may contribute to the realization of a dynamic survival, a personal and/or communal orientation toward both continuity and transformative action. As chapter 2 will suggest, such recognitions and realizations may signal, too, the writers' engagement with traditional understandings of language.

The following chapters focus on major themes or characteristic modes in contemporary Native poetry (indeed, in contemporary Native literature), in order to explore how the poets' responsiveness to borderland experience affects their approaches to the issues they address. I begin, in chapter 2, by examining contemporary Native writers' theoretical and thematic treatments of language. In chapter 3 I discuss how awareness of borders—geographic, historical, cultural, internal—raises questions about the meanings of community, the makeup and role of the audience, and the poet's or poem's relation to both. Chapter 4 examines some treatments of place (and of displacement) and shows how, in the work of some poets, border consciousness and relationship to particular places interact. Chapter 5 considers the healing powers of dream, vision, myth, and memory. And in chapters 6 and 7 I consider some poets' uses of storytelling, and reclamations of documentary history. Each chapter demonstrates, too, how the poets' attentiveness to contests and exchanges of language creates dialogic discourses to evoke the subtleties and complexities of the issues they address. Inevitably, the chapters' topics overlap, for all are vitally related. Audience and community are part of storytelling, spirit and language are inextricable, and so on.

By defining chapters 2 through 7 in terms of themes that are important across contemporary Native culture, I am able to show how, for a diverse group of poets, the confluence of borderland consciousness with issues of community, place, spirit, language, storytelling and history makes for poetry that is deeply committed to resistance and continuance, and for language that is richly and variously dialogic. At the same time, this structure has allowed me to include some poems in which borderland conflicts and concerns and dialogism are muted or very differently inflected or maybe, arguably, even absent. I've included such works because they contribute provocatively to understanding these central, organizing issues. The presence of such poems (which may be different poems for different readers) might prompt alternative conclusions to some of those I offer. This is as it should be, for this project can be only a part of a process that will continue as more readers become engaged with American Indian poetry. What I offer in chapter 8, as another step in that process, is a description of some characteristic elements of the poetry I have studied here, elements that, taken together, suggest the shape of a contemporary American Indian poetics.

CHAPTER 2

"Still Talking Indian"

. . . spirits we can't see
are dancing joking   getting full
on roasted caribou, and the praying
goes on, extends out.
          —Joy Harjo, *She Had Some Horses*

Language, in traditional Native American cultures, and for contemporary Native writers who make it their subject, "extends out": it is a source of relationship, healing, and survival. Such a vision of language is at the empowering core of the poems discussed in this chapter and in those that follow.

Traditional indigenous beliefs about language emphasize the sacredness and the efficacy of the word. Pawnee/Otoe writer Anna Lee Walters tells us that in Otoe tradition, the "totem voices . . . swirled visibly overhead in the immenseness of the universe, and this is how the clans knew they lived" (13). Simon J. Ortiz affirms that language is "a spiritual energy that . . . includes all of us and is not exclusively in the power of human beings" ("Song/Poetry and Language" 11). The verbal and the sacred are not simply related, they are "indivisible" (Momaday, "Native Voice" 8). Language is thus creative, and "intensely pragmatic"; the word has "performative power" "to structure the universe."[1] With its spiritual power, its grounding, through story, in particular places, and its concrete efficacy, language has, too, the power of "placing the speaker in communication with his own being and with the whole world" (Gill 23).

What, I think, most distinguishes this conception from the beliefs in the power of language shared by other poets and writers are the conviction of the sacred reality of language, its power not just to move but to make, and the particular contexts—cultural, geographic, historical—in which such beliefs have their deepest meanings. For contemporary Native American writers that contextual web, complicated by colonization, borderland experience, and the multifarious influences of literacy in the Western tradition, is consequently marked, too, by heteroglossia and dialogism. Thus, to cite just one piece of suggestive testimony, Harold Littlebird tells us that he writes in part because he hears and understands,

but can't speak "either of [his] languages, either Santo Domingo or La-
guna" (Bruchac, *Survival* 167).

The contemporary American Indian writers who most persistently
and searchingly make language their subject are N. Scott Momaday
(Kiowa) and Gerald Vizenor. They differ radically from each other in
voice, tone, and style. Momaday's voice is orderly, measured; often rever-
ent, even magisterial in tone, he conveys stability and serenity. Vizenor,
in contrast, presents himself as an agent provocateur, a player with "trick-
ster discourse" who uses disruptive, irreverent language to draw atten-
tion to the comic and the disorderly. If Momaday establishes and confirms
truths, Vizenor as often draws attention to "truths' " fallibilities. Yet they
hold in common, I believe, their most important convictions about lan-
guage. Thus their different practices reveal the range of possibilities inher-
ent in a common vision, and together their texts suggest the implications
of language that are most widely compelling for contemporary Native
writers. At the same time, their differences can help guard against critics'
constructing theoretical prisons on the foundation of their words.

The key text for reading Momaday on language is his essay "The
Man Made of Words." Language here is one with being, memory, and
imagination; it is power and vision. Hence it necessarily has a moral
dimension; hence, too, language makes survival possible. Such convic-
tions are evident in Momaday's recollection of the old Kiowa woman
Ko-sahn:

> My eyes fell upon the name Ko-sahn. And all at once everything
> seemed suddenly to refer to that name. The name seemed to human-
> ize the whole complexity of language. All at once, absolutely, I had
> the sense of the magic of words and names. Ko-sahn, I said, and I
> said again KO-SAHN.
>
> Then it was that that ancient, one-eyed woman Ko-sahn stepped
> out of the language and stood before me on the page . . . "You have
> imagined me well," [she said,] "and so I am. You have imagined that
> I dream, and so I do. I have seen the falling stars."
>
> "But all of this . . . imagining," I protested, ". . . is taking place in
> my mind. You are not actually here . . ." It occurred to me that I was
> being extremely rude . . . She seemed to understand.
>
> "Be careful of your pronouncements, grandson," she answered.
> "You imagine that I am here in this room, do you not? That is worth
> something . . . If I am not here in this room, grandson, then surely

neither are you" . . . Then she turned . . . and receded into the language I had made. (164)

But the core of Momaday's essay is in the story of the arrowmaker (174), a story the importance of which is signaled by his frequent references to it.[2] In a sense this story has given him his being: "I have no memory that is older than that of hearing it" (171). The arrowmaker detects the presence of an unknown person outside his tipi, but continues his work, " 'talk[ing] easily, as of ordinary things,' " with his wife, while saying to the one outside, " 'If you are Kiowa, you will understand what I am saying, and you will speak your name.' " Receiving no words in response, he continues testing his arrow until "his aim [falls] upon . . . his enemy," he shoots, and the enemy, identified as such by his silence, dies. The story is "about language"; its point "lies . . . in what [the arrowmaker] says—and indeed that he says it." The man's "reality consists in language . . . language is the repository of his whole knowledge and experience, and it represents the only chance he has for survival . . . The arrowmaker," then, "is preeminently the man made of words. He has consummate being in language . . . a world of definite reality and of infinite possibility" (171–72). The essay's circling structure, its repetitions and renewals, its balanced and parallel syntax, its lists and its interplay of abstract and concrete diction, are integral to the narratives and commentary, making the whole an organic manifestation of Momaday's convictions about language.

For their compactness and relative clarity I have chosen two stories that appear in *Landfill Meditation* to represent Vizenor's vision of language. In these stories, too, style and structure—puns, neologisms, large- and small-scale repetitions, and resistance to closure—contribute to our sense of that vision. "Almost Browne" (1–10) draws attention to language's creative, liberating vitality.[3] The title, which is also the protagonist's name, foregrounds both dialogic play and the provisional quality of language. But if language is always somehow incomplete, it is also very real, as Almost tells us:

Listen, there are words almost everywhere . . . Words are in the air, in our blood, words were always there . . . Words are in snow, trees, leaves, wind, birds . . . we are words, real words, and the mongrels are their own words. Words are crossbloods too, almost whole right down to the cold printed page. (8)

As in "The Man Made of Words," language and imagination are bound together in creativity. In his first-person narration Almost creates himself. Even damaged language feeds the imagination, while imagination recovers and renews language: Almost learns to read from books burned in a library fire. As he says, in a passage that recalls Ko-sahn's appearance to Momaday, "The words became more real in my imagination . . . Finally, I could imagine the words and read the whole page, printed or burned" (8). As Almost plays with words and tells his own stories, he acts out "survivance . . . the end of domination in literature."[4]

In "Ice Tricksters" (22–34) Vizenor celebrates the playfulness of the supreme artist of language, the trickster. "Uncle Clement," nicknamed "Almost,"

> never told lies but he used the word almost to stretch the truth like a tribal trickster . . . The trickster . . . frees the world in stories . . . Almost told me . . . "The almost world is a better world, a sweeter dream than the world we are taught to understand in school." (24)

The trickster's imagination releases language's power for creativity and survival. Through the recurring plays on *almost* and the interchangeable use of *he* and *she,* as the characters create a carved-ice Fourth of July trickster, becoming tricksters themselves in the process, Vizenor again demonstrates language's liberating potential.

The concrete reality of language is brought out by the child narrator, Pincher, who "pinched [his] way through childhood," pinching everything, even words. In this he is not alone; his relationship to language also binds him to his family and culture, as we see when he recalls the winter ride to the hospital during which his grandmother died:

> we pinched summer words over the hard snow and ice. She smiled and said *papakine, papakine* over and over. That means cricket or grasshopper in our tribal language and we pinched that word together . . . Later she whispered *bisanagami sibi,* the river is still, and then she died . . . at the wake in our house, my grandmother pinched a summer word and we could see that. She was buried in the cold earth with a warm word between her fingers. That's when my uncle gave me my nickname. (23–24)

We see here, too, language's dependence upon the relationship between speaker and listener, writer and reader: the audience, whether individual or communal, must actively participate in creating meaning. Momaday implies as much in "The Man Made of Words": before Ko-sahn's response, "the words" he had written "did not seem real" (164).

Vizenor's stories and Momaday's essay reveal the contours of significant common ground, yet their views of language also diverge. Momaday's commitment, voiced several times in "The Man Made of Words," to the idea of "racial memory," or "memory in the blood," as a fundamental source of knowledge and hence of language and story, seems to bespeak an inclination toward fixed certainties and to coexist uneasily with his also oft-repeated belief that "we are what we imagine."[5] His commitment to "racial memory" is related, and draws attention, to characteristics that distinguish his approach to language from Vizenor's (and, I think, from those of many contemporary Native writers). The profound certainty implied in the "blood's" imagination seems to inform his most characteristic voice, which I have described as orderly and magisterial, and Arnold Krupat considers "committed to hegemonic monologue," "authoritative," marked by "a tendency to subordinate all other voices."[6] Momaday's continuing use of the phrase "the American Indian," as the subject of generalizations about history, culture, and relationships to place and language, is consistent with such characterizations, and stands in marked contrast to a phrase like Vizenor's "postindian warriors" (*Manifest Manners* 1–44). The two phrases contrast not only as the familiar does with the neologism but also as the all-encompassing singular contrasts to the plural. And implicit in that singular is an act of ordering, of control. In his vision and use of language Momaday is, I believe, strongly disposed to resolution and, consequently, not particularly receptive to disorder or to open-ended multiplicity of meaning.[7] His dismissal of "deconstruction" seems indicative, as does his apparent belief in the permanence of the arrowmaker's story: notwithstanding "a certain latitude to imagine," the story, he says, in response to a question about possible alterations by future storytellers, "is what it needs to be . . . and it ought to remain that and I'm sure it will . . . you can't change it because it's there" (Woodard 137, 117, 119).

Vizenor's pursuit of multiple meanings, evident in "Almost Browne" and "Ice Tricksters," and his embrace of "postmodern conditions" define a contrasting orientation. In a statement suggestive of affinity with Bakhtin, he tells Laura Coltelli, "I lean a bit . . . toward the margin . . . I choose words intentionally because they have established multiple meanings" (175). Describing the postmodern conditions of Native American literature, he assumes an openness to multiplicity and to the unknown or even inconclusive:

> first, no story is the same. The conditions are postmodern because of their connection to oral expression which is usually a kind of freefloating signifier or a collection of signifiers, depending on who's present. The meaning of such stories . . . depends on a number of interesting, lively, immediate, temporal, and dangerous . . . conditions . . . dangerous in nature and *in language* . . . "dangerous" as hunting . . . because your life depends on seeing and catching something . . . it's an encounter with the unknown . . . that may come together, alive or present in the telling or the hunting. (McCaffrey and Marshall 53–54)

The analogy to hunting, his phrase "postindian *warriors*" (emphasis added), and his statement that "a mixed-blood" like himself must find meaning "where the contention is . . . where the energy lies" reflect Vizenor's "agonistic" conception of language and draw a clear contrast between his sense of (dialogic) linguistic struggle and Momaday's preference for resolution (Coltelli 174).

The contrast between these writers' orientations toward language is evident in the tension between two key ideas: Momaday's conception of the arrowmaker (and, potentially, any person) as having "consummate being in language" and Vizenor's concept of "survivance." *Consummate being* implies wholeness, completeness; indeed, Momaday says of his arrowmaker, "language is the repository of his whole knowledge and experience" ("Man Made of Words" 172). On the other hand, Vizenor describes survivance as "a conditional experience," an inventive, seriously playful response to the fact that "life is a chance" and to "postmodern conditions" (McCaffrey and Marshall 53–54). Whereas for Momaday a sense of completeness is evidently of most vital importance, for Vizenor what is primary is struggle, challenge—and, inevitably, change. But these orientations are not, I think, necessarily opposed. If survivance might make "consummate being" imaginable, a vision of wholeness may be, in part, what sustains the effort of survivance. Paula Gunn Allen observes that "an impulse toward wholeness . . . characterizes the act of writing; this impulse is the essential nature of thought and is the primary motivat-

ing principle of the imagination."[8] Survivance is both "tribal existential-
ism" and "the end of domination in literature" (McCaffrey and Marshall
55); these phrases suggest that what links Momaday's and Vizenor's posi-
tions, however differently nuanced, is the commitment to individual and
communal integrity.

Another kind of conflict may appear to exist in the tension between
traditional views of language as real, efficacious, and grounded in particu-
lar places and, on the other hand, the vision of language as fictive, as an
unstable invention, that Vizenor's trickster discourse most persistently
foregrounds and others, too, evoke. Robert Davis, for example, in "Sagi-
naw Bay: I Keep Going Back" and his several Raven poems, demonstrates
that language locates us, but, with Raven in control, it's likely to be a
shifting and unstable location. Ortiz says both "It is language that brings
us into being in order to know life," and "Our language is the way we
create the world."[9] Ortiz's statements suggest not conflict, however, but
reciprocity: language creates us; we have the power to imagine, remem-
ber, and tell, and thereby to create language. And Momaday himself may
help reconcile the apparent duality when he says that "we are what we
imagine. Our very existence consists in our imagination of ourselves."
The imagined self must be both fluid and stable, made (up) and real, for
language "is a world of definite reality and of infinite possibility" ("Man
Made of Words" 167, 172).

Vizenor and Momaday both see their language as coming from oral
tradition, and a reader of "The Man Made of Words" or Vizenor's stories
can easily recognize that each is so grounded. As we juxtapose their ways
of writing from this inheritance and their comments on their projects, the
more conservative tenor of Momaday's endeavor and the more explor-
atory nature of Vizenor's are both illuminated. There is, we might say, no
"almost" in "The Man Made of Words," as there is no certain closure in
"Almost Browne."

The arrowmaker and the trickster, different as they are, stand on the
common ground from which Momaday's and Vizenor's conceptions of
language spring. Vizenor affirms that common ground when he alludes
to the arrowmaker, as he does, for example, in the preface to *Wordarrows:
Indians and Whites in the New Fur Trade*: "The traditional tribal arrowmaker
turns his arrows on his teeth with absolute awareness and personal recog-
nition. With the same familial dedication the wordmaker shapes his
words in the oral tradition" (vii). Vizenor quotes Momaday at length,
then explains that his own book's subtitle alludes to "those who act for

others outside the allegorical tipi . . . enemies to the arrowmakers . . . The arrowmakers and wordmakers survive in the word wars with sacred memories" (viii).

Trickster and arrowmaker both have their origins in oral culture; both are "wordmakers"—Momaday imagines that the arrowmaker was the first teller of his own story. Both are vulnerable, and both use language to survive. Where they diverge is in their survival strategies, especially their uses of order or disorder: while the arrowmaker fends off the chaos of invasion and attack, using words to maintain order and acting within the conventions of his language and his craft, Vizenor's tricksters use language to disrupt the order imposed on tribal people by alien institutions. Again, what empowers these figures is their grounding in the oral, and hence in place, culture, history. The belief that, in turn, contemporary Native writing responds to oral traditions, unites Vizenor and Momaday and is implicit in the convictions about language that they share with other American Indian writers.

Foremost is the belief that language is efficacious and creative, inseparable from imagination. So conceived, language expands possibilities; with imagination it enables one to break down walls and "break . . . out of boxes."[10] Ray Young Bear, Linda Hogan, Joy Harjo, and others act on this belief, as they open this world to the realities of dream, myth, and vision, for the efficacy of language implies the power to make the dream, the vision, the mythic moment, happen anew, and thereby to make it accessible to communal knowledge and connection. Carter Revard, in "Discovery of the New World," and Wendy Rose and Chrystos, in the poems discussed in chapter 3, also act on their belief in language's efficacy as they break down expectations and stereotypes, to reveal new possibilities of perception and of political reality. And so do Paula Gunn Allen, Louise Erdrich, and Maurice Kenny, as they revise and reclaim history, in the poems I discuss in chapter 7. In every instance the writers demonstrate the liberating potential of language.

Without language one is powerless; with it one can effect change. Linda Hogan recognizes language as essential to the vision that makes action possible: "I couldn't see what was happening to me or what had happened to my family culturally or politically because I did not have the language." Ortiz affirms that telling the truth is "a political act." And Lance Henson assumes language's reality as action when he says, "Poetry is revolutionary. It must be to survive. It has to establish new boundaries . . . it must . . . move forward."[11]

Henson's, Hogan's, and Ortiz's statements imply a vision of language as resistant or, as Vizenor says, "agonistic" ("Trickster Discourse" 196)—a vision, to repeat, grounded in the sense of language as efficacious and thus linked, too, to Momaday's less struggle-oriented understanding that language makes things happen. Blackfeet/Gros Ventre writer James Welch may be closer to Momaday when he questions the appropriateness of writers' engaging in "militant" activism,[12] and in his "Blackfeet, Blood and Piegan Hunters," language's power for survival has been all but lost. If Welch's speaker recognizes that "children need a myth that tells them be alive," his hunters have been persuaded by their own sadness that such a myth must now tell them to "forget the hair that made you Blood" (36). But Welch's renegade, in "The Renegade Wants Words" (41), refuses to forget; defiant, he only grieves that no one has acknowledged his history or even explained his failure.[13] Hanged under a "sky so blue / the eagles spoke in foreign tongues," he heard only his crimes enumerated; "no one spoke of our good side." Expecting "no mercy," he still wants "a word—the way we rode / naked across these burning hills." Dead, the renegade still resists, and in his resistance claims language, to reclaim himself.

Demanding words, Welch's renegade implicitly recognizes language's power to create and locate us and our own capacity for imagining and locating ourselves through language. As Vizenor says, "we imagine ourselves, we create ourselves, we touch ourselves into being with words" (Coltelli 158). Language's power so to locate us lies in its connection to place, culture, community, and family. Bound as it is to the life-giving world, language so binds us, even as it may free us. Harold Littlebird understands this when he talks about the people of Paguate, his mother's pueblo, a site of open-pit uranium mining: "A lot of them don't really understand ["what that uranium is about"], but they hold on. They hold on through the language" (Bruchac, *Survival* 160). Native writers "hold on" as they revise or defy the meanings of "Indian," and as they recreate and reclaim connections to nature, history, and community—as, for example, Jim Barnes, Robert Davis, Simon Ortiz, and others do when they address issues of place and the meanings of home, of dislocation and return, of transience.

Traditionally, connection to family and community is inseparable from connection to place and culture. Contemporary poets use language to reweave those links. Simon Ortiz does this in his story poems, as does Carter Revard, in "Wazhazhe Grandmother." So does Cherokee Gladys

Cardiff, in "Where Fire Burns," which recalls Vizenor's boy and grand-
mother pinching words:

> it is like gathering nuts
> . . . .
> cracking the vowels and consonants
> of a language I need to know,
> trying to get the taste of them.
> Because of our son
> . . . for our daughter . . .
> . . . .
> I gather these names and places
> . . . .
> words that say
> *tsita'ga,* "I am standing,"
> *da nita'ga,* "They are standing
> together as one."
>   (Green 61–63)

As Warm Springs/Wasco/Navajo writer Elizabeth Woody says, "A song in
one throat draws up the drums. / The hand moves. With one heart, we
move. / The song is in each place, seen and unseen" (*Seven Hands Seven
Hearts* 48). And Anna Lee Walters, recalling her Otoe/Missouria grand-
mother, affirms the power of language for connection and continuance: "It
was through her words that she lived as she did, touching the other dimen-
sions of the universe in a verbal and mystical way" (26).

In his poems about Raven, the Tlingit trickster-transformer/creator,
Robert Davis examines the implications of language's power to create and
locate us, by drawing attention to the complex meanings of Raven's prom-
ising and disturbing power. A consummate maker and manipulator of
language, a dazzling "smooth talker" (14), Raven plays a vital role in the
creation of place, identity, and meaning. This role is especially evident in
"Saginaw Bay: I Keep Going Back," which I discuss in chapter 4. Davis's
six poems dedicated to Raven, four at his book's beginning and two at the
end, reveal Raven's (and Davis's) affinity for the multiplicity so cultivated
by Vizenor. In these poems we can see as well language's resistance to
complete control. Thus we see that language voiced or influenced by
Raven may be playful but can also be perilous, a power to engage watch-
fully, cautiously. In Davis's world we are always chastened by the knowl-

edge that Raven is mercurial, that his play is necessary but not always fun for those with whom he plays. Raven's power can be disconcerting as well as liberating. Language frees, but to what purpose or condition? Sometimes to discomfort or disorientation—which may be construed as re-creative disruption but is nonetheless painful. Davis shows this more jarringly than Vizenor does, perhaps because he's not so inclined to emphasize either the obviously comic or satiric or the "compassionate" qualities of the trickster.[14]

The perplexing power of this "ravaging mentor" 's language ("Raven Arrives" 3) is the central fact of the first poems Davis devotes to Raven. In "Raven Tells Stories," the speaker pleads, "Raven, gather us to that dark breast, / . . . Answer / us our terror of this place we pretend to belong . . . lull us with lies," so that when

> your mouth opens to tell this,
> we will not notice
> your tongue black,
> your mouth full of shadow.
> (1)

The human imagination is directly, creatively engaged with Raven in "Raven Laughs": "We imagine your graceful glide / braving the way before us." Raven brings the people and the world to life and light: "Our trusted benefactor you name us your People, / but turn our backs for a second / you're off," and they are left listening "for that close betraying cackle" (2). These poems draw attention to language as reassuring but also as deceptive and disturbing, thus as inviting interpretation; Raven's meanings are not absolutely fixed.

In "Raven Moves" Davis makes explicit the poet's dependence on Raven, the language maker, and on the cultural history to which Raven is central. It is a difficult and empowering knowledge:

> If I make words, they are Raven's echo.
> If I move, it is in that rhythm, Raven's heart
> . . . .
> In the back of my mind
> long-ago night ritual
> men crouched in a circle
> drumming the earth.
> (4)

"Raven Is Two-Faced," at the end of *Soulcatcher,* again draws attention to language's doubleness, to the necessity but also the limits of interpretation and to the poet's participation in this fabric of meaning and implication. Raven has "made certain everything / about him has two sides," and

> There's no way out;
> you can turn this poem
> inside out
> trying to interpret
> its other meaning.
>   (50)

This poem seems to embody an important aspect of language under the influence of Raven and thus to draw attention to the doubleness (at least) potential in all language.

In "Raven Dances," his book's final poem, Davis evokes the almost heartstopping power of Raven and implicitly of language, as he recreates one of the rituals recalled in "Raven Moves." The transformative power of ceremony is manifest as the mythic and the mundane ("a dead, lingering day, / edgy flock of ravens") merge, creating both awe and the necessity of creative understanding, or interpretation. "Ravens nod" as a "child dances and screams"; "his back [is] feathered, / black lines run down his cheeks." And as "he hops and glances about," ravenlike, "Ravens flash in his eyes, / beat him to the ground." Through the dance, and identification with the mythically empowered regalia, the boy has become Raven, entered into Raven power. There is "a crunch / of shattered skull / and . . . black shadows escape, / leav[ing] you with . . . a small human dance rattle."[15] The poem ends by drawing attention to the ceremony's powerful impact on the poet, who must now, we may infer, engage this power in an effort of interpretation: "You withdraw and find / your head too is full / with raven wings beating" (55).

As the end of "Raven Dances" stunningly reminds us, living language depends upon a responsive audience. And as Vizenor's stories and Momaday's colloquy with Ko-sahn also demonstrate, contemporary Indian writers, like their forebears in oral tradition, see the teller/poet and audience/reader as jointly engaged in the creative process. Mohawk poet Maurice Kenny speaks from such an understanding when he voices his wish to "draw . . . a reader's very rich imagination into my imagination."

And Klallam writer Duane Niatum elaborates: "I've tried to create these stories in a way that the reader has a lot of space to work . . . I think creating art is reciprocal. It requires almost as much energy from the reader" (Bruchac, *Survival* 148, 200).[16]

Their characterizations of language as efficacious and liberating, grounded in place, culture and politics, and dependent upon a responsive audience imply important affinities not only between these writers' practices and oral tradition but also between traditional understandings of language and Bakhtin's theory. Such affinities suggest, as do Blaeser's observations about the dialogic quality of oral tradition, and the importance of dialogism in sustaining community, that we might recognize dialogism, in some respects, as an indigenous concept. Similarly, indigenous theory's emphasis on language's grounding in specific contexts offers a bridge to border theory.

Carter Revard's "How the Songs Came Down" illustrates many of the convictions about language shared by his contemporaries. Language calls attention to itself in this long poem—in Revard's complex syntax and use of spacing, for example, and in the joyous wealth and variety of the poem's vocabulary and allusions. It begins and ends in intimacy, which anchors language in the social and the personal, even while it enacts language's freely ranging power. In the end we know language as created and creative, a source of identity and continuity:

> That lullaby our Ponca aunt would sing us that we always
>   asked for . . .
> . . . .
> . . . she would sing us
>   over and over, but she never told us there on
>   the cool dark porch under the full moon
>   what the Ponca words were saying; it was a song
>   her blind great-aunt had made up after
>   they had been forced down from Nebraska onto
>   the Oklahoma reservation and she made it
>   one night to sing her brothers when the whisky
>   was almost drowning them, its words
>   said
>   Why are you afraid,
>   no one can go around death!
> She tells her children lately now, Aunt Jewell, some of

> those real old things,
>   now that the time has come
> to pass them on, and they are ready
>   to make new places for what she
>   would sing into
>   the moonlit darkness like
>   a bronze and lively bird.
>
> (52)

Language functions as a creative, connective, flexible power that both shelters and depends upon a participant audience, the children who "are ready," now, "to make new places for what she / would sing."

With his reference to "Ponca words" Revard reminds us of a crucial fact about his and the other poets' language: they all write in English; they all write in (response to) borderland conditions. As Hogan says, "this poem is written in the language / the presidents speak. / That is another reason to learn a new tongue" (*Seeing* 8). In *The People Named the Chippewa* Vizenor identifies the consequences and some of the methods of the "harsh privileging of English over tribal languages."[17]

> When a tribal person is expected to understand several thousand years of tribal histories in the language of dominant societies, his identities are a dangerous burden. Two generations ago the Anishinaabeg, and other tribal cultures, were forbidden to speak their language and practice their religion. Now, in ethnographic monographs, tribal people are summoned to be proud of their invented Indian and Chippewa heritage as it appears in narrative histories.

Vizenor's words recall Davis's "At the Door of the Native Studies Director": English displaces Tlingit; years later Tlingit becomes an artifact and a commodity in the English-controlled academy. Vizenor continues, "The cultural and political histories of the Anishinaabeg were written in a colonial language by those who invented the Indian, renamed the tribes, allotted the land, divided ancestries by geometric degrees of blood, and categorized identities on federal reservations" (19). In the history that Vizenor and Davis recount, and Hogan and Revard allude to, we can recognize the imposition of what Louis Owens would call territorial control; however, this history is also an incitement to resistant dialogism.

Chrystos defines the high stakes in the contest of languages: "*When*

they take our languages"—replacing them with "white words prison bars . . .
little words . . . nosy & noisy"—*"they take our lives . . . afterawhile / I just
stopped talking"* (*Dream On* 73, 129). In "The State's Claim" Ortiz exposes
the dominant culture's institutional power to oppress through dishonest
distortions of English—specifically, here, by using the term *right of way* to
deny the Acoma people's right to their lands. Ortiz directly confronts the
silence imposed by such distortions and their effects: "You don't want
that silence to grow . . . because that growth . . . stunts you . . . And so
you tell stories" (*Woven Stone* 260). In the face of the linguistic-political
impositions of European-American culture, silence is dangerous and the
liberating power of language doubly necessary.[18] The idea of language as
resistant and liberating unites traditional understandings of language's
efficacy with dialogism and Bakhtin's beliefs about the social/political
power of language. It is because language is powerful that it is infused
with competing intentions.

Recognizing this power, and the necessity of contesting the domi-
nant culture's intentions, Native American poets devise ways to speak
their people's history and survival, even in English, as Elizabeth Woody
suggests in the title of a single poem: "The English in the Daughter of a
Wasco/Sahaptin Woman, Spoken in the Absence of Her Mother's True
Language" (*Luminaries* 107). Davis, too, while he mourns loss—"The old
ones tell a better story in Tlingit. / But I forget so much"—struggles to
connect and to speak: "I know my own name . . . Listen, I'm trying to say
something . . . always our stories have stayed alive in retelling" (20–21).
The insistent "Listen" reminds us of the need for a responsive audience, a
necessity that must contribute to the poets' careful workings out of ways
to speak and write Native truths in English. Concern about audience, in
fact, seems to explain Momaday's lack of interest in learning Kiowa: "I
couldn't write better than I do if I spoke Kiowa," he says, and "there is no
point in trying to write in Kiowa, because I wouldn't be understood"
(Woodard 115). Lance Henson is fluent in his Cheyenne language and
sometimes integrates it into his poetry, thereby implicitly affirming its
vitality and its contestatory power. When Cheyenne is translated into
English, he says, "the English pales in comparison to the Cheyenne." Yet
he shows how complex the contest of languages can be, as he continues:
"English is a *good* language, just as to a warrior the soldiers who fought
the Cheyenne were *good* soldiers. English is an enemy, but it's the way we
communicate. That conflict is something I haven't resolved yet. I don't
know if I can" (Bruchac, *Survival* 112–13). Mohawk poet Karoniaktatie

plays with English as a direct response to its displacement of his tribal language: "English is meant to be fooled around with . . . I fooled around with the language because English and America fooled around with me and my life" (Bruchac, *Survival* 140). Karoniaktatie's "fooling around" reminds us of Vizenor's use of trickster discourse to disrupt the expected structures and meanings of a language that has made itself known to Native peoples primarily as an engine of colonization.

An elder in a story by Anna Lee Walters defies linguistic colonization when he voices his faith in continuity: " 'Now I sit here, sixty years later, telling you exactly the same thing my old folks told me . . . The only thing that's different is I'm talking in a foreign language, one forced on us, but nevertheless, I'm still talking Indian. It's ironical' " (41). One might perhaps add, "it's dialogical." Simon Ortiz has expressed misgivings about translating from Acoma, the language "that has sustained me through my years of writing," to English, yet he too affirms the certainty voiced by Walters's character, when he reminds us of Native people's history of appropriating European languages to their own purposes. Ortiz believes that Indian people's survival depends in large part on "the consciousness we have of ourselves," which includes "the language we use . . . not necessarily only native languages but the consciousness of our true selves at the core of whatever language we use, including English."[19] Such a statement implicitly acknowledges the creative, liberating, dialogic power available in language. Wendy Rose reminds us of the communal possibilities of such power when she observes that, having been "forced . . . to learn English . . . for the first time in history, Native peoples are united by language."[20]

Rose, Chrystos, and others, in the poems discussed in chapter 3, draw our attention to the complex implications of knowing language as relational, communal, creative, and liberating. They suggest some of the difficult negotiations that can be involved in bringing into life-sustaining action "the consciousness of our true selves," as they explore the process of connecting with, but also sometimes challenging, diverse audiences and communities: how, and with whom, might they be united? how, and to whom, might they be empowered to speak?

CHAPTER 3

Who Speaks, Who Listens?
Questions of Community
and Audience

Many contemporary Native poets find themselves compelled to address questions about the nature of community and audience and the writer's relationships to both. Such questions may involve issues of accessibility versus authenticity,[1] of what may ethically be shared with non-Indian or nontribal audiences, of the writer's obligations to Native communities and relation to non-Indian culture. Karl Kroeber illuminates the challenge implicit in concepts of community and audience for contemporary poets when he observes that the status of traditional Indian poems as "sociocultural synecdoche[s]" implies both the centrality of performance and the identity of "the total group, tribe, or nation as the appropriate 'audience' for each individual poet-singer" (104–6).[2] Borderland history and ongoing experience raise the question of how contemporaries can write in response to traditions grounded in a sense of wholeness and connectedness which for many has been eroded. How do cultural and political change impinge upon conceptions of community and audience that are central both to the oral tradition and to the continuity of tribal or pan-Indian identity and integrity? How can contemporaries sustain, recover, or revise empowering relationships to community and audience? For self-defined political poets Chrystos and Wendy Rose, such questions are especially compelling, given their marginalized positions vis-à-vis community and audience and their commitments to multiply-nuanced change. The poets whose work I will discuss at the end of this chapter—Gail Tremblay, Lance Henson, and Ray Young Bear—address similar issues from diverse positions and perspectives. For all, questions about community and audience are fundamentally, too, questions of survival, and in this conviction all manifest the commitment to relationship central to diverse American Indian cultures and more generally identified by Bonnie TuSmith as a value that consistently distinguishes American ethnic writers.[3]

My purpose is to make it as clear & as inescapable as possible,
what the actual, material conditions of our lives are.
—Chrystos, preface to *Not Vanishing*

the bottom line is contributing to our communities and adding
to the total strength that makes for survival
—Wendy Rose, interview with Carol Hunter

Chrystos and Wendy Rose negotiate relationships with their audiences
that both reflect traditional Native assumptions about the roles of audi-
ence and community, and diverge from those assumptions. Traditional
oral cultures rely upon the common ground shared by poet-performer
and audience—"a sacred vision of the universe" that "helps to shape the
community's social organization" (Zolbrod 2), "a dynamism, at once both
guardian of the values of speech and creator of the forms needed to
maintain social cohesion" (Zumthor 26). Such commonalties allow the
traditional singer or storyteller to expect an audience's active engage-
ment.[4] While both Chrystos and Rose aspire to similar relationships with
their Indian (and sometimes other) audiences, their political purposes
and the heterogeneity of the reading audience mean that they often ad-
dress readers or listeners with whom they have little in common, yet
whom they also aim to move.

     Louis Owens builds on Bakhtin's observations about the vexed rela-
tionship between " 'a poet . . . cut off from the social unity of his group' "
and the reading public, to elaborate on "the predicament of the contempo-
rary Native American writer," in relation to the audience:

> The effect is a richly hybridized dialogue aimed at those few with
> privileged knowledge—the traditionally educated Indian reader—as
> well as those with claims to a privileged discourse—the Eurocentric
> reader. One effect of this hybridization is subversive: the American
> Indian writer places the Eurocentric reader on the outside, as
> "other," while the Indian reader . . . is granted . . . a privileged posi-
> tion. On the one hand, by consciously identifying her- or himself as
> "Indian," the writer seeks to establish a basis for authoritative, or
> externally persuasive discourse; on the other hand, the writer must
> make that discourse internally persuasive for the non-Indian reader
> unaccustomed to peripherality. At the same time the writer is appro-
> priating an essentially "other" language and thus entering into dia-

logue with the language itself. The result of this exquisite balancing act is a matrix of incredible heteroglossia and linguistic torsions and an intensely political situation. (*Other Destinies* 14–15)[5]

The meanings of collaborative relationship with the audience thus become problematic for Rose, Chrystos, and other Native writers because of the multiple and divergent audiences they address, the complex relationships among those audiences or between the poets and some of their readers, and the inevitable linguistic complexities. Such complications result from and reflect borderland experience: how does the Native address the non-Indian, the mixed-blood address the traditional community, the feminist woman of color speak to white feminists, the oppressed speak to the oppressor, the "object" of study speak to the academic? Powerful and creative responses to such questions may well depend upon the writers' commitment to language's connecting, contesting, and liberatory potential.

Rose (whose background includes Hopi, Miwok, and Euro-American ancestors) and Chrystos (Menominee and Euro-American) respond to and create fluid, sometimes ambivalent relationships with audience and community. For both, these relationships derive from complex dynamics of ancestry and affinity, and contribute energy, power, and tension to their poetry. Both live on multiply defined borders, in relation to Native cultures and communities, and to the dominant culture. Those borders aggravate oppositions (Native vs. white, indigenous peoples vs. anthropologists), yet they can highlight sometimes overlapping, if contested, spaces and identities (lesbian and Indian, Indian and anthropologist). Both come from mixed backgrounds, and urban experience. Distanced from the languages of their tribal ancestors, both are intensely aware of using a language that was imposed fairly recently on those ancestors, yet is now their own "native tongue." Each identifies herself in terms of pan-Indian affiliation. Chrystos is a lesbian, and Rose often defines herself in relation to the academic world; both affiliations, as reflected in their writings, are experienced as doubly marginalizing. With their access to traditional communities rendered problematic by geography, mixed parentage, and other factors, these poets must simultaneously create and negotiate relationships with community and audience that will accommodate their needs for connection (or distance) and empower them to change the world.[6] Borderland politics, intense border consciousness, and multiple marginalizations inflect their efforts to locate themselves in relation to communities and audiences, and in turn concerns with community and audience foreground heteroglossia and dialogism in their poetry.[7]

Each of these poets identifies herself variously within her work, and expands the meanings of her multiple identities by implicitly or explicitly speaking for similarly situated others. Both voice their identities as Indians in varied ways—for example, in terms of collective experience, in connection with sorrow and anger, or in celebration. For Rose the fact of mixed blood is unavoidably bound up with her Indian, particularly her Hopi ancestry. Concerns about mixed origins seem less important in Chrystos's poetic self-identifications; rather, she names herself a woman of color, lesbian, political activist. Such self-identifications, often overlapping, hardly represent the full range of either poet's self-conceptions; they are the facets of claimed identity most noticeable in poems that foreground issues of community and audience. What these multiple, interwoven aspects of identity, all together, most clearly convey is the fluid dynamics of identity, and hence of relation to audience, community, and language, that Rose and Chrystos both create.

Their multiple self-identifications might be construed as instances of poststructuralist, postmodernist representations of the nonunitary self, but I would argue that they more surely reflect the complex border consciousness that Rose and Chrystos share, as a given of contemporary Native American experience.[8] Likewise, the realities of life in contested borderland spaces, or in Owens's frontier or territory, almost inevitably imply that these self-identifications will be associated with conflict. Further, their multiple self-conceptions sharpen the poets' awareness that their audiences are likewise multiple: from their shifting locations, they recognize and address different audiences, as they seek to affect, and sometimes to join, diverse communities. Among the dilemmas created by their awareness of the marginalizing effects of borderland experience are questions about how and to whom one may speak and what may be said.

Both Rose and Chrystos respond directly to the potential for conflict inherent in borderland conditions. Rose's poems often expose conflicts between components of her mixed identity, and between her academic and Indian affiliations. Chrystos, on the other hand, is more likely to emphasize the possibilities for conflict between her various identities and affinities and the communities with which she would ally herself (e.g., Native and lesbian, white feminists and women of color). Again, borderland conditions exacerbate, and border consciousness clarifies, such conflicts. Their complex self-conceptions and multiple conceptions of audience and community assure that heteroglossia will surface audibly and the dialogic will become a defining characteristic in the poetic language of both Chrystos and Rose. These multiplicities also assure that the conflict of competing intentions (Bakhtin, "Discourse in the Novel" 294), the "serious contest of codes" (Saldívar 259) will be foregrounded—as both consequence and means of the struggle to establish collectivity with their various audiences and communities.

Chrystos and Rose don't necessarily assume commonality with those with whom they would claim community or those whom they address; rather, they emphasize the need to create commonality through struggle, sometimes even with audiences "like them" (e.g., women, Indians). When they indicate a primary audience, it is often an audience of others, identified in opposition to the poet or speaker: "you" may be racist white feminists, superficially sympathetic non-Indians, academics engaged in various kinds of appropriation—and the poem's effort may be to shake or shame or persuade "you" into new recognitions and behaviors. On the other hand, both poets directly address audiences less clearly "other": Native resisters, elders, or ancestors, for example. Each also addresses the communities with which she would ally herself, from which she seeks nurture and recognition, in order to make common cause. (I am focusing on audience as conceived in their overtly political poems; audience is conceived quite differently, for example, in Chrystos's love poetry.)

For many Native American writers, issues of audience and community are vexed by the question of "What is ethical to tell?"[9] Can tradition be offered as a means to commonality with an eclectic audience? These writers might, for example, honor tradition by acknowledging in their writing the stories that are their sources, and in so doing continue the oral tradition that is the ground of Indian cultural survival. On the other hand, cognizant of the opportunities for misunderstanding, misrepresentation, and appropriation offered by every translation and sharing of tradition, they might honor tradition by protecting the old stories and alluding to sacred or otherwise culturally vital materials cryptically, indirectly, partially, or not at all. Out of such tensions, many Native poets have created careful balances between protective reticence and imaginative re-vision.[10]

Their somewhat ambiguous relationships to Native communities complicate these issues for both Rose and Chrystos. Chrystos is adamantly silent about traditional stories and spirituality; as she says in the prefatory statement to *Not Vanishing,* "Our rituals, stories & religious practices have been stolen and abused, as has our land. I don't publish work which would encourage this—so you will find no creation myths here." On the other hand, Rose, who often alludes cryptically or indirectly to traditional Hopi lore, sometimes adapting such material as a way of claiming her place, responds to questions about the accessibility of Indian poetry to non-Native readers by referring to the context of American society at large: "I think that a person does need to stretch the imagination a little bit, perhaps, or to learn something about Native American cultures or Native American thought systems or religion, or philosophy. Just a little bit . . . This is a plural society and all of us have to work at it a little bit to get the full flavor of the society" (Bruchac, *Survival* 263). Protective of tradition, Chrystos still resists the self-censorship that would keep her silent about contemporary conflicts within her communities. As she confronts these issues, she suggests the problematical relationship to community that she shares with Rose. "What is ethical to tell? This is especially complex when one is part of oppressed groups, who stand to have any negative information used against them" ("Askenet" 241). She continues,

> I've been relatively silent about a number of issues . . . because I've feared alienating Native People and/or Lesbians. These issues . . . the full implications of being a person not really welcome in either group . . . What do these silences mean? How can I break out of them respectfully? . . . In opening these areas to scrutiny, am I violating my culture? Is that culture the actual tradition or merely a mirror of colonization? ("Askenet" 242)[11]

Rose writes from the outsider's need to redefine community in ways that will enable her to heal the isolation and hostility engendered by her marginalizations. She speaks of feeling "alien" among whites yet knows that she "wouldn't really fit easily into Hopi society" and that she is also cut off from her mother's Miwok people: "When I think of my mother's people, I think of confusion, tragedy, death, fragmentation, bones, and things that are gone forever." Thus, while she urges writers "to look within our own communities" and to "be more responsive to our own people," she is also, like Chrystos, committed to "acknowledging and identifying with . . . the struggle of indigenous people the world over." Coming from Rose, what might seem a fairly simple statement about "roots" becomes, if not problematical, at least multiply suggestive: "The vehicle for finding my Hopi and my Miwok roots has been existing within a community in which these things are important and are known, being part of contemporary Indian life."[12] This statement, I believe, contains simultaneously regret for the loss of community, resolve to survive that loss, and affirmation of the community that is now being created and sustained by contemporary Indian people, those who are and those who aren't formally tribally affiliated.

For both poets, then, relationships with Native communities are complex, potentially problematical, marked by tensions that may be either productive or debilitating. Such multivalenced realities produce parallel complications vis-à-vis their audiences, who, unavoidably, are implicated in questions of community: both poets, after all, speak to and about those with whom they would ally themselves; both, too, address others who are variously defined but who almost always include white European-Americans, with a whole history of responses to indigenous cultures and communities. For Chrystos and Rose the audience conceivably encompasses both those with whom the poet would affiliate herself most deeply and those against whom she feels compelled to protect her chosen or inherited communities.

When they address audiences at whom they are angry, their poems may raise questions about anger's uses and effects—especially, perhaps, if we readers recognize ourselves among the recipients of the anger. Chrystos often voices single-minded outrage; Rose, too, sometimes opts for this approach.[13] As Oneida poet Roberta Hill Whiteman says, "we need to be purified by fury" (66); acknowledging and articulating anger is a step toward solidarity and survival. But poets and critics of many origins remind us that voicing anger can only be a step, if the aim is to empower the dispossessed and change the world. Thus whoever we are, we may look to politically engaged writers to use their anger creatively, to show us how to move beyond the static knowledge either of guilt or of oppression. Both Rose and Chrystos offer many lessons.

Rose demonstrates how powerful anger can orient the poem toward revision and redefinition, in works like "I expected my skin and my blood to ripen" (*Lost Copper* 14–15), "Three Thousand Dollar Death Song" (*Lost Copper* 26–27), and "Notes on a Conspiracy" (*Going to War with All My Relations* 11–13). Each begins with an epigraph from the written records of the long assault on Native peoples; in the body of each poem a Native-identified voice speaks of the physical and emotional realities denied by

the epigraphs, which come from the world of anthropological collecting—
auction catalogs and museum invoices. Rose's anger hits home as each
poem shocks us into recognizing that its two voices refer to the same events
or facts, which are veiled and marginalized by the objectifying prose of the
epigraph but which the body of the poem brings to the center of attention:
rape, massacre, robbery, grief. Any reader who has, in museums or galler-
ies, casually or studiously observed Native "artifacts" must be drawn into
complicity by the juxtaposition of epigraph and poem: we have on some
level benefited from some of the practices implied, for our aesthetics, or
"appreciation," have been "enriched" by the collecting and cataloging of
the objects on which we gaze. But each poem's body forces a recognition
of the bodies and lives of Native peoples, and the horrors that made some
of these artifacts "available" to collectors.

Among the effects of such poems is an all-pervasive dialogism and
dialogue. The contrasting discourses of epigraph and poem embody the
competing intentions and meanings of heteroglossia, and open the possi-
bility of dialogue, as the reader responds. Heteroglossia may thus func-
tion in part not only to mark conflict but also to instigate communication
and change, by involving readers in ways that recall, too, traditional
understandings of language's dependency on a responsive audience.
Thus the poems succeed both in condemning reprehensible actions and
attitudes and engaging perhaps historically implicated readers in change.
Significantly, they facilitate engagement through reflection and question-
ing that encompass both mourning the dead and damaged, and strug-
gling to re-imagine and reclaim Indian history and lives. For example, in
"Notes on a Conspiracy" the spirit of the dead, referring to the colonizers,
exclaims, "How little we knew! We should have asked / where is the
dust of your mothers? / What happened to your own land? / Why did
you come so far from your homes?" The questioning continues: "And we.
Where is our strength that was acorn and blue jay . . . When will we
dance—you remember the one— / where we bring up the sun with a
shout?" The poem foregrounds dialogism by pointing out how language
was and is used as a tool of oppression—"They blame us for their guilt. /
They say we are now a privileged few"—but dialogism is complicated by
the poem's questions, which, recalling the title, invite us to consider
whether the Natives themselves, in some terrible way, might have been
implicated in the "conspiracy," or in its continuing effects. Even so, and
without softening the sharp knowledge of death and loss, the poem's
shifts among past, present, and future imply the possibility of a revital-

ized Indian present and future—this spirit of the dead is not dead, after all: it is speaking.

Poems like "Notes on a Conspiracy" establish part of the context of struggle that is central to much contemporary Native poetry, and is a major source of Rose's and Chrystos's concerns with audience and community. The experiences of invasion, destruction, and oppression that such poems directly recall, underlie the struggles for relationship, recognition, and authority and the questions of how and to whom to speak.

These questions and struggles are powerfully present in a poem by Chrystos that reflects the concerns of her essay "Askenet" as it confronts the difficulties of community, and illuminates the conflicts potential within identity politics, when identities collide.

"YA DON WANNA EAT PUSSY"

that Chippewa said to that gay white man who never has
Ya don wanna eat pussy after eatin hot peppers   he laughed
I stared   in the white sink memorizing rust stains
He nodded in the general direction of the windows behind us
    Two Native women chopping onions & pickles
    to make tuna fish sandwiches
    for these six men helping to move
                (*Not Vanishing* 36)

Repetition of the first (and title) line draws attention to the offensive language; the succeeding lines emphasize its divisive power:

He said   *Ya didn hear that did ya*   Good
She answered   *I chose to ignore it*
I muttered   *So did I*
Ya don wanna take offense at an Indian man's joke
    no matter how crude
in front of a white man
Close to my tribe   he probably guessed we're lesbians
said that   to see what we'd do
which was to keep on doin what we had been doin

The situation effectively silences the women. Yet the poem allows Chrystos, by mimicking the Chippewa's speech, to draw attention to the dialogic doubleness of her own language, and thus to re-empower herself as an offended woman. On the one hand, her explanation (to the reader) indicates her desire to protect the possibility of community with the Indian man; on the other, she distances herself from him and mocks him, by using his speech only here, and her explanation implies a gesture of connection to a non-Native audience. At the same time, "close to my tribe" raises painful questions: in what sense is he close? Is the speaker herself close to her tribe? Does his closeness give him the power to exclude her, or imply that there should be a bond between them?

> That gay white man stopped talking about how much he loved
> hot peppers
> That Chippewa said   *Not too much for me   Don eat fish*
> probably another joke we ignored   I said
> *The grocery was fresh out of buffalo & deer*

With "probably another joke," Chrystos again draws attention to heteroglossia and the divisions it implies; in the next line's rejoinder, she implies the doubleness of *we ignored*. The poem ends with the gay man's direct entry into the uneasy searching of the multiply oppressed for community, or at least recognition, across the dividing lines:

> Much later that gay white man called that Chippewa a drunk
>   we both stared at a different floor
>   in a different silence   just as sharp
>   & hot

In Wendy Rose's earlier poetry, collected in *Lost Copper,* the desire for connection with Native communities often awakens tensions, as the speaker is marginalized by her mixed origins. Images of fragmentation are common, as are suggestions that language is problematical for one whose connections to community are ambiguous or broken.[14] Thus, "It is I . . . who vanishes, who leans underbalanced / into nothing; it is I . . . without song / who dies and cries the death-time" ("Vanishing Point: Urban Indian," *Lost Copper* 12). And "Builder Kachina: Home-going" (*Lost Copper* 126–27) figures the poet-speaker (or her Hopi father) as "a shred of brown cotton" blown west from the Hopi village of Hotevilla to California. Though it was thirty years ago,

. . . the scars are still fresh
in me. They speak in my flesh,
they rasp and shake in my bones,

. . . .

Must I explain why
the songs are stiff and shy?

She feels unbearably divided between California, which "moves my pen" and "Hotevilla dash[ing] through my blood." In "The Endangered Roots of a Person" (*Lost Copper* 50–51) Rose navigates between fragmentation and the possibility of healing through language and ritual. The poem begins, "I remember lying awake / in a Phoenix motel . . . coming apart accidentally / like an isolated hunk of campfire soot / cornered by time into a cave." "Sometimes," she acknowledges, "Medicine People shake their hands over you," and once "[t]he Hand-trembler said / I belong here. I fit in this world." Yet only a tenuous reassurance is suggested by the final image of the speaker "piecing together the flesh / that was scattered in the mesa wind / at my twisted-twin birth."[15]

"The Well-Intentioned Question" (*Lost Copper* 6–7; *Going to War* 55–56) elaborates on some of the consequences of a mixed and ambiguous inheritance. Asked her "Indian name," the poet responds by drawing attention to the multiple, competing meanings of an apparently simple but in fact heavily dialogized question. Rather than answering in the manner undoubtedly expected, she characterizes her unrevealed and perhaps literally nonexistent "Indian name" in ambiguous terms that subtly draw attention to her vexed relationship to the community, the source of names. Her "Indian name" seems to signal her marginalized status: she is observed by "obsidian-hard women / sighting me with eyes / Coyote gave them;" and the final lines imply a permanent isolation, as her "Indian name listens / for footsteps / stopping short of my door / then leaving forever." In the course of the poem *Indian name* becomes dialogized: the asker's expectations, the traditional implications, and the meanings of both to the speaker all come into complex conflict. Her "Indian name" does not include her in an Indian community; further, the asker of the "well-intentioned question" and the reader, also awaiting the answer, may be implicated—not having received the expected exotic or validating answer, do we leave forever, believing that the speaker is neither "really Indian" nor worthy of further interest?[16]

In some of these poems Rose does move toward imagining re-integration into a sense of Hopi or Indian identity and community. Thus in "Vanishing Point" the urban Indian's urgent repetitions of "It is I" (repetitions that render the statement and identity itself dialogic) culminate as she claims a role that might be protective, heroic, ironic, or all three simultaneously:

> . . . It is I who die
> bearing cracked turquoise & making noise
> so as to protect your fragile immortality
> O Medicine Ones.
>
> (*Lost Copper* 12)

Most reassuring is the final stanza of "Builder Kachina: Home-going," where the Hopi father speaks:

> Carefully
> the way we plant the corn
> in single places, each place
> a hole just one finger around.
> We'll build your roots
> That way . . .
> . . . .
> What we can't find
> we'll build but
> slowly,
> slowly.
>
> (*Lost Copper* 127)

Referring to "Builder Kachina . . . invisible / yet touching me all over / with his sound," Rose at once demonstrates the poem's promise, and exposes the heteroglossia latent even in a word like *Kachina* (of course, simply transliterating this concept into a word pronounceable in English has already implied that potential). Builder Kachina, as she notes (*Lost Copper* 127), represents not a traditional conception of the Hopi spirit people, but her own creative response to a "somewhat flexible" tradition. The tradition, she implies, gives her a means of connecting with the community, through language. Yet the last three lines, "we'll build but /

slowly, / slowly," remind of the need for care and caution, and of the likelihood that disruptions and uncertainties will recur.

Chrystos might be thought of as trying to circumvent or break through tensions like those Rose represents, when she claims community by simply asserting that it exists. Thus "I Walk in the History of My People" (*Not Vanishing* 7) begins,

> There are women locked in my joints
> for refusing to speak to the police
> My red blood full of those
> arrested   in flight   shot

Community is founded on a history of pain, realized by the speaker in her own body's ills and in her memory, and confirmed by difference: "In my marrow are hungry faces / who live on land the whites don't want." Similarly, in "Going Through" (*Dream On* 90–91) Chrystos claims kinship with those who are gone:

> These are the hills where bear hunted sweet berries
> We women rubbed our hair with their grease
> This was a song requiring many harmonies
> a sky blue as a drum   flute sweet as spring.

Again, community implies pain, founded as it now is in loss felt not only by the human speaker, but also by bereaved nature. Native traditions have the capacity for introducing into heteroglossia and dialogism an element probably unforeseen by Bakhtin, the speaking voices of nature: the voices of trees, a river, and wild roses are layered into the lament that is this poem's most effective claim of community: "River turns in her sleep / *Where are my sweet salmon?*"

That community, continuity, and resistance demand complex effort is the burden of "I Like to Think" (*Dream On* 68), in which Chrystos engages her audiences on several levels:

"I LIKE TO THINK"

> of the Black miners in south africa
> continually
> I like to remember that they are always

Black

. . . .

I need to remember their wages
aligned with the price of diamond & gold jewelry
& so do you
I need to know
they plunder what is their own land
I like to think about the days they spend in total darkness
. . . .
I like to remember the misery of death
under the gleam of necklaces   rings   cars   knives   spoons
I like to think how much we have in common
. . . .
I like to remember all the white owners
of Navajo rugs   Zuni jewelry   Lakota shirts   Pueblo pottery
. . . .
& the price of those things when whites sell them
to each other after buying them from us for dimes
or taking them

The poem's repetitions become a chant, with transformative power. The repeated "I like to think" seems to insist on the dialogic nature of the sentence and of language, without doing us the favor of translating—*we* need to think. Similarly, Chrystos complicates the contrast between solidarity and exploitation by her use of spacing:

I need to remember that the Native design towels
I want to buy at Macy's   fill a white man's pocket

The temptation to complicity is not only verbally acknowledged but is also visually represented, conveying a brief shock. This recognition of possible betrayal justifies the simplicity of the immediately following final lines, and makes the ending complex:

I like to think of our relationship
boiled to a simple phrase
They take   We give
They take more

While the poem ends by sharply distinguishing "us" from "them," it goes beyond articulating anger in part, I think, because its address to the audience is inclusive. If in the end it speaks most directly to an Indian audience, exhorting them to recognize the grounds of solidarity, and the dividing lines, as those of race and exploitation for profit, its first direct address to the reader—"and so do you"—does not exclude any from the "you" who "need to remember." While different readers' relationships to the poem change, as the meanings of *we* and *they* shift and separate, the non-Native and white readers have still been given the work of remembering. We may not be invited into the community of color-based oppression and resistance the poem seeks to build, but we are all, I think, invited to consider how we wish to align ourselves in relation to that community—will we listen, remember, learn how to support, exploit?

If, by the end of "I Like to Think," Chrystos intimates the possibilities of creating common cause within and across communities of color, even the possibility that white readers might be engaged in solidarity, Indians' ongoing marginalization by the dominant culture remains a pressing reality for both poets. Rose brings consciousness of such marginalization into sharp relief in early poems that draw on her experience as an anthropology student. Issues of community, audience, and language remain problematical in the university, which arouses both anger and ambivalence as the aspiring student recognizes herself as the exploited object of others' scholarly gazes. In "Anthropology Convention" (*Lost Copper* 22) the speaker identifies with the anthropologists' objects of study:

> From the day we are born
> there are eyes all around
> watching for exotic pots of words
> spilled from our coral and rawhide tongues.
>
> O we are
> the Natives.

Other poems indicate the consequences, for a Native student, of aspiring to enter the academic world. "Matriculation" (*Lost Copper* 32–33) shows her compelled to test and disrupt the language and stories she hears:

They really got mad
when I picked up the books
and like laundry began
to shake them clean.

She likens her instructors' lectures to earlier colonizing adventures:

The rattles and groans
of the speeches you give
might in another time have been
the wood and rope of tallships
. . . .
You discover me
again and again.

Yet she soon realizes, "You don't / see me." Indeed, she is hardly there
to be seen, for the university she has entered is an example of Owens's
"territory": "that space which is mapped fully imagined as a place of
containment, invented to control and subdue the wild imaginations of
imagined native peoples" (" 'The Song Is Very Short' " 59). That she will
not succumb but will, rather, turn the university's borderland territory
into a frontier, is promised as she shakes the books out, and confirmed
most powerfully in some of the university poems from *Going to War*.
Now she becomes "a red ghost" ("Handprints," *Lost Copper* 36–37), search-
ing in the university for "a woman / built from earthen blocks / who is
not / specimen" or "evidence / for 'affirmative / action' "—searching
for herself.

Not surprisingly, becoming an "Academic Squaw" (*Lost Copper* 30),
like being of mixed origins, subjects her to splitting and breaking:

Like bone in outer space
this brain leans to a fierce break;
with crooked muscles and names mis-said
we ethno-data heroically bend
further and further, becoming born
from someone else's belly.

Rose notes that the word *squaw* is, "in modern usage, a derogatory term"
(*Lost Copper* 30); using it ironically, she underlines her awareness of the

high stakes involved in dialogism's competing intentions—a recognition that comes painfully to the "red ghost" and is implicit in all of her confrontations with the academy's stories of Native lives. One consequence, the silencing of the Natives' own stories, is realized with personal immediacy in "How I came to be a graduate student" (*Lost Copper* 38): "It was when my songs become quiet. / No one was threatened." The Indian who would enter the academy, these poems tell us, becomes vulnerable to, and implicated in, tensions and ambivalences analogous to those that confront the mixed-blood person. Both experience discomfort and alienation as internal realities and as externally imposed conditions, as borders drawn by history and politics are reinforced and reflected internally, with devastating effects. In both contexts her identity as an Indian is contested, and she must respond defensively to influences that would undercut her affiliation with living Native communities. Reading Rose's *Lost Copper* university poems together with Chrystos's poems of struggle for a multiracial activist community, throws into clear relief behaviors Chrystos's intended audience might not recognize in themselves, but from which she attempts to shake them.

Chrystos's "I Am Not Your Princess" (*Not Vanishing* 66–67) responds to a non-Native audience romantically eager to know, honor, and help the Indians—perhaps the same questioner who asked Rose the "well-intended question." Insisting that we acknowledge her individual identity and integrity, Chrystos at once distances herself from generalizations and affirms solidarity with Indian communities by insisting that she cannot speak for them, only for herself. She begins by drawing attention, uncharacteristically, to her own mixed origins: "Sandpaper between two cultures which tear / one another apart I'm not / a means by which you can reach spiritual understanding." She makes clear that it is not mixed origins as such, but history, culture, and the limits of individual experience that make her unable—and unwilling—to fulfill her implied questioner's desires. Thus, while she offers a recipe for fry bread, it comes accompanied by a language lesson, but not the lesson of an "Indian name" or prayer for which the listener might have hoped: "This is Indian food / only if you know that Indian is a government word / which has nothing to do with our names for ourselves." Rather, it is a lesson about heteroglossia's angrily contested meanings, which are brought into visible dialogic conflict along the borders between "the government's" and "our own" names—and between Native individuals and communities and those who wish to exoticize or homogenize them. Refusing to "chant for you . . . sweat with you or ease your guilt with

fine turtle tales," she refuses to collaborate in the appropriation of Na-
tive language, voices and stories—as she does, too, when she warns us
"Don't assume . . . that I even know names of all the tribes / or can
pronounce names I've never heard." She insists that we not impose our
stories and needs on her, in effect appropriating her, as a Native person,
to our agendas: "Look at my heart   not your fantasies   Please don't
ever / again tell me about your Cherokee great-great grandmother."

While voicing frustration, she also conveys a desire to reach and
instruct the audience, despite her doubts: "I don't think your attempts to
understand us are going to work." She's not, though, advising us to give
up, as much as indicating that our expectations are wrong: she would
rather, I think, that we recognized her as an individual and respectfully
left her alone or supported her own self-determination. And she conveys
this hope in a way that allows the audience their own self-respect and a
way of revising expectations, by claiming the common ground of "human
weakness   like your own . . . work to do," washing "the same things /
you wash," and by repeating the fry bread ingredients at the end, with a
disclaimer both modest and assertive: "Remember this is only my rec-
ipe   There are many others." The poem thus acknowledges an impor-
tant, though limited commonality, which can be the basis of respect with-
out smoothing over anger or pain.[17]

In "Just Like You" (*Dream On* 48–49) Chrystos challenges her audience
to extend the recognition of commonality and share a particular political
perception. Where the audience is by the end of this provocative poem
may be open to question, but that may be the necessary nature of work that
truly challenges things as they are. The poem takes off from the common
fact that like her reader, the speaker gets "a lot of junk mail." As she
peruses a newly arrived "american eagle outfitters catalogue," her re-
sponse defines her in ways that may separate her from her readers. In the
first place, she admits that she has "many complex bitter feelings about the
words / american & Eagle in conjunction"; still, she opens the catalog and,
as she reads it, suggests that the dialogism at work in those opening lines
may also be latent in the visual images. In "romantic patagonia / four
spray-starched ken and barbie dolls" are depicted, "icons . . . so clean . . .
[in] bright blue, red and yellow . . . ready to go sailing on someone's
rosewood & brass yacht." Juxtaposed to this "beach ball collage" she sees
"four brown-skinned women," three of them shoeless. "I'm sure they
were unpaid," she states and then focuses on "the only person looking
straight at the camera," a small girl in this group of women. The child holds
a slingshot; the poem concludes, "she looks as though she'd like to put a

rock / right through the camera lens / just like me." By the end, the title's statement prompts a question—*are* poet and audience just alike in their assessments of the junk mail that linked them? Are their ties any more substantial than junk mail? The poem's judgments and contrasting images create gaps that readers must negotiate. In the process they must engage in dialogue and recognize dialogism. If they end by agreeing with Chrystos, then poet and reader together may have built a small piece of the foundation of an activist community. The indeterminacy of the readers' responses, however, highlights some of the difficulties of establishing such alliances.

Chrystos's strategy in "Just Like You" is to foreground realities that the dominant discourse generally admits only as background, contrast, or atmosphere for the images and messages of a white Western culture of consumption: what has been marginalized is brought to the center, and allowed to displace the catalog's brightly colored "icons," challenging the exploitative gaze of the camera. Similarly, in "I Like to Think" she brings the Black miners of South Africa up from underground in order to incite a critique of the institutions that marginalize them for profit. In both instances she is breaching borders drawn by those in power, borders that create territories where the disenfranchised can be controlled in part because they've been made invisible to readers, consumers, and all who do not share their lot. Any reclamation of suppressed stories implicitly subverts such territorial intentions by questioning assumptions about what is worthy of the center and what is of only "marginal importance"; that is one of the effects, too, of Rose's early university poems, and as I will discuss later, Rose's more recent work develops complex modes of bringing the "marginal" into the center.

In "The Women Who Love Me" and "Lesbian Air" Chrystos redresses, with engaging energy and evident joy, the marginalization documented in "Ya Don Wanna Eat Pussy":

They're the Lesbians mothers don't want to meet
who make shy girls blush from their feet up
They're out here on the same razor I walk shouting
the goddam emperor is naked & so is the empress
. . . .
Just remember when you open your mouths to trash us
we're the ones carving out the tunnels
so you'll have room to breathe

(Dream On 104–5)

The border, that "razor I walk" on, is the site of brash and liberating speech, which Chrystos makes sensuous, kinetic, political, and ordinary:

> Ah the theory of Lesbianism is a lot of words that not all Lesbians understand or want to   It is the wanting of women we share . . . Our tongues meet we can never have too much of each other as we speak on palestinian land rights, as we march against racism, as we demand abortion rights for women who might hate us as we stand for them . . . as we write Lesbian traffic tickets, as we predict Lesbian earthquakes . . . We are our mother's infinite variety   We are Lesbian redwoods . . . we are Lesbian lizards . . . we are the Lesbian sky. (*Dream On* 142–43)

These poems draw attention to language in a way that challenges borders by foregrounding and enriching the heteroglossia of "Lesbian." Addressing "the women who love [her]" and those who are nervous, homophobic, or not lesbians, they both celebrate lesbians' presence, and challenge us to recognize that presence in all of our lives, however we define ourselves. Thus she engages an inclusive audience in the project of bringing the marginalized into the center. In doing so, she also implicitly questions the exclusivity of "the center," inviting us to consider the validity of acknowledging multiple, coexisting centers.[18] Though "Lesbian Air" ends with affirmations that recall Native cultures' emphasis on connection with nature, neither poem draws attention to a specifically Indian context. Yet reading them with others that do directly address issues of relationship to Indian communities, we can see these two as working toward inclusiveness in Native contexts, as well as more generally.

Like Chrystos, Wendy Rose redefines margins and centers, both to empower self and community, and to instruct her audiences. She does so in poems from *Lost Copper* like "I expected my skin and my blood to ripen" (14–15) and "Three Thousand Dollar Death Song" (26–27) as well as in the early university poems. In *Going to War with All My Relations* she voices a more complex, less defensive ambivalence about the academy, but what predominates is the voice of authority—the voice of one who will no longer allow herself to be appropriated as an object of study, because she no longer assumes that such appropriation is inevitable, for herself or others. While this authority does not exempt her from soul-searching or from difficult encounters, it does empower her to respond effectively to people and assumptions that earlier paralyzed or simply angered her.

Again, "If I Am Too Brown or Too White for You" (*Going to War* 63–64) seems to embody Rose's creative vision of an empowering alternative to the complicity in self-marginalization often imposed by mixed origins and abetted by the academy.[19] As such, it may be read as enabling her to claim the authority manifest in later poems. The capacity for affirming integrity in the midst of flux, or even integrity *as* flux that she celebrates in "If I Am Too Brown or Too White for You," allows Rose to take the stance she does in the poem that follows it in *Going to War*, "Margaret Neumann" (65–69). Here she approaches her complex relationship to her German great-great grandmother from a meditative position in which a Native identity is both a given, assumed without needing to be defended, and fluid, "clouded" by history. And her relationship to the audience, mediated by the figure of her ancestor, is similarly complicated and rendered collaborative.

Margaret Neumann, a participant in the California gold rush, inevitably implicated in the shedding of "Bear Creek blood, blood of Mariposa, / Yosemite blood, Ahwahnee blood," is introduced as a "wild girl" with "dangerous dreams," a characterization that associates her with some of Rose's own self-depictions. Not only "wild" but "transformed . . . at the border," Margaret is recognized, too, as a subject with a fluid identity, an ancestor in the process of becoming, an audience (Rose addresses her directly) who might hear the heteroglossic layers of language, with whom dialogue might be imaginable.

> Into the muscle and flesh
> of what you called wilderness
> you drove the brown horses
> . . . .
> You brought to life
> the anxious temblor
> in my heart.

Language and its layers of intentions both justify and expose invasion and cataclysmic disruption. Single-minded condemnation, then, would be inadequate linguistically and emotionally. Rose imagines her ancestor as a living spirit, a participant in the process of imaginative creation and recreation:

Are you the astonished one
or am I? . . .
    . . . that you
are my ancestor
learning to imagine me.

Meeting Margaret in mythic time, where present and past coincide in
transformative simultaneity, Rose recognizes her ancestor's complex real-
ity, which is her own truest inheritance, and imagines this distant relative
into dialogue.

The relationship she creates is one of reciprocity, a balance that im-
plies an ongoing rhythm of recognition and recreation:

If you are a part of me
I am also that crazy acorn
within your throat
around which pioneer stories
rattle and squirm
If you are the brave heritage
of Gold Rush California,
I am also the bone
that buzzes behind your breast.
If I am the tongue made indigenous
by all the men you would love,
I am also the ghost
of the pioneer's future.

The poet imagines an embrace of contraries, a resolution provisional in its
commitment to difficult emotional realities and to dialogic process, yet
convincing in its empowerment of the multiply identified speaker. These
lines, after all, both compellingly imagine the European ancestor's discom-
fort and give precedence to the speaker's present indigenous and mixed
reality—implying both an ongoing discomfort and the restorative power
of revision and recreation. Again, Rose draws attention to contested
meanings as "pioneer stories / rattle and squirm"; again, her images
make concrete, and concretely disturbing, the acute dialogism compelled
by border consciousness.

Yet "touching the silver / at the center" of both of them, Rose is
moved to an imaginative act of faith—"I believe you would understand"—

founded on an implicit confidence in the power of her and her ancestor's historically grounded imagination:

Do you remember
the sacred signs
. . . .
in the German Black Forest?
Do you remember the tribes
that so loved their land
before the roll
of Roman wheels?

The poem ends successfully on these two questions, not because the answer is a foregone conclusion, but because Rose has imagined an ancestor, and by extension a contemporary audience, capable of hearing and responding. Having created the possibility of dialogue by imagining her ancestor as a participant, she can leave the poem's ending truly open. She has not transcended ambivalence, but she has conceived of a dialogic process in which she need not be trapped or paralyzed by any of the components of her multiple identities. This enables a more creative, more productive, because less defensively reactive, relationship with her various communities and audiences than was evident in the earlier poems on mixed-blood or academic experience. Such an accomplishment, I believe, also grounds the poems about the academy, and others that question and redefine margins and centers, in *Going to War with All My Relations*.

"Excavation at Santa Barbara Mission" (*Going to War* 6–8) bears the following epigraph: "*When archaeologists excavated Santa Barbara Mission in California, they discovered human bones in the adobe walls.*" In the course of the poem, the artist-archaeologist must confront the (literal) foundation of her expectations about the dig and her relationship to the site; she can deny neither her position as a "hungry scientist" nor her kinship with the bones she unearths. The process of self-recognition raises questions of complicity that the poem cannot evade. The possibility of conflict is implicit from the first lines: "My pointed trowel / is the artist's brush / that will *stroke and pry* . . . the old mission wall" (emphasis added). The poet explains her eagerness: she "wanted to count [herself] / among the ancient dead / as a faithful neophyte . . . in love / with the padres / and the Spanish hymns." As the "excavation" proceeds, she discovers the problematical and conflicting meanings of such counting and replaces the

Spanish hymns with a different song. Her own blood mixes with the bones she uncovers, and the bones' fragility is matched by her own growing helplessness as she hears "the whistle / of longbones breaking / apart like memories." Her hands "empty themselves / of old dreams"— her own? the dead Indians'?—even as she knows herself "a hungry scientist / sustain[ed] . . . with bones of / men and women . . . who survived in their own way." The limits of that survival, however, and the anguish of her own realizations, are evident in her final, chanting lines:

> They built the mission with dead Indians.
> They built the mission with dead Indians.
> They built the mission with dead Indians.
> They built the mission with dead Indians.

The fourfold repetition (itself reminiscent of much traditional Native American poetry) asserts the literal centrality of the Indian dead in the walls and confirms the poem's primary accomplishment, placing them in the center of consciousness for the speaker and her audience. Doing this, she has redefined Santa Barbara Mission and revised the way we must speak of it in the future. In its creation of a process of self-recognition and acknowledgment, this poems recalls "Margaret Neumann"; in both the process is arduous and the implications for community complex.

The multiple meanings Rose finds in "bones" link "Excavation at Santa Barbara Mission" to other poems that question or revise margins and centers. Bones are more now than the remnants of victimization or appropriation found in the earlier university poems and in "Three Thousand Dollar Death Song." At Santa Barbara, bones are fragile and broken, yet not simply dead remnants. They are "scattered like corn." Mixed with the speaker's blood, "breaking / apart like memories," they intimately evoke physical and spiritual connection and loss; "shivering into mist," they transform the poet's vision even as they dissolve; brittle and crumbling, they are yet a strong foundation, for they *are* the walls of the mission. The poem exposes the heteroglossia of *bones,* for the word is now infused with past and present intentions that imply dialogic possibilities. The walls made of bones figure both colonialism's brutal imposition of territorial borders, and the difficult revisions that may be possible in the contested spaces of the present. Such revisions are necessary if Indian people are to survive.

The revisions of "Excavation at Santa Barbara Mission" most immedi-

ately affect Rose's knowledge of herself in relation to the past; "Musko-
gee" (*Going to War* 48–49) affirms her relationship to the past and to the
"Mother Ground," through the creation of a contemporary multiethnic
Indian community. *Muskogee,* a Creek word, names both the people and
their language. In this poem Rose uses the cultural differences between
herself, "this desert girl," and the people of the Roundhouse, the oaks,
and the Trail of Tears, to emphasize strength and continuity: "there is
still / the song that carried me east to sacred ground," a song of earth,
history, and relationship, as she has been taught by the Muskogee elder
she addresses. Singing, she remembers the people's affirmation of their
own center, through fidelity to memory, ritual, and dream:

> . . . when they made you walk away from your land
> she only rolled over, tricked them good
>
> for the center is still the center, the fire
> carefully kept, Mother Ground still alive.

Strong in this song and in her memory, she now sees bones as the inti-
mate signs "of how we are related through the red earth here" and of
"Mother Ground's" continuing protection. She thus can imagine an or-
ganic relationship that accommodates cultural difference within a pan-
tribal community.

Perhaps partly enabled by the self-recognition (albeit ambivalent) of
"Excavation at Santa Barbara Mission," and the empowering knowledge
of relationship in "Muskogee," Rose speaks with authoritative assurance
in two poems that redefine margins and centers in the context of academe:
"For the Campus Committee on the Quality of Life" (*Going to War* 57–58)
and "For the Complacent College Students Who Don't Think People
Should 'Live in the Past' " (*Going to War* 61–62). The first reprimands, with
morally grounded energy; in the second, Rose reaches out to help her
students see their own possible connections to those they would criticize.
"For the Campus Committee" is prefaced by a lengthy epigraph that
forcefully catalogs the indignities visited upon the speaker's diversely
identified students, indignities presumably ignored in the committee's
proposal of *"coffee hours and bowling teams."* The contrast between such
projects and *"sickle cell crises . . . rocks thrown at . . . mixed-blood children,"*
sterilization *"merely for crossing a border,"* struggles against alcohol, and
BIA checks that don't arrive, demonstrates the marginalization of the

oppressed and the heteroglossia of "Quality of Life" as it is understood by
the relatively comfortable and by the students for whom Rose speaks.
Epigraph and poem work together; while the epigraph lists the literal
indignities, the poem itself identifies the effects of institutionalized disre-
gard for the disenfranchised. What is at stake is survival.

> . . . we have stripped ourselves bare for you
> and you eat, just that simple thing
> unable to taste the sweet blood or feel
> against your teeth the bone . . .

In the poem's second half Rose does with *bones* what Chrystos does
with *Lesbian,* in "Lesbian Air." Bones become literally and figuratively the
lives of the ignored, oppressed, and marginalized, which Rose brings
back into the center by giving them ubiquity and dialogic vitality.

> O we are the bones
> a forest of bones
> . . . .
> bones of clay, obsidian, redwood
> . . . .
> . . . weak and hurting bones,
> . . . .
> bridges of bones, fences, horizons, barriers
> of bones . . .
> bone prisons, bone colleges, encampments
> of bones, we are the bones
> of what you forget, of what
> you thought were just lies
> we are the bones
> that stop you from feeling better
> . . . .
> the bones forever
> floating out of reach.

These "bones" signal, too, both the futility of attempting to improve "the
quality of life" unless those in power attend to the students' grievances
and the students' own refusal ("floating out of reach") to have their needs
or identities defined by campus committees. Their implicit appeal to the

audience is grounded in the claim of a relationship that is as persistent as it is uncomfortable for all—"you" consume and ignore "us"; "we" "fol-low . . . you home . . . direct . . . your dreams," and will not let "you" rest. The audience is left, as in Chrystos's "Just Like You," without the comfort of a formula or a promise, to consider, to choose, perhaps to act.

In "For the Complacent College Students" Rose offers her audience the possibility of dialogue, if the students will accept her invitation to consider imaginatively the implications of their own experiences. The provisional quality of the offer is evident in the beginnings of the poem's four sections: "do you see," "and if someone thinks," "and you wonder," "and now you wonder." Rose first takes us adroitly through a demonstra-tion in which the killing of ivy "on the old brick wall" becomes an analogy for cultural genocide: the roots are severed, the flowers "pressed and dried . . . catalogued, thoroughly studied, / or thrown away . . . as if they had never lived / except on display."

The poem's second, more directly personal half depends entirely upon our willingness to imagine ourselves as similarly vulnerable to being cut off at the roots—or perhaps already cut off: "and you wonder at the name / your mother's mother wore." Rose evokes the vehicles of her own Native people's dispossession, to reach the inheritors of the westward expansion: "you wonder . . . at the wagon or the sailing ship she rode." Perhaps she is able with equanimity to offer such likely touchstones of her students' dreams and uncertainties because she has wondered similarly about herself and her ancestors, in "Margaret Neumann." Indeed, she is inviting her students and readers to engage in such questioning explora-tion for ourselves, as she suggests: "and now you wonder / if you are she and she is you . . . prayer or prophecy or mere suggestion . . . the woman's face / you never knew that you rub with warm water / in the morning." Rose is asking her "complacent" students to undertake something analogous to her own "excavations" at Santa Barbara and her poetic conversation with her German great-great grandmother. In so do-ing, she addresses assumptions perhaps unstated in the students' critique of those who "live in the past": that such people and their pasts are insignifi-cant to and less real than the students' immediate present—that in fact they deserve to be marginalized. As she revised the implications of "live in the past," subtly playing on the power differentials inherent in the phrase's dialogism, she also reveals the commonality of our need to know ourselves in terms of our pasts; thus by imagining the students' own concerns, she recenters the issue and the unnamed people whose efforts to recover their pasts presumably prompted the students' scorn. As Chrystos did in "Lesbian Air," Rose here, by demonstrating the possible centrality of the marginalized, implicitly disrupts the dominant assumption that there can be only one center and the creation of borders to disenfranchise those who are excluded.

"To Make History" (*Going to War* 79–80) similarly engages and instructs its audience in a process of creation that is also a process of establishing relatedness. While it does not explicitly address marginalization, if we juxtapose it to poems that resist the dominant historical versions of Indians' lives, we can read it as inviting alternative stories, as it creates a concept of history that (rather like indigenous concepts of language as grounded and relational) involves the integration of the maker, the story, and the natural world. "To Make History" thus destabilizes margins and centers, by emphasizing the making, and not just the reception, of history. The poem marks a shift from Rose's early university poems, where she and her readers could only react angrily or sadly to versions of history imposed on them by finished texts. Now Rose offers an alternative image to the walls of Santa Barbara, and an alternative activity for poet and audience: while "Excavation" deconstructed a historical monument, the evidence of the dominant culture's version of history, "To Make History" constructs an image. Making history is figured here as weaving a blanket: "The strongest memory is the warp / carrying structure and order to the sky." The process requires delicacy and care, for the product and the maker are both fragile:

> Take care not to go too fast
> or the body of the blanket
> will burst like breaking bones.
>
> Your hands get wilder, bleed and blister.

Reminiscent of the images in "Excavation at Santa Barbara Mission," these lines imply that to aim at the objectivity assumed by conventional academic anthropology and history would be self-deluding, even harmful. What the poem offers instead is participation in the interwoven dialogic layers of natural, human, and visionary realities. Erasing the lines between the codifiers and the objects of history, it offers an ethos in which people tell their own stories. With the spider's web, the mesa, and the four directions, the final lines may suggest Hopi origin myths and surely imply a promise of order and connectedness:[20]

> Backlit spider webs encircle the day
> fragile and tough as morning. Listen
> to the singing, the mystical thing
>
> finished and folded and spinning away.
> Lie face down on the mesa, hands and feet pointing
> to the four corners of everything
> and now it is done
> now it is done.

Invoking mystery and ritual, continuity and completion, Rose renders "history" dialogic. Most radically, I believe, she invites her audience to participate in the ongoing creation of history: if "now it is done," still "the mystical thing" is "spinning away": ritual offers both closure and the promise of continuity.

Chrystos offers a similar invitation to participate in the remaking of history (and of the world), in "Urban Indian" (*Dream On* 151):

> I drum an old song on the hood of an abandoned stripped car
> . . . .
> calling down horses . . . calling down deer . . . calling down loons
> calling down turtles
> . . . .
> as green our mother takes herself back . . . fine dust is all
> that's left of these prisons & pain
> I am dreaming on this
> Dream on with me

Her dream-song is analogous to Rose's blanket-web; as Rose does in "To Make History," here Chrystos affirms a community of creative continuity and invites all who would, to join.

"Ceremony for Completing a Poetry Reading," the final poem in *Not Vanishing* (100), is one of Chrystos's most sustained evocations of an inclusive, desired community. Like "To Make History" and "Urban Indian," it used Native cultural references to suggest the poet's spiritual and historical ground, but without implying exclusivity. Chrystos is certainly not reversing her criticism of non-Native appropriations of Indian

spirituality. But at least within this poem's hopeful invitation to reciproc-
ity, she implies that cultural specificity need not mean creating borders
that cut off the realization of common joy, mutually sustaining engage-
ment. Here the desired community and the desired audience may be both
one and various. The poem's double premise is stated in its first lines:
"This is a give away poem / You've . . . made a circle with me of the
places / I've wandered." From these premises, the poet invites us to
"Hear / the stories . . . Let me give you ribbonwork leggings . . . Come
closer." She details the gifts and asks our permission to bestow them—
which, by reading on, we grant, and receive thereby "the seeds of a new
way . . . the sound of our feet dancing . . . the sound of our thoughts
flying . . . the sound of peace moving into our faces & sitting down." As
in many other poems, repeated phrases create the effect of incantatory
efficacy, evoking the forms and aesthetics of traditional Native song, and
thus revealing the dialogism of the poem's language—realizing rhythmi-
cally the speech and intentions of indigenous singers in the language of
colonizers and their descendants (among them many of her readers).

It would be a mistake to read "Ceremony for Completing a Poetry
Reading" (or "To Make History") as replacing or softening the grief, an-
ger, and resistance voiced in poems like "For the College Committee,"
"Just like You," "I Walk in the History of My People," or "Three Thousand
Dollar Death Song." What this poem does, rather, is to intimate the
possibilities that justify the poets' sometimes impatient challenges to their
diverse readers, the possibilities for community that our more adequate,
active responses might welcome into being. Not only a justified and self-
defending anger at the continuing destruction, but a vision of life-
sustaining alternatives, moves Chrystos and Rose to words of resistance.

Many other contemporaries also address issues of community and audi-
ence. To demonstrate the varied approaches, I have chosen poems by Gail
Tremblay, Lance Henson, and Ray Young Bear, writers whose cultural
affiliations are also diverse. For all of them, as for Chrystos and Rose,
issues of survival and the need for life-sustaining alternatives to personal,
cultural, and communal disruptions are deeply integral to their work.

Onondaga/Micmac Gail Tremblay's "Indian Singing in 20th Century
America" opens with an affirmation of connectedness that sustains its
speaker-singers: "We wake, we wake the day, / the light rising in us like
the sun— / our breath a prayer" (14–15). At every step of this quiet,
communally-voiced poem, traditional knowledge provides a grounding,

reassuring balance against the disruptions imposed by the non-Indian world. "We stumble" becomes "we dance," while "earth breath eddies between factories," and "we work / fast and steady," remembering that "each breath alters the composition / of the air." The rhythms of dance and memory reflect the continuity of natural cycles and enable the singing Indians to sustain personal, communal, and spiritual connectedness through change: "we're always there—singing round dance / songs, remembering what supports / our life." This poem seems to be primarily for, as well as about, an Indian community; the "we" is embracing, affirming, and only secondarily concerned with confronting representatives of the non-Indian world, who are referred to obliquely or anonymously and are eventually subsumed in the dance of light, spirit, memory, and change. As the first and title poem of Tremblay's book, "Indian Singing" provides a current of hopeful assurance for poems in which she addresses more directly some of the painful realities of twentieth-century Native life.

The need for such assurance is evident in Tremblay's "Urban Indians, Pioneer Square, Seattle" (32). For these displaced contemporaries audience is problematical: "Walking the streets, we watch the people stare, / then quickly look away when they see us notice / them." Unsympathetic observers both judge the dislocated Indians and fail to see them, except for "their own visions of what they'll let us be." Yet to return home to a communal audience is impossible, because of the migrants' sense of responsibility:

>   . . . At times,
>   we think about returning home—there is no work
>   there, and relatives already have trouble making
>   ends meet, but at least there'd be cousins
>   to tease. Most of the time we know such journeys
>   are impossible, to see us beaten like this would
>   make our loved ones cry . . .

For these urban Indians, the question "what is ethical to tell?" has turned inward: the question is not whether to give communal knowledge to outsiders, but whether to give pain to one's community. Their own tenuous sustenance is in memory, associated with "good days," and in the effort to maintain traces of community in a life-threatening context: "We look after one another / when we can, and wonder, if the world don't / change soon, how much longer will any of us live."

Lance Henson's "we are a people" (20) is a serene expression of communal assurance, grounded in a people's knowledge of their oneness with place, spirit, and history: "days pass easy over these ancient hills"; though the "moccasin path" is "overgrown with rusted cans and weeds," Henson knows that

> there is no distance between the name
> of my race
> and the owl calling
> nor the badgers gentle plodding
>
> we are a people born under symbols
> that rise from the dust to touch us
> that pass through the cedars where
> our old ones sleep
>
> to tell us of their dreams

This is the same confidence in communal continuity that sustains Tremblay's Indian singers. Like "Indian Singing" too, "we are a people" seems to address the people about whom it sings, in reassurance, as much as it might address a non-Cheyenne, non-Indian audience, in assertion. In its direct simplicity, its resistance of hierarchy, its calm concentration on the fundamental facts, this poem implicitly puts the sorry history of assaults on Native people into perspective by leaving it out of the poem. Lest I seem, as a non-Native reader, too ready to discover a message of transcendence, or to ascribe an easy optimism to the poet, I note that Henson, a traditionally identified Southern Cheyenne, is far from ignoring the agonies that this poem omits: across the page, "we are a people" is faced by "morning star," which tells part of the story of the 1878 Fort Robinson massacre of Cheyennes trying to return to their northern homes (21); an earlier piece is entitled "anniversary poem for the cheyennes who died at sand creek" (14). What I think Henson is doing in poems like "we are a people" is demonstrating that Indians need not always define themselves or their communities in terms of non-Natives. From this perspective, borders and heteroglossia, as markers of cultural conflict, become virtually irrelevant; undeniable as conflict and competition may be, here Henson claims sustenance in the conviction that, grounded in spirit and history, his people can define themselves independent of others' impositions.

Ray Young Bear's sometimes cryptic and always allusive poetry seems to manifest a similar conviction, in the freedom with which the poet draws on personal and traditional references without evidently feeling compelled to provide clarification. In "Emily Dickinson, Bismarck, and the Roadrunner's Inquiry" (*Invisible Musician* 21–26) Young Bear, a "traditional-minded" Mesquakie, creates a complex fabric of ambivalence and ambiguity, as he plays on questions of community and relationship with other Algonquin peoples and across Native and Euro-American cultures. Young Bear's persistent ambiguity also, I think, reflects an implicit response to the question "what is ethical to tell?"[21]

Young Bear's note on this poem indicates his interest in relationships among Indian peoples.[22] Hence we may assume that his primary audience is other Indians, and specifically other speakers of Algonquin languages. Yet the poem's title, some of its allusions, and its final lines suggest that Emily Dickinson, another cryptic American poet acutely aware of the difficulties of relationship, is also Young Bear's audience and subject, as he reaches for and questions the possibility of community. Thus Young Bear's poem would represent a variation on Rose's and others' acknowledgments of bicultural influences on contemporary Native writing, with the implied concomitant dialogical potential. His allusions to Dickinson include not only references to the "ruffled blouse" and the "tainted photograph" (both recalling how Dickinson was re-created to suit late Victorian expectations) but also subtler echoes of her language, imagery, and thematic preoccupations. For example, one might easily connect the addressee's implied preference for "the philosophy / of being Insignificant" with Dickinson's famous announcement, "I'm Nobody!" (Such a connection need not diminish Young Bear's attribution of the philosophy of insignificance to his grandmother, who "let . . . me know that we are all insignificant in the gigantic world around us" [Moore and Wilson 211]. Recognizing the double reference does increase one's sense of the poem's ambivalent ambiguity.) Likewise, the following lines from Young Bear's poem echo Dickinson's evocations of transience and ineffability, most particularly in her poem numbered 1602 ("Pursuing you in your transitions"):

> she precariously engaged herself
> to different visions
> . . . .
> Whenever we were fortunate
> to appear within each other's prisms[23]

Like much of Dickinson's poetry and like many indigenous stories, this poem resists interpretation or translation; as Robert Dale Parker says of Young Bear's first book, it has "a contemplative intensity that often risks the indecipherable" (89). The poem seems private, esoteric, yet at the same time it is addressed to "you" and is permeated by first-person-plural references that may suggest parallel audiences, while raising the question of who they might be.[24] Unelaborated, culturally specific allusions, like those that provide much of the imagery and emotional grounding in Young Bear's poetry, "instill . . . linguistic distance itself as a subject of the text" and, further, "incorporate . . . the warning that the site of the shared discourse—the literary text—is not the site of shared mental experience, and should not be seen as such." Such allusions can thus be read as embodying "the curious tension of cultural 'revelation' and cultural 'silence' "[25] and as foregrounding both dialogism and the complex issues of audience and community.

Given the poem's combination of inviting suggestiveness and resistance to discovery, I offer only a speculative reading of possible readings, shaped by my interest in how this work might bear on issues of relationship to audience or community. The poem's primary realities seem to be the speaker's effort to communicate, his memory of common origins, and his sense of distance and difference, despite the common past. It begins,

> I never thought for a moment
> that it was simply an act of fondness
> which prompted me to compose
> and send these letters.
> Surely into each I held
> the same affection as when
> we were together in a canoe
> over Lake Agassiz in Manitoba,
> paddling toward a moonlit fog
> before we lost each other.
>
> (21)

The desire to communicate is evident in the first four lines, which represent the poem as letters composed out of complex motives; it is apparent later, in a perhaps punning reference to "our correspondence," in the request to "please accept advice," and, near the end, in the confession that "I had no words to offer." The common past evoked in these

introductory lines is also implied later, in the exclamation that "our dia-
lects are nearly the same!" and the implication that "our Creation stories"
are too.[26] Most pervasive is the present sense of distance and difference
between the poem's speaker and his audience, which is conveyed in the
statement that "I would be out of place / in the tundra or the desert" (22),
in his "vigil" for "boats disappearing over / the arête horizon," and his
reference to "your dissatisfaction / in my society" (23).[27]

Its clusters of imagery and assertions seem to offer a number of
(perhaps simultaneously) possible readings for this complex and sugges-
tive poem. It may be addressed to other Algonquins. Or, having recog-
nized the slight possibility of returning to a mythic, indigenous unity
("No business politicizing myth," he whispers to himself), Young Bear's
speaker perhaps turns to the tenuous possibility of alternative affinities:
the poem's last words, "Dear Emily," might support this reading. Or, in
response to that same recognition, the speaker might be trying to recon-
struct mythic images, as a grounds for communal continuity in the
present—thus the many apparently indigenous and mythically sugges-
tive references.

The difficult ambiguities of memory, relationship, and communica-
tion shadow the whole poem, which might be read as a series of efforts to
make some kind of clarity from the layered uncertainties. One passage
that serves to represent the uncertainty and the effort comes toward the
poem's end:

> All of a sudden it is difficult
> to draw and paint your face
> with graphic clarity,
> when the initial response is to alter
> your age.
> Automatically, the bright colors
> of Chagall replace the intent.
> When the Whirlwind returned
> as a constellation
> we asked for cultural acquittance,
> but when the reply appeared as herons
> skimming along the updraft
> of the homeland's ridge,
> we asked again.
> It was never appropriate.

We were disillusioned,
and our request became immune
to illness, misfortune and plain hate.
Or so we thought.

(24–25)

The tonal disruptions of the passage's first and last lines constitute an uneasy frame for the implicit questions and discordances that arise between them. Impersonal confession ("the initial response" masks "*my* initial response") is succeeded by first-person recollection of recurrent, inappropriate asking and disillusionment. The plea for "cultural acquittance" seems to follow from the events that precede it in the passage but precisely how is unclear. (Intentionally unclear, from the standpoint of Young Bear the poet, though I would guess painfully and unavoidably so from the standpoint of the speaker in the midst of recollected experience.) Again, audience is indeterminate: the *you* in the opening lines could be Emily Dickinson, Algonquin contemporaries or mythic ancestors, or even some other singular addressee.[28]

"Automatically, the bright colors / of Chagall replace the intent." Like Dickinson, Chagall might be a kindred spirit for Young Bear the contemporary writer. But if Chagall's images of the traditional world of the stetl—in dreamlike, manifestly modern compositions—could make him an enabling precursor, the replacement of "the intent" by his "bright colors" apparently does not give "graphic clarity." Or does it? Is the replaced "intent" that of clarity, or that of "alter[ing] / your age"? And is the automatic appearance of Chagall's "bright colors" then liberating? intrusive? evidence of internalized cultural loss? enriching? Chagall and his colors may represent community for the contemporary artist, but they also may disrupt his relationship to his audience(s) and his traditional community.

Each possible reading suggests an unresolved concern with community and audience; the poem seems to reach for but also to question the possibility of community *with* the audience. Mythic and other cultural references may offer grounds for connection, even while they may also divide the speaker from some of his listener-readers. A member of a conservative Native community, someone both grounded in living tradition and involved in the dominant culture, Young Bear may be addressing the dilemma of disclosure ("What is ethical to tell?") in part by the choice of esoteric and dreamlike references that allow him to tell without telling.[29] (Such indirection aligns him again, perhaps ironically, with Dickinson: "Tell all the Truth but tell it slant.") Young Bear suggests some of the tension involved in such a double stance when, in an interview, he both pointedly refrains from discussing the "powerful image" of the salamander, and describes his realization that "I am here for a purpose, and that purpose is to . . . be my grandmother's messenger, to disseminate pieces of our culture" (Moore and Wilson 209). Perhaps inevitably, such a double stance highlights the potential complications of audience and of community.

Native American oral cultures—which all of these poets invoke and honor—traditionally integrate storyteller or singer, community, and language. Membership in community is fundamental to integrity, to voice, and to power; one speaks most fully and truly in and with one's community. Chrystos, Rose, and the other poets I've discussed here aspire to such relationships, even if often in contexts that revise tradition. Rose, Chrystos, and Young Bear, particularly, show us that the effort can be fraught with risk and uncertainty, and others bear out this truth: contrast, for example, the confidence of Tremblay's "Indian Singing in Twentieth-Century America" and Henson's "we are a people" with the bleak effort to keep going in "Urban Indians, Pioneer Square, Seattle" or the stark image of "the old women . . . lifting their broken hands" in "morning star" (Henson 21). Their poems clarify both the difficulties and the gifts of community, and the crucial importance, for Native American survival, of maintaining, reclaiming, and recreating communal bonds. As the poems discussed in the next chapter will demonstrate, whether in affirmation or ambivalently, such bonds are often inextricable from relationship to place.

CHAPTER 4

"That's the Place
Indians Talk About"

The importance of place in Native American traditions cannot be overestimated. Ancestral landscapes offer not only familiarity, shelter, and sustenance but also spiritual and cultural grounding. A people's geography is the site and source both of their stories and of dynamic reciprocal relationships with the spirits that inhabit the natural surroundings. Thus the creation stories of indigenous American peoples often describe the origins of particular places and geographical features, and associate those particulars with the mythic interventions of gods, spirits, and first people. Thus, too, landscape supports a traditionally grounded people's sense of self-in-relationship, and access to sacred sites is crucial to full identity and to spiritual well-being.[1]

Sioux writer Vine Deloria observes that, in contrast to the Western inclination

> to see land as a commodity and think first of its ownership . . . the traditional Indian understanding of land focuses on its use, and the duties people assume when they come to occupy it. When an Indian thinks about traditional lands he always talks about what the people did there, the animals who lived there and how the people related to them, the seasons of the year and how people responded to their changes, the manner in which the tribe acquired possession of the area, and the ceremonial functions it was required to perform to remain worthy of living there . . . Obligations demanded by the lands upon which people lived were part of their understanding of the world; indeed, their view of life was grounded in the knowledge of these responsibilities. (261–63)

Leslie Marmon Silko (Laguna), in "Landscape, History, and the Pueblo Imagination," suggests some implications of such an understanding. Her observations on traditional artists and storytellers apply to contemporaries like Simon Ortiz (and ring true, as well, for writers from other Native traditions): "Pueblo potters, the creators of petroglyphs and oral narratives never conceived of removing themselves from the earth and sky. So long as the human consciousness remains *within* the hills, canyons, cliffs, and the plants, clouds, and sky, the term *landscape*, as it has entered the English language, is misleading," for it "assumes the viewer is somehow *outside* or separate from the territory he or she surveys. Viewers are as much a part of the landscape as the boulders they stand on" (84). Further, "location, or 'place,' nearly always plays a central role in Pueblo oral narratives. Indeed, stories are most frequently recalled as people are passing by a specific geographical feature or the exact place where a story takes place" (88).

Five hundred years of encounters between Natives and non-Natives have embued Indians' relationships to land with anguish but also with resistant determination, as Indian people have sustained the shocks of displacement by purchase, treaty, war, federal education policy, "removal," "termination," and "relocation," and have struggled to retain or to return to their home places. The Trail of Tears and the post–World War II Relocation program are only some of these massive displacements. And the battles for control of the Black Hills and Taos Blue Lake, and for the American Indian Religious Freedom Act and the Native American Free Exercise of Religion Act, are likewise only a few of the contemporary campaigns for the integrity of Natives' relationships with their lands.[2] Anishinaabe activist Winona LaDuke speaks for many when she says "Native communities are not in a position to compromise, because who we are is our land, our trees, and our lakes" (43).

The history of Indian peoples' integration with ancestral landscapes and the repeated assaults on such relationships contributes to the intensity with which contemporary Native writers refer to place. Inevitably, the meanings of place and the imaginable responses to the land now vary in countless ways. For just one example, Joy Harjo demonstrates both the continuing emotional power of lost land and the commitment of displaced peoples to new home grounds. In "New Orleans," the poet's memory, "deep in the blood . . . swims out of Oklahoma, / deep the Mississippi River"; her "spirit comes here to drink," and she knows that "there are ancestors and future children / buried beneath the currents," and "stories here made of memory" (*She Had Some Horses* 42–43). At the same time Oklahoma, "which has come to mean home to many tribal peoples . . . never leaves us. The spirit is alive in the landscape that arranges itself in . . . poems and stories . . . [and] the tribal peoples of

Oklahoma bear a responsibility to that place, to the community of earth and language that has formed us" ("Oklahoma: The Prairie of Words" 43–44). Both "New Orleans" and the essay about Oklahoma bear the deep knowledge of place as contested.

Considering treatments of place raises the question of how border consciousness might be apparent when literal, geographical borders are potentially involved. How might awareness of borderland issues impinge upon depictions of literal places, and how might the emotional, spiritual, or political significance of those places affect awareness of borderland issues? Though traditional Native American communities were and are land based, that seems less likely for many contemporary Indians; pan-Indian communities don't share one identifying place, in the way that their ancestors did, and urban Indians may or may not remember and return to ancestral places. By contrast (and this does not at all negate that they might also consider themselves members of pan-Indian or sometimes urban Indian communities), Robert Davis and Simon Ortiz identify themselves explicitly in terms of place, and in terms of the terrains and histories of those places. So does Jim Barnes, though with quite different effects. In Davis's and Ortiz's poetry, surely in part as a result of their ongoing relationships to particular places, we see borderland conflicts that are in fact contests over control of land and resources. Varied as they are, the responses to place discussed in this chapter are perhaps most fundamentally representative in their variety and in the poets' evident, shared conviction that place matters.

"Like myself, the source of these narratives is my home. Sometimes my father tells them, sometimes my mother, sometimes even the storyteller himself tells them" (168).³ In this poem title from *A Good Journey* Ortiz establishes the deep connection between place and language, and reminds us of the place-oriented oral tradition of Acoma Pueblo that nourishes his poetry. He affirms this association of personal identity with place that he shares with other Native Americans in "Some Indians at a Party" (219–20), which is made up of a series of place names, answering the question "Where you from?" The last is "Acoma / the other side, ten miles from Snow Bird," on which the poem concludes, "That's my name too. / Don't you forget it."

"Canyon de Chelly," from *A Good Journey,* affirms the intimate, necessary connection to land and place; this poem's specific location, in Navajo country, confirms that for Ortiz such connection needn't be limited to one's origin place. "Lie on your back on stone," the poem begins, "the stone carved to fit / the shape of yourself." As it ends, the poet's small son touches an ancient root by the canyon wall, and Ortiz again confirms the sustaining relationship: "I tell him: wood, an old root, / and around it, the earth, ourselves" (201–2). As the earth embraced us in the first lines, now in these closing lines we, "ourselves," protectively surround the root. Together, the images reveal a mutual embrace, a mutually necessary and supportive relationship.

In "A New Mexico Place Name," and "The State's Claim," place is the object of conflict, which is reflected in resistant dialogism. "A New Mexico Place Name" (207–9) focuses on Cochiti City, a housing development built on bulldozed sacred land of Cochiti Pueblo and promoted by "salesmen / from Southern California." Ortiz defines the "crux" as "a question / of starving or eating," acknowledging the economic basis of a painful conflict among Indian people. He repeats *city* in various contexts, drawing attention to the word's diverse, dialogized implications: "COCHITI CITY" appears three times; Ortiz also uses "the old city," "the / CITY," "a model / CITY," and "the model city." The conflict over what this "New Mexico Place" is and how it should be used echoes in these varied repetitions. Other instances of charged language occur when Ortiz and some friends visit the development "armed with a tape recorder and questions" and are met by a "cool," smiling manager whose "handout" of brochures they reject. Leaving, one of them takes a picture of Indian men working at the site, a photograph he'll later title, "Indians Building a New Way of Life."

As a result of the renaming and "development," the people are gradually silenced. Early in the poem, a Cochiti man points out the endangered sacred place: " 'Right there,' he says, / a halting in his voice"; in the manager's office, the "young and angry" men's "insistent questions . . . [have] no chance, realistically, of being answered." Later, they are equally unsuccessful in talking with a Cochiti man and "a pretty Indian girl," both employed by the development—the former walks away, summoned by a salesman, and the latter "refuse[s] to talk." Finally Ortiz comments that, leaving the site, "It wasn't a strange feeling at all that there wasn't much to say . . . On the way back to Albuquerque, we drank in silence." If the source of Ortiz's narratives is his home, conversely the silencing of Native voices here has its source in the disruption of a sacred place and of a people's relation to it.

Ortiz again draws attention to resistant dialogism as a manifestation of conflicts over place in "The State's claim," the full title of which draws attention to borderland tensions: "The State's claim that it seeks in no way to deprive Indians of their rightful share of water, but only to define that share, falls on deaf ears" (254). A headnote attributes this sentence to *"an April 1974 editorial comment in the Albuquerque Journal."* This title establishes the conflict of intentions between the people of Acoma and the emissaries of the dominant culture—the U.S. government and its commercial beneficiaries, "American RAILROADS, ELECTRIC LINES, GAS LINES, HIGHWAYS, PHONE COMPANIES, CABLE TV" (255). The poem's sections, each named for one of these interests, recount in the voices of Ortiz, his family, and Acoma neighbors, the history of successive claims to the right of way by powerful outside interests, and suggest the consequences for the people and the land. That Native people tell these stories keeps the slippery implications of "The State's claim" always in view, by exposing the state's reliable unreliability and providing resistant voices speaking in essence a different language—straightforward, concrete, personal. Thus both in substance and in manner the poem draws attention to its profound dialogism, and to the high stakes in the contest of languages.

That the Acoma people are virtually compelled to use the state's terms to explain their losses to themselves further complicates our awareness of multiple perceptions and intentions. Ortiz relates one instance early on. As a child, he heard his father explain the railroad's action as an exchange of land. Only later did Ortiz realize that the U.S. government "had given"

> the railroad the right of way
> through our land and also allotted
> them land so that what the railroad did
> was "give" that land in exchange to us
> who were the right of way.

This passage adds layers of implication to the next one, in which he recalls explaining to his younger siblings the building of the electric lines: "At that age, / I didn't know much of anything . . . I probably told them some lie" (256). In the passage dedicated to the phone company juxtaposition highlights the humorous possibilities of heteroglossia while effecting an un(der)stated criticism. Ortiz begins by explaining how a cousin won some money in a phone quiz: Asked "Who is the father of this country?"

He said, "Without thinking about it,
I answered 'George Washington.' "

I don't think my Grandfather ever used
a telephone in his life . . .

As in "A New Mexico Place Name," depredations on the land and
disruptions of the people's relationship to their ancestral place disrupt
language and communication:

The elder people at home do not understand.
. . . .
The questions from their mouths
and on their faces are unanswerable.
. . . .
They ask, "The Americans want my land?"
You say, "Yes, my beloved Grandfather."
. . . .
There is silence because you can't explain
and you don't want to . . .
. . . .
You don't want that silence to grow
deeper and deeper into you
because that growth inward stunts you,
and that is no way to continue.

(259–60)

In the course of the poem Ortiz has committed acts of dialogic resis-
tance, for example by using Acoma place names to counter the imposition
of an American name for his home, and by offering a community's
voices, including those of "beloved old man Clay," "Old Man Tomato,"
his father, his cousin, and the elders, to counter "The State's claim[s],"
past and present. Now, faced with the silence brought on by the loss of
land and the state's language, he goes further, exhorting his audience,
particularly his Native audience, in an intimate second-person address.
"You want to continue," he affirms,

And so you tell stories.
You tell stories about your People's birth

and their growing.
. . . .
You tell the stories of their struggles.
(260)

Ortiz tells such a story in the extended web of prose and poetry that
makes up "Our Homeland, A National Sacrifice Area," in *Fight Back;* he
begins;

> Aacqumeh hanoh came to their valley from a direction spoken of as
> the northwest. The place they came to had been prepared for them,
> and the name, Aacqu, therefore means that: Which Is Prepared.
> When they arrived in the flat valley sheltered by red and orange
> cliffs, they knew they had found what had been prepared by their
> leaders and instructions from earlier generations of the people. (338)

The story of the people's birth, growth, and struggles is a story of the
land, their relationship to it, and their efforts to maintain that relation-
ship; the stories of this place, Ortiz reminds his audience, are fundamen-
tal to struggle and to survival. "You tell that kind of history, / and you
pray and be humble. / With strength, it will continue that way" (260).

"The State's claim" embodies a communal dialogism (also evident in
"Like myself, the source of these narratives is my home") which demon-
strates one limitation of Bakhtin's theory in relation to works by Native
writers like Ortiz. In communal dialogism, family members, ancestors,
neighbors, even the land itself, speak together, each voice implied, em-
powered, and contextualized by the others; instead of contest or competi-
tion, we hear a harmony of unified, though not identically voiced, inten-
tions. And this harmony, proceeding from a shared relationship to place,
carries an authority which, though it is conferred in part by the presence
of ancestors or elders, is not the "authoritative discourse" of "the fathers"
to which Bakhtin opposes the individual's "internally persuasive dis-
course" ("Discourse in the Novel" 342–46).[4]

In "That's the Place Indians Talk About," from *Fight Back* (321–24),
Ortiz makes clear the distinction between the authority of communal dia-
logism and that of the "authoritative word (religious, political, moral . . .)
that . . . demands that we acknowledge it . . . [that] is, so to speak, the
word of the fathers" ("Discourse in the Novel" 342). In this poem the (great
white) fathers' discourse is quietly challenged by the presence of multiple

voices (including the implied voice of the hot springs), first signaled in the
transition from Ortiz's first-person prose introduction to the body of the
poem. Ortiz begins, "At a meeting in California I was talking with an elder
Paiute man . . . He spoke about Coso Hot Springs, a sacred and healing
place for the Shoshonean peoples, enclosed within the China Lake Naval
Station." He then gives the poem over to the old man, who begins by
establishing the importance of the springs and the presence of other
voices:

> We go up there and camp.
> . . . .
> And we would stay
> for the days we have to.
>
> The Coso Hot Springs would talk to us.
> And we would talk to it.
> The People have to talk to it.

Throughout, he emphasizes the dialogue between the people and the hot
springs:

> You take a flint like this,
> . . . .
> And you give it like this.
> When you pray.
> When you sing.
> When you talk to the hot springs.
> You talk with it when it talks to you.

This communal reciprocity of intentions is voiced in a dialogic that encom-
passes past and present, people and place; when it is disrupted by the
imposing presence of the white fathers, one effect is a subtle but clear
foregrounding of heteroglossia. Now, the old man says, when

> The People go up there to talk with the hot springs,
> to use the power, to keep ourselves well with,
>   . . . there is a fence with locks all around,
> and we have to talk with the Navy people
> so they can let us inside the fence to the hot springs.
>
> . . . .

We don't like it, to have to do that.
We don't want to talk to the government fence,
the government Navy.
That's the place the Indian people are talking about now.

These lines reveal the heteroglossia of "have to," while they make an earlier statement like "we would stay / for the days we have to" clearly dialogic, for it challenges the "fathers'" presumption that only the Navy "can let [the Indians] inside" (a claim that would make the relation of people and place dependent upon the interlopers' authority). But the communally cohesive and therefore authoritative discourse of people and place withstands the discourse of the "fathers"; the effectiveness of the communal struggle is forecast as the Paiute elder continues:

We keep going up there,
for all this many years, we have to.
To keep talking to the power
of the power in the earth, we have to.
That's the Indian way.
. . . .
                . . . and pretty soon
we will talk to the hot springs power again.
That's the place Indians talk about.
                                        Listen.
that's the way you hear it.

The poem continues for another half page, but the Navy and the fence do not reappear; in effect their words have been enclosed and erased by the place, the prayers, and the Indians' talk. By giving virtually the whole poem to the old man, Ortiz both makes himself part of the audience and implicitly models the attentive listening necessary to reciprocity.[5] The relationships between the people and the hot springs, and the poet and the old man, in turn, make possible the power and the assurance with which they engage the ongoing struggle to "overcome the official line, with its tendency to distance itself from the zone of contact" ("Discourse in the Novel" 345).

"We Have Been Told Many Things," says the title of the poem that immediately follows "That's the Place Indians Talk About," "but We Know This to Be True" (324). Again, a title conveys the competing intentions underlying the exchanges of language between Ortiz's Acoma people and the representatives of government, industry, and the dominant non-Native culture. The tensions that pervade contested spaces are implicit in this title, even in the difference between the passive voice of the first clause and the active voice of the second. The "many things" the people have been told are not enumerated; they can be readily inferred from Ortiz's earlier collections and from poems that surround this one in *Fight Back,* poems that describe Indians' experiences of exploitation and prejudice in the context of the New Mexico uranium mining boom. What Ortiz emphasizes in "We Have Been Told Many Things" is not the deceptive and manipulative words of the "liars, thieves, and killers" but what the Paiute elder knew, what "we know . . . to be true":

> We are not alone in our life;
> we cannot expect to be.
> The land has given us our life,
> and we must give life back to it.
> . . . .
> the land and the people.
>   (324–25)

The mutually necessary, mutually supportive "self-reliance" (Ortiz's term) of land and people supersedes the conflicts implied in the title and foregrounded elsewhere.

An earlier piece (from *A Good Journey*) elaborates upon this relationship of people and land in more intimate terms. "Back into the Womb, the Center" (209–10) begins with a drive toward Cochiti Canyon,

> onto a mesa which very gently
> upsloped, and Dave pointed
> to a distant white space of clay,
> saying, "Right there is the beginning."

In this first evidence of heteroglossia "the beginning" signifies the beginning of the canyon, the beginning of a story, the place of that beginning, the first place, the womb.

> At the mouth
> the canyon begins without notice.
> . . . .

and you don't notice at all
that you're going deeper in.

After driving further, "about a mile up," Ortiz tells us,

> . . . I looked up
> and the immensity of the place
> settled upon me without weight.
> I knew that we were near
> one of the certain places
> that is the center of the center.
> Later on, when I walked
> a mile up, I found the crotch
> where the canyon enters
> the mountain, the crotch
> where there is a clump
> of thick brush, and I felt cold.

Ortiz has reached a place of personal and cultural origins invested with immense mythic power; this place constitutes an affirmation that enables the poet to pray, as he concludes:

> It is strange this time,
> and I have to pray this way.
> "Do you mind if I sit on this stone
> and lean against this mountain
> and listen to the silence of everything?
> Do you mind if I go back 10,000 years?"

Ending the passage in the present tense, Ortiz gives the experience an immediacy that implies a continuous present, a time that in language and in relation to the land, can be sustained. As he speaks to the place itself, attentive to the moment's concreteness and its silence, he again demonstrates the reciprocity with land and place that enables survival.

The second part of "Back into the Womb, the Center," in prose, immediately follows the prayer, and reveals the pain caused when that intimate, reciprocal relationship is disrupted. This passage recalls an experience shared with thousands of other Indian children, including the poet's father: leaving home for boarding school. Ortiz tells us, "The way we went was this way. From Grants past our home in McCartys where my mother said, 'There's our home. Look.' I looked but tears blurred my eyes" (210–11). During a mass in the chapel shortly after his arrival, he fainted.

> I just fainted, that's all, into the subtle chasm that opens and you lose all desire and control, and I fell, very slowly, it seemed. I found myself being carried out by my father . . . He talked with me for a long time, slowly and gently, and I felt him tremble and stifle his sobs several times. He told me not to worry and to be strong and brave.
>
> I wonder if I have been. That was the first time I ever went away from home. It's a memory of it, that time.

The passage suggests both return and loss—the "subtle chasm" might recall the canyon, the "certain place" of beginning. Yet the faint also represents a loss of self, in the loss of "all desire and control"; the boy *finds himself* in his father's arms, being carried away from the chapel (the central defining reality, we might suppose, of Saint Catherine's Indian School), yet his father's barely suppressed emotion confirms that the reprieve can only be temporary. As the final sentences tell us, this experience of profound dislocation is the result of his removal from home; this is a story of the devastation he felt on leaving his place. The effects continue in the adult's uncertainty as to whether he has been "strong and brave." The last line, "It's a memory of that time," both provides a necessary distance from the experience, and prevents its being forgotten: as memory this loss of home is part of the history that must be recollected and told, if the people and the land are to continue.

"A New Mexico Place Name," "The State's Claim," and "That's the Place Indians Talk About" focus on literal border conflicts, in which the contested space is land—its ownership, its use, but more fundamentally (and more culturally revealing), its meaning. As these poems imply and "We Have Been Told Many Things" makes explicit, for Ortiz and for traditional people the land, their place, is a relative, a party to a dynamic relationship of responsibility and reciprocity. To the developers, the utilities, and the Navy the land is a commodity. This is the contrast between traditional Indian beliefs and Western assumptions about land identified by Vine Deloria. That such conflicts can create internal border conditions and contested spaces is evident in each poem's recognition of the potentially silencing effects of struggles over land. Very clearly, in each, succumbing to silence would be succumbing, in Owens's sense, to territorial control of both land and spirit. Each poem offers dialogism as a way of resisting the landgrab and its effects. One's relationship to place can be affected by borderland tensions even when control of the land is not the immediate issue. We see such effects in "Back into the Womb, the Center." Here questions of return to or departure from particularly meaningful places are subtly shadowed by the poet's awareness of ongoing conflict—as represented, in the first section, by government buildings and a dam, and in the second by the train, the chapel, and the trip itself.

Ortiz's evocations of the land, his prayers to holy places, his responses to Acoma's landscape and history, are one with his people's knowledge that their identity and history are grounded in their ancestral place. It is this knowledge that makes continuation possible and struggle not only necessary but worthwhile. Even paved over with cement, as in "Washyuma Motor Hotel" (97–98), the spirits of the ancient people survive in the land, their voices powerful and empowering. These realities, in turn, imbue Ortiz's voice with assurance. Thus, despite names like Church Rock and Laguna, Ortiz knows that

> . . . for sure those are Indian lands
> and the People who live there
> are Indian People.
> Hanoh stu tah ah.
> We are Hanoh. People. Hanoh. People.
>   (330)

Robert Davis's poetry, similarly grounded in an ancestral place, is imbued by that place with a sense of constant multidirectional transitions; his landscape offers an unstable familiarity, a shifting ground. For Davis, a self-consciously mixed-blood writer who locates himself in the home and culture of his Tlingit father, place is both solid and mutable, the ground one walks on and the ground, too, of a compelling and vexed communal history and a still vibrant mythology; place is thus both utterly and incompletely reliable in his poetry. Yet his poetry, like Ortiz's, reverberates with the creative possibilities integral to a place-grounded culture. (It is tempting to think of how geographical difference could contribute to contrasting senses of place. Ortiz belongs to a place whose appearance can suggest stability and changelessness—even ruins stand for many hundreds of years. In Davis's Alaska landscape change is palpably constant, in fog, rain, the tides, the smell of water-soaked earth and wood. Yet my perceptions are those of an Alaskan; my description of change as "constant" is intentionally paradoxical; and, as a traveler in New Mexico and Arizona, I have seen the changing effects of light and shadow on apparently changeless landscapes.)

Davis's home is Kake, a Tlingit village of 700–800 people located on Kupreanof Island in southeast Alaska. In 1869, as a result of Native retaliation for the killing of a Kake man by a U.S. Army sentinel in Sitka, the *U.S.S. Saginaw,* under Commander R. W. Meade, destroyed several Kake villages. (During this same period Meade, engaged in mapping the area, named a number of local features, including Saginaw Bay, for his ship.) In the early 1900s, influenced by Protestant missionaries and their local converts, Kake villagers destroyed their totem poles, the carved and painted cedar symbols of family and clan stories and status; from then until perhaps the late 1960s traditional Tlingit culture was suppressed in Kake, surviving, when it did, underground.[6] Davis himself is the son of a white mother, who came from Michigan to Alaska as a teacher and was adopted into the Tsaagweidi clan (Eagle moiety) of Kake; by matrilineal descent this is also Davis's clan. His father, also a teacher, was a Kake Tlingit of the Raven moiety. Davis describes himself as "a Neo-traditional artist/storyteller," one of whose responsibilities is "to begin naming and acknowledging our grief, as a first step toward healing. Because writing is a catharsis, and healing always moves outward, to others, and finally, hopefully, to the earth herself." He believes in a "continuous creation theory: everything is in perpetual renewal." Tradition and ritual "are necessary because they ground us and affirm who we are in relation to where we have been." But because "we are more than just our pasts . . . [f]orm and content of older ritual are modified as they accommodate newer circumstances . . . [and] the old and the new become one thing in the present."[7] Davis's poems thus acknowledge and incorporate elements of myth and history in a continuous—and difficult—act of coming to terms with past and present which is also a process of coming to terms with a particular, powerful place. In this place the instability of that "one thing" composed of the old and the new makes for a poetry of shifting borders and recurrent questioning.

In two parallel stanzas "What the Crying Woman Saw" (*Soulcatcher* 26)[8] evokes the tensions known by those who find themselves divided or

negotiating between different places, times, and cultures. These stanzas
evoke two pasts, each appealing, each binding time to a particular place,
each inaccessible:

> We could not go back
> . . . .
> Michigan farm, earth-smell following rain,
> fresh-mown grass and lilac on the breeze
> . . . .
> We could neither go back
> to a time of fishcamps, of boardwalks
> in a small Tlingit village . . .
> . . . .
> everything quietly alive.

Each place was peaceful, each associated with nurturing fertility. Unable
to return, to locate himself completely and unambivalently in either past
(or place), the speaker must imagine some new mode of being in time and
place. The poem's third and final stanza both begins and reflects on that
process:

> He was one of the first to marry a white woman.
> It must have been hard, some things he never talked about.
> I don't know.
> Did you imagine the darkest-eyed, brown-skinned boy
> one day stuck at a typewriter
> remembering time two different ways?

The speaker first extends his present dilemma into the past, by referring to
an earlier generation's cultural border crossings. (Davis probably refers to
his own parents, especially his father, but the lines might suggest others'
histories as well.) The older man's silences prompt the speaker's recogni-
tion of his difficulties; the painfully simple "I don't know" evokes the loss
of communication, an ironic continuity of past with present, the speaker's
self-awareness, and his only partial ability to articulate the older man's
experience or his own. The poem's final question, perhaps addressed to
the "crying woman," conflates the two generations, in an effort to imagine
a new place and mode for the "brown-skinned boy." The juxtaposition of
one day and *two different ways* throws into relief the at best partially resolved

dilemma of accommodating cultural, temporal, and personal differences. Rather than in a geographical location, the poem places the boy "at a typewriter," where he is "stuck": language, which proved inadequate to his father's experience, must now be made to serve both memory and the present. The doubleness of this poem's memory implies doubleness of language, but only in the last six lines (quoted above) does Davis directly link the problematical nature of language to the geographical-cultural dislocations the poem emphasizes; this link becomes the focus in the poem that immediately follows, in his book, "At the Door of the Native Studies Director" (see chapter 1).

The eight-part "Saginaw Bay: I Keep Going Back" (14–21) situates the theme of cultural, familial, and personal location and dislocation in the mythic and historical past and traces it into the present and future in a continuous, recursive process of recollection and struggle. The poem begins in heteroglossia. Saginaw Bay, named for the warship that attacked the village (a ship named for a bay in Michigan that was in turn named "from the Ojibway, 'the place of the Sac' " [see Abate]), is the place to which Davis and his poem "keep going back" in search of self, history, and language. The first remembered home of the Tsaagweidi clan, it was created by Raven, the Tlingit trickster/creator, who is introduced in part I. Language, as we have seen in Davis's Raven poems, is both a means of creation and a sign of changeability: "cocksure smooth talker, good looker, / Raven makes a name for himself . . . stirs things up." Having brought light to the world,

> Raven turns his head and laughs in amazement
> then dives off the landscape,
> dividing the air
> into moment before and instant after.

Moving on, he infuses "Kuiu Island, Saginaw Bay" with language and with instability: "Its voices trying to rise through fog, / the long tongue of the sea / sliding beneath the bay." Tricky, enchanted, ungraspable and yet constant, "Raven is taken in" by the plenty of this place he has created; "Oilslick Raven / fixed against the glossy surface of infinity" becomes a fittingly elusive presiding spirit for the Kake people's history and Davis's efforts to come to terms with it.

In part II, Davis recalls his Tsaagweidi clan's almost idyllic life at the first village site, its rude disruption by "intruders" on "a swift slave raid," and the "battered" clan's move north to Kupreanof Island. "That became the village / of Kake. Those became Kake-kwaan." Thus the village was born in the change from peaceful plenty to displacement and homesickness. This is confirmed in the first line of part III: "Kake is The Place of No Rest. It is." Here the poet speaks in the first person for the first time, as he begins to recall the history of the destruction of traditional culture and his own family's complex involvement: on the one hand, "my aunt drove the silver spike / in the middle of Silver Street / sealing the past forever." On the other,

> Grandfather went out in his slow skiff
> and cached in the cliffs
> his leather wrapped possessions
> preserved like a shaman body
> that can't be destroyed, that won't burn.

The aunt's action marks the re-creation of place according to non-Native, urban conventions; the grandfather's identifies a place that will protect the material remains of indigenous culture. Part IV further complicates family history by identifying the grandfather as "a great minister" who "traveled / with the Salvation Army band, the famous Kake band . . . to play for President Harding." Davis's question, "So that must have been about when?" may suggest uncertainty not only about temporal history but also about his grandfather's location in the often-contested spaces of emotional and cultural history. Continuing, Davis tells of his father's dislocation as a student taken away to industrial school, then brings himself into family history: "Now they say I remind them of him. / But you have to catch me sober." Not until the final part, though, will he bring his personal experience fully into the poem. First, in part V, he describes the assault on place and history by loggers who "gnaw . . . at the edge of the woods" and with "high-power rifles chip / at the cliff painting." Here, too, past and present intersect, for the painting was a warning to the raiders of centuries before, "who destroyed with such precision." Next, through his uncles' memories in part VI, Davis again recalls that long ago devastation at Saginaw Bay, but now he adds the memory of a disaster that befell one party of invaders: at low tide, "at Halleck Harbor, Saginaw Bay," his uncles "found in the rubble / of boulders from the cave-in / a hundred skeletons" of "slave hunters / piling over each other / still hunting." Throughout "Saginaw Bay: I Keep Going

Back" Davis brings the past into the present through memory; in part VII, he returns to the poem's beginning to affirm the unity of past and present in this place:

> Because Raven tracks are locked in fossil,
> the clambeds snarled in roots,
> because we have been told,
> we know for a fact
> Raven moves in the world.

Place and story correspond, and the mercurial Raven becomes a certainty.

Part VIII, the final one, brings us into the recent past and the present, then hearkens back again to the time (and place) of origins, as Davis returns to the theme of language, one of Raven's means of creation and, since the beginning, changeable and filled with potential for conflict. "When I was young everyone used Tlingit / and English words at once. / Tlingit fit better." *Fit better* implies both comfort and accuracy; now, we may infer, only a few use both languages so readily.

> The old ones tell a better story in Tlingit.
> But I forget so much
> and a notepad would be obtrusive
> and suspicious . . .

The gap between *tell* and *forget* marks the loss of place-grounded history that resulted from the replacement of Tlingit by English, and the oral by written language and began with the dynamiting of the Kake totems, "storytellers blown to pieces." Then "people began to move differently, tense. / They began to talk differently, mixed." Now, as this poem's very existence testifies, the written must carry the burden if any of the old knowledge is to survive.

> I know there is a Tlingit name for that bay
> and it means "Everything Shifted Around,"
> what was once down there is up here.
> I do not remember the name
> of the Halleck Harbor shaman
> except that he was of course the most powerful
> and I feel somehow tied to him (and was he

the one wrapped in cedar mat
sunk in the channel
only to reappear
at Pt. White ascending the beach
to his own grieving ceremony?) I don't know.
I get mixed up. But I know my own name,
it's connected with some battle.

Dialogism comes to the fore in this passage. By referring to a Tlingit name known only in translation, Davis suggests the incompleteness, the inadequacy, of the subsequently cited English place names, even as he uses them to imply the reciprocal centrality of place, language, and story. He complicates his own knowledge by enclosing a compelling image of shamanic power in parentheses and voicing it as a question. What he knows is, in part, the incompleteness of his knowledge. Thus his certainty about his "own name" is confirmed by uncertainty about its relation to history— "some battle." Yet the shaman's story, and with it some of his power, does survive, even if fragmented and clothed in doubt.

Listen, I'm trying to say something—
always our stories have lived through paintings.
always our stories stayed alive in retelling.

You wonder why sometimes you can't reach me?
I keep going back.
I keep trying to see my life
against all this history,
Raven in the beginning
hopping about like he just couldn't do enough.

Davis juxtaposes the uncertainty implicit in ongoing effort ("I keep going . . . keep trying"), with conviction ("always . . . always"). In these lines he acknowledges the burden of responsibility he bears, as a sharer and remaker of language and story, and the precariousness of the story and its telling. To fulfill his responsibility in the present, he must continuously go back in time, back to the place of origin, back to the knowledge of Raven "hopping about like he just couldn't do enough"—an image of assurance and incompleteness, and thus of the grounded mutability of place and language as Davis knows them in this poem. Like Ortiz, Davis draws attention to conflicts over control of the land and the people, conflicts that, in Kake, successively involved the Navy, the missionaries, and the logging company. Davis suggests some of the internal cultural tensions as he alludes to the beginning of shame at old practices, alcohol-related problems, and the threatened loss of the indigenous language. His reflections on his own relationship to language suggest a trace of hesitancy, and tension is discernible between this hesitancy and the urgent desire for continuity through language—a continuity put at risk by the cumulative effects of borderland contests. And Davis's acute awareness of uncertainty must, I think, be intensified (perhaps ironically) by his knowledge of Kake's history: "Kake is The Place of No Rest"; the bay's lost Tlingit name means "Everything Shifted Around." (With contrasting effects, Ortiz tells us that Acoma's name means "Which Is Prepared" [*Woven Stone* 338].) Perhaps it is this recognition of instability in the place (-name) itself that keeps Davis from presenting dialogism as a direct means of resistance, as Ortiz does; instead, dialogism simultaneously implies the shortcomings of English place names and is the means whereby the poet, by writing the poem, both exposes his sense of his own linguistic limitations and contributes to his culture's continuity. (As a carver, Davis of course also contributes materially to continuity.)

Davis is continually negotiating the borders between past and present, the Tlingit and English languages, Tlingit and Euro-American cultures. These borders meet and shift in his own personal history, as they have in the history of his Kake people, from their beginnings, where "the long tongue of the sea / slid[es] beneath the bay," into the present. His own border consciousness, then, may not only complicate his relation to the place and culture to which he evidently feels most drawn, but also allow him a way of connection, via reflection.

Davis's poems show that experiences of language and place are analogous and connected. Knowing a place, specifically the village of Kake and its environs, the temperate coastal rainforest of Southeast Alaska, is knowing the mutability of a particular geography and the parallel multiplicity of place-grounded myth, history and language. As place becomes unstable (in both its changing physical realities and its history-infused meanings), it in turn contributes to the foregrounding of heteroglossia and dialogism and the consequent further destabilizing of language. Such grounded instability seems inevitably, in Davis's work, to produce ambivalence. Another kind of ambivalence about place appears in the poetry of Jim Barnes, for whom places left behind become sites of desire or regret, reminders of the not unwilling traveler's sometimes tenuous connections to personal and cultural pasts.

Barnes celebrates his English and Welsh, as well as his Choctaw origins. In his accounts of childhood, the significance of things Indian is subject to change: in his 1983 *MELUS* interview he says, "in my immediate family we did not speak Choctaw . . . I delighted in learning names of things in Choctaw . . . the food I ate at [a Choctaw friend's] . . . house didn't taste like the food at my house which was more typically English or Welsh . . . We would have *chongus chompooey* at Tom's house, but Mom never made it" (57–58). "On Native Ground," though, tells us that "I was raised in Choctaw country . . . I was raised on the language and the foods . . . I have eaten *chongkus chom pooey* . . . and *tom fuller* . . . and hickory nut soup—to my infinite delight" (92). The facts have not changed, nor the pleasure, but the emphasis has. In the interview, he carefully qualifies his "Indian" experience:

> I identify with those things that have become associated with the Native American movement, but I would identify with those anyway. I love the land, the earth, the sky, the natural things and I have reverence for them . . . I know it is popular for some Indian writers to proclaim their Indianness, but I don't feel the need to, nor do I feel any need to proclaim my Welshness, because, after all, I am an American . . . It makes me feel good to be included with poets I know are more Indian not only in blood but maybe in outlook than I am. But again I don't know what an Indian outlook is, because I am a mixture of so many things. I am glad to be there in the anthologies. (59–60)

Fundamentally, Barnes resists regional or ethnic categories: asked whether he sees himself as "an Indian voice," he responds, "No. I see myself as a poet." Asked whether Indian writers have "a role to play in carrying out . . . or maintaining traditions," he says, "Yes, I think the Indian writer is like any other writer. First, he should be committed to the art itself and if in his art he can make the general reading public more aware of other cultures, that is a plus" (interview 59, 60). His is an aesthetic of the universal:

> Whenever the universal grows out of the specific and vision is achieved, you can tell yourself here is art and it should be preserved . . . we must not be misled. The writer is first a writer, second a Native American, a Black, a Chicano . . . A writer, whoever he may be, if he believes in art as art, will bring everything to bear upon his art, ethnic or otherwise ("On Native Ground" 93, 94)

In his commitment to "everything" Barnes isn't all that different from Wendy Rose, but his conclusions are different. More inclined toward a formalist poetics, he resists politics in poetry; perhaps related is the fact that he seems less intent upon examining his racial and cultural affiliations, and less apt to perceive those in terms of conflict. Indeed, though, he very frequently brings "the ethnic" to bear, not only in some of the poems I discuss here but also in others that recall or imagine Native American history personal or communal.

Not surprisingly, Barnes also rejects biographical criticism, and in "On Native Ground" he assails the idea of "the Poet-as-Speaker":

> the poet does not speak. The poet creates a voice, and that voice speaks . . . The voice is the fiction (the lie) in respect to the poet's life . . . he has to expound these facts [from his experience] in a certain way to create a universal. He must *think* he is speaking, and he must make it real. (95–97)

On the other hand, and Barnes's dismissal of poetry as autobiography notwithstanding, his numbered but nonchronological "Autobiography" poems suggest at least a readiness to test the dividing line and to exploit the creative possibilities its subtlety (and permeability) offers.

"On Native Ground" begins with words that identify place, its recollection, and its loss, as vital sources for his work:

> I was five years old the last time I heard the mountain lion scream.
> That was in Oklahoma, 1938, when times were hard and life was good—and sacred. But a year later the WPA [Works Progress Administration] had done its work: roads were cut, burial mounds were dug, small concrete dams were blocking nearly every stream. The Government was caring for its people. Many were the make-work jobs. A man could eat again, while all about him the land suffered. The annual spring migration of that lone panther was no more. The

riverbanks that had been his roads and way stations bore the scars of
the times, the scars of loss.

In my mind the rivers must always run free. But in truth today I do
not recognize them. They are alien bodies on a flattening land where
everything has been made safe, civilized into near extinction . . .
Green silence in the heavy heat of summer is no more.

The Fourche Maline River and Holson Creek flow through much
of what I have written . . . My sense of place is inexorably linked to
these two streams and to the prairies and woods between them. (87)

Much of Barnes's poetry is a poetry of transience, and thus of loss, of
departure, of elegy. Still, he ends the first section of his essay with these
words: "We have been called a nation of tourists. But I suspect, deep
down, some of us somehow know where home is—and what it has
become" (91). In reading Barnes's poems, it is important to honor his
reservations regarding the role of ethnicity and autobiography in poetry.
At the same time, we must acknowledge what the poems show us. For
Barnes place is compelling, and place and the past are often intimately
intertwined, especially on home ground. There the past evoked in the
poems is partly, and importantly, though by no means only, an Indian
and a Choctaw past.[9]

Often, in Barnes's poetry, a particular place becomes the site of a
search for connection to the past, or of questioning whether connection is
possible. This is the case in "Near Crater Lake" (*Season* 7), where

Between hill and river the trail
forks, edges deep in stone only
shadows know, and only the stones
can say which way my fathers took.

The stones' testimony is somewhat reassuring, yet it also draws attention
to the speaker's limited knowledge; he is moved, here, to prayer that
draws attention to loss and the fleeting nature of his knowledge:

old fathers, tell me once again
why the path forks and the river
runs fast with fish to homes beneath
another sky, homes beneath the sea.

"A Season of Loss" (*Season* 27) begins with a moment that could have led to "Near Crater Lake":

We left the horses in the draw
and climbed the painted ledge to see
the blue and distance home but saw
an autumn sun set fire to trees

on ridges we had yet to pass

Behind the speaker the ledge offers a still image of lost knowledge: "At our back a glyph grew perfect: / hard in stone a hand drew back to throw"; between the sunset's "fire" and the stone's silent witness, the speaker ventures an impulse of connection, silent too, perhaps disappointing in its evanescence, but admirable in its spare integrity:

. . . Only human,
we touched thoughts, hands, eyes,
assured ourselves of the moment,
and leaned together hard against the sky.

"Call It Going with the Sun" (*Season* 64–65), a poem located by its first line in the place Barnes has identified as central to his sense of place, is dominated by qualification and nonstop undercutting of the impulse to return and the effort to recover the past. The landscape offers both a lesson and an image for the seeker's effort:

Where Fourche Maline runs into Holson Creek,
first it almost does then backs off and makes
a circle so that an almost island
sits as though the river's god forgot his job.

Riddled as this poem is by self-subversions, it is almost as if Barnes is moved here to disrupt articulation and any illusions of power or permanence that human language might facilitate. Thus,

Now it has faded
. . . or just about . . .
. . . .

> . . . I cannot think
> this a field of corn. How can I reach
> Caddoes or pre-Columbians said to
> have lived this land? I came to fish but think
> of paying rent . . .
> . . . .
> . . . I drift. The current's vague.
> . . . .
> I remember cornfields, but find a forest.

Such discourse demonstrates language's self-disruption as self-conscious heteroglossia or dialogism: the competing intentions belong to the same speaker. And as place becomes almost ephemeral, certainly unreliable, so does language. By the poem's end not only memory but the place itself, and the object that embodies both, are disintegrating: "A stone axe in my hand is cold / comfort. Crumbling, it's hardly worth the trip."

Yet fleeting moments of knowledge offered by places like the ones evoked in these poems seem to vindicate the impulse to return and the effort to connect. And two other poems from *A Season of Loss*, "The Long Lone Nevada Night Highway" (37) and "Autobiography, Chapter X: Circus in the Blood" (51), demonstrate Barnes's ability to wrest moments of connection from transience itself. In the former the fact of being in transit is literally what stops two drivers in a moment and place that create a kind of intimacy:

> Strangers we were friends for a long moment
> on that long lone Nevada night highway
> at the wreck (two dead on blankets or carcoats
> on the gasolined pavement under our stars[)]
> . . . .
> the long Nevada night highway is like that.

There is, Barnes implies, something wondrous in the stranger-friends' instant, mutual recognition and concerted efforts. Thus "what finally shocked" them was "only this":

> . . . that after the taking
> of numbers, after the siren's wail, after
> the sanding of blood and the sweeping of glass,

after the conjectures, the sighs, the regrets,
what would there be to hold us to this spot
on the lone Nevada night highway where the stars
blanketing earth were ours and we were one?

Repeating slight variations on the title three times in the poem's twenty-two lines locates transience and stops it, while human disaster and response make this almost featureless place theirs, a site for connections and then for the shock of parting. Of course, the fact that this respite is caused by death on the road, and that the two stranger-friends continue on their different ways, reminds us that transience, not its opposite, is the given here.

Barnes personalizes and elaborates upon such a recognition in "Autobiography, Chapter X" (*Season* 51), where an inherited predisposition to "nomadic ways" is the speaker's surest basis for connecting with his father. The combination of celebration and effort makes the poem ambivalent—and ambivalence is Barnes's hallmark tone in his reflections on place and mobility.

There's a circus in my blood I've waited forty years
    to know, my father's hollow glance weighing on
    my shoulders like a sledge . . .
    . . . .
So here in this nonesuch bigtop in slow August, I
    surprise myself into a certain knowing . . .
        . . . a lust forever to move
    from place to place . . .
Henceforth I swear I will delight when I can name the
    earth new under my feet . . .
    . . . .
And I will try to know the dancing in my blood, how
    it reels, steps, stops, and how on occasion it
    swings me out of tune . . .
    . . . .
And I will praise my father for his shifting the shape of
    ways, for letting me know the permanence only of
    road; will praise my father and swing my heavy
    hammer to guy this my own ephemeral sky.

Again, being on the road is the given. Place is present, if it is, by implication, in the speaker's resistance to being placed. The figure of the circus tent embraces both the concreteness and the temporary essence of his inheritance and this moment. Likewise, the poem's final one and a half lines both celebrate and resist this recognition. Perhaps one might ask whether, in poems like "Near Crater Lake," Barnes betrays a tendency to idealize the past he envisions in association with remembered places; I would suggest that, with the kind of resistance he manifests here (a resistance implied in other poems as well), he offers a sure counterpoint to any such idealizing. Barnes's tone makes this poem somewhat reminiscent, in its critical self-awareness, of "Call It Going with the Sun." Here, though, we find the possibility of a kind of joy, an animation that allows a comic resilience to show through the critical self-exposure.

Perhaps the remembered and imagined power of place to sustain a sense of self is one reason for Barnes's recurrent poetic returns, however much he sometimes undercuts such efforts. Such a validating power evidently inheres in the childhood place he recalls in "Fourche Maline Bottoms" (*Sawdust* 47):

> *Kid*, they told me, those raucous neighbor boys,
> *you won't find nothing down in them bottoms*
> *worth a shit.* I showed them nothing but thumbs
> and fingers waving ears. I knew what poise
> to take and still avoid their wrath. The joy
> of finding arrowheads beneath the crumb-
> ling leaves was something I could never come
> to trade for any neighbor's game. No toy
> could ever do what flint or milky chert
> could do for my own small mauled imagination.
> For seven years I sifted coal-black dirt,
> found arrowheads so keen I knew I'd seen
> into my own ancestral past where hurt
> and harm stood taller than neighbor boys had been.

The contrast between the neighbors' voices and the speaker's knowledge anchors the poem in certainty, obviating any possibility of the self-mockery that shadows some of the other poems' searches for identity in connection to place. In Fourche Maline Bottoms and in possession of arrowheads sifted from that dirt, the speaker knew an assurance unlike the sensations of Barnes's more adult (and more doubtful) wanderers and questioners. The arrowheads attest both to a continuing ancestral presence and to the speaker's own belonging, earned by his tenacity and loyalty, to place and to people. The sonnet's sestet subtly modulates what might otherwise be a tone of pure satisfaction, as the speaker characterizes his "small" (child's) imagination as "mauled" and concedes he knew even then that "hurt and harm" had loomed in the "ancestral past." Yet such recognitions are restorative, such knowledge the stuff that enables survival: the flint and chert he found in the leaves and dirt of Fourche Maline Bottoms strengthened the boy's imagination so that he could see into the past; his knowledge of the past, similarly, enabled him to recognize the insignificance of the neighbor boys and stand up to their disdain. (It bears noting that in the first eight poems of *The Sawdust War* Barnes evokes in a sustained way a child's grounding in place; the child's consuming interest in a far-off world war throws into relief his existence in the place that is home.)

Place is compelling in Barnes's poems in part, too, because, as is also true for Ortiz and Davis, it is so inextricably (and for Barnes as for Davis, problematically) related to knowledge, memory, and language. In Barnes, place can serve to chasten our presumptions about language, to correct language's delusions, to suggest the verities beyond speech that we cannot capture yet must attempt to name. These seem to be the implications of his references to "tales told by shadows" and "a sense hard to name," in "After the Great Plains" (*Sawdust* 35), a poem that affirms the paradoxical power of a changeable place, even over travelers passing through. Sometimes the speaker's transience prompts reflections on language's shortcomings. In "Autobiography, Chapter XVII: Floating the Big Piney" (Niatum 57), place is movement and change; the speaker floats on the river, which becomes an image both of language's changeability and its limits: "How the river cools your blood is something you can't / explain: you search the bottom stones for words / unscientific, words fleshed with the sound of sense." As in other poems, place, the river, reminds him of lost human connections; further, on the river, "all words are lost and . . . all you have to offer is / pause, the silence of the water and the small / knowledge that the river takes you over all." Place subsumes language, affording us only a "small knowledge," an ambiguous assurance.

The section of *The Sawdust War* entitled "In Another Country" (87–116) offers a kind of celebration of fully intentional transience, as it expresses a cosmopolitanism that is in accord with Barnes's aesthetics of the universal and his resistance of ethnic or regional categories. These poems of a temporary residence in Italy suggest a process of becoming familiar with the unfamiliar through inquiry and adjustment.

> We expected thick moss
> and castle walls
> and olives
> . . . .
> . . . But this is Lombardy . . .
> . . . .
>   . . . so full of
> centuries we
> want to trust
> the Alps . . .
>
>   (88)

In "Castle Keep" (108) place is an invitation both to meditation and to hazard:

> Three hundred feet above the lake, the fort
> is turning back from stone to soil. The high
> wall crumbles daily onto the grass by
> the retaining wall we sit on . . .
> . . . .
>   . . . This place
> takes hold of us and draws our eyes around
> precipitous ways. The risks we take on
>
> climbs would make a sane man dizzy. We run
> the trails that lead us to more than ruins.

Yet if these Lombardy poems sometimes suggest the possibility of finding oneself at home in transit, Barnes disrupts any inclination to read them as resolving the themes of place and transience. He does so, for example, with humor that draws on the relation between place and language: in a jewelry store, "I say / we are just looking, and feel my Italian sink" (94).

Barnes shares with Ortiz and Davis a recognition of the emotional and spiritual power of place. Beyond this recognition, probably the most important commonality evident in these poems is their recognition that place and language are related. In "Call It Going with the Sun" place conspires with the poet's own tendency to undermine illusions of connection or permanence by subverting articulation, and in "Autobiography, Chapter XVII: Floating the Big Piney" Barnes give us the river as an image of language's chageability, its evanescence, its unreliability ("all words are lost"). In contrast, in Ortiz's work, the fact that language is responsive to land, through story, makes both reliable. "The source of these narratives is my home," we are told, and in "That's the Place Indians Talk About" there is no doubt that language connects the people and the place. In a sense the ability to speak depends on and is confirmed by the land, and language, rightly used, protects and serves the land. Barnes's perception of the connection between place and language is closer to that of Robert Davis. In "Saginaw Bay: I Keep Going Back" memory and language are both fragile, thus incompletely reliable. Language's instability has counterparts in the history of the place and its physical character—this is a landscape highly subject to change, as evidenced in Davis's references to the tides, fog, mud flats, and river. Since it depends to a considerable degree on language, relationship to place is also open to uncertainty, redefinition, and change.

For Barnes the sense of language's limited certainty is compounded by the fact that his speaker is far from, or only passing through, the places to which his poems refer. Though Barnes identifies himself in terms of a particular, powerful place (recall "On Native Ground"), his relationship to that place, unlike those evoked by Ortiz and Davis, appears to exist primarily in the imagination.[10] Blaeser's comments on Vizenor's relationship to place, and the relationships he creates for his protagonists, apply as well to Barnes's depicted relationship to his Oklahoma childhood home. Vizenor's characters, Blaeser says,

> may have an imaginative rather than an actual connection to place. Having himself experienced how easily actual places can be altered, Vizenor's literary accounts portray a storied 'interior landscape' that persists beyond removal and survives physical destruction of the place . . . the only immutable connections Vizenor's protagonists can afford are interior . . . Vizenor's emphasis on the interior connection serves his attempt to universalize his stories, to deliberately extend their significance beyond the mere tribal. (*Gerald Vizenor* 201)

Perhaps in part because of its dependence on language, Barnes seems to emphasize the often tenuous quality of such an imaginative connection. While Vizenor and his characters appear to revel in the possibilities of imaginative connectedness, Barnes's reflections on place often tend toward the elegiac, as he recounts past losses and draws attention to the fleeting quality of present connections. (And this tone differs not only from Vizenor's—and Ortiz's—but also, despite the ambivalence they have in common, from Davis's.)

Barnes rarely draws attention to the kinds of borderland conflict (including place-related conflict) so compellingly addressed by the other poets discussed thus far. Perhaps the conflicts most important to his sense of place were the unidentified, unnamed contests that must have preceded the irreparable loss he mourns in "On Native Ground"—the loss of wildness occasioned by the WPA projects of the 1930s. In any case his perceptions of place are filtered through the facts of loss and mobility, and the memory of losing the most precious and formative place seems more compelling than present conflicts over landscapes one is simply traveling through might be.

Thus in these poems the closest thing to border consciousness may be the regretful recognition that place can make one's awareness of temporal and cultural distance and difference acutely painful. "Near Crater Lake," for example, draws our attention to the different meanings the place has, for the speaker and his "old fathers," and to the unbridgeable gap between what the speaker "can say" and what his ancestors "knew." "Ghost Fog" (*Season* 57) evokes a similar disjunction, the effect of which turns on Barnes's knowledge of historic borderland conflicts. Camping on Tule Creek, where in 1874 the cavalry slaughtered "between 1,000 and 1,400 Indian horses" (11), he smells "smoke of ancient campfires," hears the wailing of a bereaved mother, and then is abruptly "set . . . straight": "Here was now: a trucker, damn his tunneled eyes, / barrelling-ass down the Amarillo-Lubbock run." Since the speaker has evidently been feeling remorse about digging for artifacts at this site, the speeding truck jolts him out of several kinds of suspect self-absorption.

As the lines from "Ghost Fog" suggest, even with his skepticism about poetry's political uses Barnes does not altogether eschew allusions to cultural or political conflict; however, such references, when they appear, are as likely to come in poems where place is not a primary focus. Thus his characterization of "contemporary Native American poetry":

"You've seen it ragged against a field, / but you seldom think, at the time, / to get there it had to walk through hell" (*American Book of the Dead* 85). "Right Place, Wrong Time" (*Season* 15) may allude to an event (fictional or historical) that occurred in the rural Southwest, but the key location is the hanging tree, called "the sacred tree" by an "old left-over Sioux" who prayed and sang while the hanged man "danced, / & circled round & round." Given Barnes's typical understatement, the only clue that this is more than a piece of entertaining local lore, that here the poet's characteristic resistance of tranquillity might indirectly express cultural resistance, is in the poem's repeated "they say," which offers the possibility of a second way—a dialogic way—of hearing the story. Having said this much, I am wary of pressing further; I want, after all, to meet Barnes's poems on their own terms. Yet noticing such traces and modulations (as well as absences) of border issues in Barnes's poems, along with the ways in which his treatments of place correspond to or differ from others', may help map common ground, and open new possibilities for the poets' works to function mutually as context and commentary.

Like Barnes, Simon J. Ortiz has many poems in which the dominant fact is being on the road. Unlike what we see in much of Barnes's work, though, a strong certainty of connection to home persists in Ortiz's travel poems. This is so even in "A San Diego Poem: January–February 1973" (165–68). Here Ortiz confronts the disorientation of air travel and arrival in "someplace called America," where he finds that "the knowledge of where I am is useless"; yet the final section of this sequence is the much-excerpted "Survival This Way," in which he affirms: "Mountains and canyons and plants / grow. / We traveled this way . . . 'We shall survive this way.' " Similarly, in the more recent poems of *After and Before the Lightning* (some of them discussed in chapter 6), though Ortiz places more emphasis on the arduousness of the journey, he demonstrates the sustaining power of a complex groundedness in place and home. Because "the traveling that is a prayer" (*Woven Stone* 38) implies eventual return, even on the road Ortiz's experience is not primarily one of disconnection.

What Robert Davis's poems evoke seems closer to some of the experience Barnes suggests; ambivalence distinguishes the poetry of both from that of Ortiz. Yet, like Ortiz, Davis writes from a clear sense of being land based. While Davis questions the meanings of place, he does so from the problematical place itself. I don't mean that he must be there to write. But even when, as in "At the Door of the Native Studies Director," he recalls physical dislocation, he voices at least an ambiguous possibility of return.

And in "Saginaw Bay: I Keep Going Back," "going back" is the means to the poet's struggle to understand the web of place-grounded relationships that is his life. Davis's seems a poetry more of transitions than of transience—which is not to claim definitive arrivals: his transitions may be "between," as much as "to" or "from."[11]

The dominant facts in much of Barnes's place-oriented poetry are transience, dislocation, and loss. Perhaps in part as a response to those emphases, his is a poetry highly attentive to form and its restraints, inclined to reticence, sparing in its treatment of the personal. Poems by Roberta Hill Whiteman, Louise Erdrich, and Joy Harjo offer more fully dramatized, less reticent treatments of dislocation. (These three writers also have varying kinds of relationships to particular geographic places; each of them, moreover, like Barnes, comes from a tribal people who have experienced removal from ancestral lands as a consequence of Indian-white conflict over land.)[12]

Gail Tremblay's "Relocation" lays out some of the commonalities implicit in Whiteman's "Reaching Yellow River," Erdrich's "Family Reunion," and Harjo's "The Woman Hanging from the Thirteenth Floor Window." Tremblay's speaker tells us,

> Need made the move inevitable.
> The careful plans, the accidents of choice
> made by strangers made it certain
> . . . .
> . . . We moved away, went to a city
> in the center of the continent and found
> no work that could delight our hands
> or stimulate our minds We struggled
> to see the magic in the land—to find
> the plants that healed. The neon lights
> of bar signs made it difficult to see
> the stars, to know the seasons
> when the ceremonies must be held.
>
> (16)

Oneida poet Roberta Hill Whiteman's "Reaching Yellow River" (26–28) dramatizes a struggle for return and healing; it ends in a homecoming which is also death. As the protagonist travels, grasping "a fifth / with his right hand, the wind with his left," his destination becomes more than a geographical place, the home he has left; he moves, finally, toward the recognition and acceptance that will enable him to join his ancestors. The shift toward a spiritual homecoming in death is signalled as he acknowledges his cultural dislocation:

> I never got the tone
> in all the talk of cure.
> I sang Honor Songs, crawled
>
> the railroad bridge to Canada.
> Dizzy from the ties,
> I hung between both worlds

Whiteman's searching speaker draws attention to the disorienting effects of borderland experience, which left him literally and emotionally dangling. But in a cathartic moment of illumination, he breaks out of alienation:

> The dark heart of me said
> no days more than these.
> As sundown kindled the sumacs,
>
> stunned by the river's smile,
> I had no need for heat,
> no need to feel ashamed.

Lost as he has been, getting by, barely, on drink and bravado, he has still been on something like a vision quest, and is now granted a vision that—though he doesn't know how to explain it—frees him from shame, perhaps the dominant experience of his life. Thus images of light replace the signs of uncertainty and despair, and thus he can go on, hearing the spirits who attend him.

> Then their appaloosas nickered
> in the dawn and they came
> riding down a close ravine.
> . . . .
> I became a hollow horn filled
> with rain, reflecting everything.
> The wind in my hand

burned cold as hoarfrost
when my grandfather nudged me
and called out
my Lakota name.

That Whiteman's protagonist has, in his death, reached home is signalled by the familiarity of his grandfather's touch and the sound of his Lakota name.

In Chippewa Louise Erdrich's "Family Reunion" (*Jacklight* 9–10), too, death might be the dislocated protagonist's destination, but this is ambiguous, partly because of the poem's more fully suggested social/cultural context. Erdrich's language is permeated with the multiple intentions of heteroglossia, which compete for meaning and precedence on the surface of the poem, in references to the turtle, Metagoshe, alcoholism, the car, Ray's names, and the angels.

A younger female relative recounts the rather dubious yet undeniable homecoming of hard-drinking Ray, whose road home ends "in a yard full of dogs. / Them's Indian dogs, Ray says, lookit how they know me," and the speaker concedes that "they do seem to know him." Yet she reflects that "Four generations of people live here. / No one remembers Raymond Two Bears." Not only Ray but his relatives, too, may be lost, even on the home place. But, the next lines say, "So what. The walls shiver, the old house caulked with mud / sails back into the middle of Metagoshe." Erdrich asks, in her interview with Joseph Bruchac, "Don't you, when you go on Indian land, feel that there's more possibility, that there is a whole other world besides the one you can see, and that you're very close to it?" (*Survival This Way* 80). In these lines the poem and its inhabitants enter a realm of mythic possibility, even as they are definitively located in Erdrich's Turtle Mountain Reservation. Metagoshe is the home of the snapping turtle that is caught on a fish line, a reminder, perhaps, of the turtle on whose back the earth was created in many woodlands "earthdiver" creation stories.[13] But Ray apparently does not recognize the animal's importance, for he "pries the beak open and shoves / down a cherry bomb. Lights the string tongue." The decapitated snapper, however, is neither killed nor, as Ray intended, cooked. Rather, the speaker tells us, it "has dragged itself off . . . into a small stream that deepens and widens into a marsh." Evidently the turtle has made it home, and this probability must complicate our understanding of Ray, whose "odor" is "rank beef of fierce turtle pulled dripping from Metagoshe."

The poem's final stanza offers a conclusion that opens, rather than completes, the possible meanings of this wanderer's return home. It begins, "Somehow we find our way back. Uncle Ray / sings an old song to the body that pulls him / toward home." As Erdrich says in "A Writer's Sense of Place," "it is arduous, it is difficult to come home" (41). The journey is now identified as a shared struggle—shared with the speaker (Ray's niece, we now know) and probably with the whole family. Ray is now "Uncle Ray," accorded his familial identity; perhaps somehow, stumblingly, he has overcome his dislocation and found himself at home, in his place. But the poem's last one and a half lines complicate the possibilities: "And the angels come / lowering their slings and litters." First, "the angels" implies a non-Native influence that has insinuated itself into the terrain which Ray and his kin must travel to find themselves. Second, the angels' "slings and litters" might—but don't necessarily—imply Ray's death. Erdrich seems to leave both possibilities open. On the one hand, this stanza may not constitute a conclusion but may instead represent a repeated experience of going "back," with the angels offering comfort and perhaps vision. On the other hand, Ray's undeniably self-destructive responses to dislocation, including his likely history of car wrecks and the fact that the final stanza's tone suggests a different destination from the dead-end yard full of dogs, may imply that the angels are coming to release Ray from his painful mortal wanderings. In either case Erdrich, like Whiteman, has imagined an end to dislocation that allows her damaged character respite, reconnection, and the possibility of vision. In both poems survival is problematical; all that is possible for Whiteman's protagonist and perhaps for Ray is an afterlife that might free him from dispiriting alienation.

In Joy Harjo's "The Woman Hanging from the Thirteenth Floor Window" (*She Had Some Horses* 22–23) ambiguity derives from the woman's history, character, and anticipated action, rather than from the powers of the spirit world. This poem is still more specifically located in terms of place, through the contrast between a present setting and a remembered home. The woman hangs from "the 13th floor window" of a "tenement building . . . in east Chicago," on "the Indian side of town," where Lake Michigan "just sputters / and butts itself against the asphalt." Hanging, she may remind us both of Whiteman's protagonist "dizzy from the [railroad] ties / . . . between both worlds," and of the speaker in Peter Blue Cloud's "Ochre Iron" (Niatum 77–79), whose sensation of his own and his people's vulnerability and dislocation is conveyed in his repeated phrase, "falling forever." "Not alone," Harjo's woman is representative, and is at least tenuously located by relationships:

> She is a woman of children, of the baby, Carlos,
> and of Margaret, and of Jimmy, who is the oldest.
> She is her mother's daughter and her father's son.
> She is several pieces between the two husbands
> she has had. She is all the women of the apartment
> building who stand watching her, watching themselves.

She remembers childhood in surroundings starkly different from the glass and asphalt of Chicago: "When she was young she ate wild rice on scraped down / plates in warm wood rooms. It was in the farther / north and she was the baby then. They rocked her." Alienated, she "sees other / women . . . counting their lives in the palms of their hands / and in the palms of their children's hands." Dangling, exposed, she at first "thinks she will be set free," but, as she hears the voices of those who urge her to jump and those who would help her, "she knows she is hanging by her own fingers, her / own skin, her own thread of indecision." Spirits may speak to her, but she herself must resolve to act; if she survives, it will not be by chance, or the intervention of others. The penultimate stanza seems to move her toward action:

> She thinks of Carlos, of Margaret, of Jimmy.
> She thinks of her father and of her mother.
> She thinks of all the women she has been, of all
> the men. She thinks of the color of her skin, and
> of Chicago streets and of waterfalls and pines.
> She thinks of moonlight nights, and of cool spring storms.

The short, declarative sentences echo her own capacity for agency, for resolution, grounded in knowledge of relationship, of origins, of place— and of the realities of her urban borderland: class, prejudice, and alienation. Then "her mind chatters," and "she thinks of the 4 A.M. lonelinesses . . . discordant, without logical and / beautiful conclusion." What comes of this thinking, most clearly, is desire: "She would speak." But she cannot speak yet. She cries "for / the lost beauty of her own life . . . sees the / sun falling west over the grey plane of Chicago." We might imagine that the reported (though unheard) voices of neighbors, her grandmother, and the "gigantic men of light," along with the implied voices of her children, husbands, and parents, constitute external traces of an internal heteroglossia with which this silent, dangling woman must contend, which she must somehow engage and make dialogic if she is to resolve her dislocation and find or make a place for herself.

As the poem ends,

> She thinks she remembers listening to her own life
> break loose, as she falls from the 13th floor
> window on the east side of Chicago, or as she
> climbs back up to claim herself again.

Perhaps tempted to give up, she at least hasn't succumbed yet. The line breaks reflect the woman's physically and emotionally precarious situation suspended between dangers and possibilities that she must face, here on the east side of Chicago, not once but repeatedly, as the poem's last word, *again,* confirms. Harjo's woman knows where she is; in that sense her dislocation may be alterable. Yet, representative and connected as she is, she is also alone, and her survival, in Chicago or elsewhere, might depend upon her ability to claim herself again and again, without any indication that going home to the place of childhood and family will ever be an option.

The poets whose work I've discussed in this chapter show us that place can be equally compelling whether one is there or not. "Location, whether it is to abandon it or draw it sharply, is where we start," Erdrich writes ("A Writer's Sense of Place" 43). Further, the power of place for these and other Native writers—Mary TallMountain, Sherman Alexie, Elizabeth Woody, Luci Tapahonso, among many others—is not simply that of beautiful or otherwise impressive landscapes, viewed from outside; it is the power of spiritual reciprocity, of story and history, of community, and of obligation. The obligation, again, isn't simply an ecological debt; it may even be implicitly an obligation to self, as it is, I think, for Harjo's "Woman Hanging from the Thirteenth Floor Window" and maybe for Barnes—or his speaker, in poems where the individual is recognized as existing in vital relationship to place, even if the connection seems to be broken or attenuated.

Simon Ortiz shows us most directly how fundamental place is as a grounding for the individual, and a source of spirit, knowledge, community, and language. Robert Davis's poetry, too, demonstrates that relationship to place is integral to a Native sense of self, even while showing that being there doesn't necessarily mean being at one with one's place— indeed, for a contemporary American Indian this relationship may be quite problematical. This is one of the burdens of Barnes's poetry, and of the poems by Whiteman, Erdrich, and Harjo. Harjo illuminates both the difficult and the sustaining aspects of relationship to place, when she describes Oklahoma as "a mythical place . . . a spiritual landscape . . . my motherland." "But," she continues, "I don't live there . . . It's too familiar and too painful . . . So my return usually takes place on a mythic level" (Coltelli 56). Linda Hogan's visionary responsiveness to the places where she finds herself, Ray Young Bear's sustaining relationship to his Mesquakie home place, and Joy Harjo's awareness of the vibrancy of myth in the mundane world make place an important, if variable, ele- ment in their work as well. That the places where they find themselves are often marked by traces of borderland conflict assures that many of the poems of vision, dream, and mythic experience, to which I turn in chap- ter 5, also share the struggle for continuance and survival.

CHAPTER 5

"To Make That Spiritual Realm More Manifest"

Linda Hogan, Ray A. Young Bear, and Joy Harjo share with other Indian writers their commitment to the struggle for survival. Survival, these poets know, requires healing, and healing depends upon spiritual suste-nance, knowledge, and wholeness. All across Native America, dream, vision, and myth are essential to spirituality; along with memory, which keeps them alive, they are thus essential to the ways of healing these poets offer. Such a healing project depends on the writer's and reader's willingness to choose, as Harjo says, "not to stay safely in what you already know" (*Spiral of Memory* 93). Their works shows that these poets have made that choice; their poems ask of readers that we do so too—especially that we suspend any tendency to compartmentalize reality, to separate the material and the spiritual, and that we instead allow our-selves to contemplate the sometimes beautiful and sometimes disorient-ing fluidity of experience. Music is one means to healing knowledge. As a medium of cultural continuity, and entry point to spiritual experience, music reverberates in these poems, renewing and sustaining life.

Recognizing the need for healing implies desire for its success, yet history may make one wary of expecting full recovery from the damage of colonization, racism, dislocation. Partly for such reasons, resolution is sometimes at issue here. But the meaning of resolution derives fundamen-tally from how the poets see the world. When reality is fluid, multi-layered, simultaneously mythic and mundane, an incomplete resolution may become a positive good, if a demanding one. Such an orientation doesn't annul the possibilities of healing; rather, it reminds us that true healing will be not into a static, comfortable completion but into life itself, into change, growth, and continuity.

Hogan, Young Bear, and Harjo together offer a rich array of ap-proaches to spiritual experience and through it to healing and survival. Hogan is a visionary poet; Young Bear explores the interpenetrations of dreamed and waking realities; Harjo illuminates mythic experience, often with hints of the surreal. Yet for these poets such designations are not really separable; dream, vision, and myth overlap, and flow into waking daily reality. At the same time, the poets' differences in background, style, and ways of characterizing their own poetic projects represent the diversity of contemporary approaches to the spiritual.

Linda Hogan writes poetry of vision. It is grounded in the phenomenal world—the world that "rises / and descends / in the black eyes of a bird"[1]—and in desire: "May all walls be like those of the jungle . . . made of the mysteries further in . . . joined with the lives of all . . . showing again, again / that boundaries are all lies" (*Seeing* 68). It is grounded, too, in history, in the "Indian people here before me" (*Savings* 9), in the knowledge that "we were once other / visions and creations" (*Medicines* 70). It is thus not only visionary and spiritual but, in the broadest sense, political.

Her poems are grounded, as well, in her heritage as an Oklahoma Indian of mixed origins. She has spoke of her "emotional recall of being a girl . . . in Martha, Oklahoma, and waking up in the morning and knowing, remembering, the feel of air, the texture of air and the quality of light and the smell of the place."[2] And her historical and creative inheritance is shaped by "the roads we had to follow to Oklahoma" (*Medicines* 59). Her Oklahoma grounding ironically also implies landlessness (a fact that recalls Revard's "Wazhazhe Grandmother"). As Hogan tells Carol Miller, "Our family allotments are now the Ardmore airport . . . The Depresson, land swindles during the oil boom . . . That's why almost all the Indians of those five tribes are landless people" (6). This history means that her poems are also moved by the ongoing struggle for survival.

Each of Hogan's three most recent books of poetry has a distinctive emphasis. As she moves from evocations of transparent beauty to more layered complexity, elements of the spiritual orientation that she shares with Young Bear and Harjo develop in concentrated clarity. Even her most intricate poems readily invite us to see what is happening. In a sense Hogan's poetry prepares us for Young Bear's obliqueness and Harjo's mythic directness. In *Seeing through the Sun* (1985) the visionary dominates, creating a tone of ecstasy or at least hopefulness, despite images of pain and struggle. Poems that celebrate the beauty and integrity of the natural world promise redemption in continuity. Characteristically, Hogan finds spiritual sustenance in the earth's natural cycles. "Morning: The World in the Lake" (*Seeing* 56), for example, affirms the possibility of immediate sensory and visionary knowledge of beauty and wholeness. In the interplay of light and water faith is reaffirmed by a constant mutability:

> My daughter rises at water's edge.
> Her face lies down on water
> and the bird flies through her.
> The world falls
> into her skin
> down to the world beneath,
> the fiery leap of a fish falling into itself.
> And then it rises, the blackbird
> above the world's geography of light and dark
> and we are there . . .

Repeated pairings—of rising and descending movements, water and sun, black and red, dark and light—as they resolve into the paradoxes of cyclic continuity, also contribute to an ongoing process of exchange between the speaker and her daughter and the natural world. It is a process analogous to the "poetic interrelationship with the land . . . a dialogics of nature" that Moore found in Maria Chona's Tohono O'odham culture.[3] In all of her poetry Hogan aspires to this kind of knowledge and its redemptive promise.

In *Savings* (1988) she emphasizes the social; there is less ecstasy and more explicit treatment of political concerns. Characteristic are "The New Apartment: Minneapolis," "Rain," "The Truth of the Matter," "The Other Voices," "Workday," and "Those Who Thunder," poems in which vision urges the reader to action that, Hogan implies, will have political consequences. Buried truths, the stuff of resistance, rebellion, and re-creation, repeatedly break out of bounds.

In *The Book of Medicines* (1993) ecstasy is virtually gone, and so are explicit calls to action. In their place we find a tone of meditative, sometimes chilling, austerity, grounded in an engaged attentiveness to nature and history. Representative poems are "Mountain Lion," with its recognition of alienation between human and animal; "Crossings," a poem of hopelessly lost connections; and "Shelter," where fish hover in the shadow of a water bird, "believing they are safe / in dark shade / that will bend and swallow them" (35). In the book's second half, though, Hogan's attentiveness to the worlds around us brings us back to a chastened certainty and the promise of life and vision. As its title indicates,

A Book of Medicines is about healing; in this sense it too is representative
of all of Hogan's writing.

She affirms her healing purpose in essays and interviews. Thus she
tells us that "what needs to be saved . . . is earth itself, the beautiful blue-
green world that lives in the coiling snake of the Milky Way" (*Dwellings*
138–39). Knowing that healing must be both spiritual and political, she
places all of her writing in its historical contexts and begins her essay
"The Two Lives" by situating her own life in relation to the day's news:

> two countries negotiating money and peace . . . the U.S. govern-
> ment preparing to invade Nicaragua, thousands of Minneapolis teen-
> agers in line to purchase tickets for a Prince concert . . . Children are
> being abused and raped in their families and schools . . . Two large
> scorpions guard jewels in Bavaria.

Acknowledging the difficulty of thinking about autobiography "in the face
of this history that goes on minute by minute," she continues, "I think
of my work as part of the history of our tribe and as part of the history of
colonization everywhere. I want it to be understood that . . . the news of
November 13, 1984, is directly connected to this history, to our stories"
(233). Spirituality indeed "necessitates certain kinds of political action. If
you believe that the earth, and all living things, and all the stories are
sacred, your responsibility really is to protect those things" (Coltelli 79), for
"to be spiritually conscious means to undertake a journey that is often a
political one, a vision of equality and freedom" ("Two Lives" 247).

In every context, healing requires us to acknowledge relationship.
Remembering "that all things are connected . . . takes us toward the
place of balance, our place in the community of all things" (*Dwellings* 40).
It enables the Indian speaker of "Friday Night" (*Seeing* 37) to find a "home
grown" solidarity with her Mexican neighbor. And in "Geraniums" (*Sav-
ings* 17) her knowledge that "Life is burning / in everything" moves Ho-
gan to challenge the reader—"you, with your weapons and badges / and
your fear of what neighbors think"—to "open the door, / break the
glass," because "you can't bloom that way."

As a way of "opening the door" and "breaking the glass," dialogism,
Hogan's work shows, may be a means not only of struggle but also of the
vision, healing, and growth. She draws attention to the dialogism of her
own language when she says "two lives lived me," and when she charac-
terizes her people, "who have not had privilege," in terms of language:

we speak separate languages and live a separate way of life. Some
of us learn [the] language [of the privileged] . . . and we are then
bilingual or trilingual and able to enter their country. But seldom
do any of them understand our language, and our language goes
deeper than words . . . all the way to meaning and heart. ("Two
Lives" 238, 237)

In *Dwellings* she describes a healing language that would be profoundly
dialogic; her description strongly recalls the traditional understanding of
language as relational, creative, and sacred:

> What we are really searching for is a language . . . that takes the side
> of the amazing and fragile life on our life-giving earth. A language
> that knows the corn, and one that corn knows, a language that takes
> hold of the mystery of what's around us and offers it back to us, full
> of awe and wonder . . . Without [such a language], we have no
> home . . . within the creation. (59–60)[4]

In "Morning: The World in the Lake," as well as in poems like
"Mountain Lion," "Travelers," and "The Origins of Corn" (*Medicines* 27,
46–47, 87), she seems to approach such a language. These poems dem-
onstrate the attentiveness Hogan emphasizes in *Dwellings* and position
the speaker in ways that support the integrity of the world and "all [her]
relations" as well. As they do so, they participate in the heterodoxy
that Blaeser finds "much contemporary Native American literature up-
holds," a heterodoxy of expansive "responsiveness . . . dialogic engage-
ment . . . [and] involvement in spiritual relationships."[5] As Hogan's
poetry demonstrates, dialogism itself can enable healing, for dialogic
language, as it contests unitary, authoritative discourse, is implicitly
open to creative interactions among multiple intentions and histories.
Indeed, the dialogics of Hogan's most visionary poems suggest an affin-
ity with Moore's "possibility of exchange without dominance or co-
optation,"[6] a phrase that might describe the relationship we find, in her
poetry as a whole, between the spiritual and the political: neither super-
sedes the other, and each contributes to the other. At the same time, her
work often reflects social and political struggle.

Struggle is implicit in Hogan's statement that her mixed background
" *'created a natural tension that surfaces in [her] work and strengthens it.'* "[7] Her

poetry is marked by counterpointed images or motifs—light and dark, buried and emerging truths, hunger or disease and medicine—that suggest such an empowering tension; at the same time the tensions evoked in particular poems may reveal struggle and the need for healing. Whether by empowering or by disturbing, such tensions can become the source and the evidence of dialogism.

The need for healing is evident precisely in terms of Hogan's mixed background, in "The Truth Is" (*Seeing* 4–5), a poem whose title seems to promise a definitive, singular truth, but which offers instead an experience of irreducible tensions. The conflict between Hogan's "Chickasaw hand" and her "white hand" is established as soon as she attempts to reassure us (and herself), by saying "Don't worry. It's mine / and not some thief's." She thus evokes the whole history of white-Native contact—personal, familial, cultural, political—which inescapably pervades the poem. But the tensions are engendered not only by conflicts between the two groups that make up the poet's ancestry. The poem voices an equally painful tension between the speaker's knowledge of history and her desire to transcend it by resolving the conflicts that destabilize, while they create, her sense of who she is. Thus the poem's rhythm is created by its oscillation between what she'd "like to say": "I am a tree, grafted branches / bearing two kinds of fruits / apricots maybe and pit cherries," and her knowledge that "It's not that way." The language that she'd like to apply doesn't work. Instead, history repeatedly imposes the language of property, violence, and politics—of "amnesty," "who killed who," "the sharp teeth of property," and the dangerous condition of being "a woman of two countries." But this language offers truth only at the cost of recognizing the language's and the speaker's capacity for (self-)betrayal. What results is a heightened awareness of a dialogics of struggle, which Hogan's repetition of the word *amnesty* illustrates. "We want amnesty," she says, after recognizing the inadequacy of the fruit tree metaphor, and follows this plaintive statement with her most direct effort to deny history: "Linda, girl, I keep telling you / this is nonsense / about who loved who / and who killed who." Later, though, having reminded herself of her historical knowledge, she returns to this desire:

> And you remember who killed who.
> For this you want amnesty,
> and there's that knocking on the door
> in the middle of the night.

Personalizing the poem's tensions by making herself both speaker and audience, Hogan brilliantly foregrounds the competing intentions of heteroglossia and the pain potential in dialogism and in vision. Her efforts to resolve the tensions by revising her language or shifting her attention ("Relax, there are other things to think about") simply fail: she's left (and the poem ends) with "the left shoe / and the right one with its white foot." What we readers are left with is a sobering sense of the meaning(s) of resolution. This is a poem whose speaker evidently wants resolution, even while she acknowledges the possibility only of an ongoing struggle. It's thus a poem likely to disappoint white readers who— perhaps like Wendy Rose's "Campus Committee"—want reassurance that "problems of the past" can be overcome as we all (but especially Natives) find a harmonious and definitive balance between Native and European cultures. For Hogan, the poem's speaker and first audience ("Linda, girl . . . Girl, I say . . ."), the lack of resolution may be read as positive, in that the truth of such unremitting tensions must create the unceasing alertness necessary to survival. And for many of her readers the absence of resolution may illuminate the need for an ongoing dialogic relationship across the boundaries of race, culture, and power.

Three poems from *The Book of Medicines* illuminate the difficult confluences of pain with the desire for healing relationship and the promise of vision. In "Mountain Lion" (27) a moment of vision clarifies the tensions arising from multilayered relationship. Spiritual and historical realities merge, as a "clearing" both physical and spiritual ("the road / ghosts travel / when they cannot rest") becomes a borderland space of recognition and mutual alienation between the speaker and the lion. "Nothing was hidden / in our eyes. / I was the wild thing / she had learned to fear." Hogan redoubles the connection and the alienation as she finds an analogy between the animal's response to her and her own response to those who reject dialogical connections. The mountain lion looks at her in "the same way" that

> I have looked so many times at others
> ·
> before lowering my eyes
> and turning away
> from what lives inside those
> who have found two worlds cannot live
> inside a single vision.

Hogan doesn't, I think, assent to this "finding," but she allows the poem and the reader to entertain it. Doing so complicates the way in which she suggests her problematical relationship to the mountain lion and to the colonizing invaders of nature and of Native cultures. The reverberating heteroglossia of "I was the wild thing" sharpens the complications, while it implies the continuity between this poem's tensions and recognitions and the more directly named borderland issues of "The Truth Is." There is, then, a mutually illuminating, productive dialogics at work between "Mountain Lion" and Hogan's more overtly politically oriented poems. This dialogics is of a piece with her political commitment to relationship with a world that is sacred. "Mountain Lion" shows how tension can be both evidence and source of dialogue and how vision may be understood as a moment of dialogic exchange. It also testifies to the difficulties of remaining attentive and responsive to the world.

Some of those difficulties are evident in "Crossings" (*Medicines* 28–29), which focuses on the pain of attentiveness when dialogic exchange fails. As in "Mountain Lion," knowledge of relationship is knowledge of loss, but here is no shared moment of recognition between the yearning speaker and those with whom she would connect: the fetal whale on its "block of shining ice," the newborn child who "did not want to live / in air," and the wild horses: "Dark was that water, / darker still the horses, / and then they were gone." (The cold that spreads through the poem from that block of ice is similar to the chill of difficult knowledge or overwhelming power, in some of Young Bear's poems.)

"Drum" (*Medicines* 69) offers visionary knowledge that resonates dialogically both with "Crossings" and "Mountain Lion" and with the joyous "Morning: The World in the Lake." This poem's two central images, water and drum, offer healing and survival, as they unite nature, spirit, and history. Like "Crossings," "Drum" begins by evoking an elemental, watery world, this one the remembered "Waters / of our mothers, / inside the blue drum of skin," where "we knew the drifts of continents / and moving tides." Here, though, Hogan continues by recalling that "we" have crossed into "a dry world," and "survived soldiers and drought . . . hunger / and . . . loneliness." Survival is made possible by love and by a visionary and prophetic memory that redeems pain as it recalls the realizations of "Morning: The World in the Lake":

we remember
that other lives fall through us

like fish swimming in an endless sea,
that we are walking another way
than time,
to new life, backward
to deliver ourselves to rain and river.

"Drum" reminds us that history has always been integral to Hogan's poetry even when not explicitly named. Poems like "Seeing through the Sun," "To Light," and "Come In" (*Seeing* 3, 35, 64), as well as "Mountain Lion," are similarly suggestive. But a pair of poems, one from near the beginning, the other from near the end of *Savings,* more fully imagine the consequences of integrating the political and the spiritual.

In "The New Apartment: Minneapolis" (9–11) memory functions as vision and, in concert with the speaker's attentiveness to a historically located setting, brings speaker and poem to a politically empowering spiritual renewal. As the apartment building and its Indian inhabitants are identified as the site and subject-victims of "all the wars / and relocation," the politically charged dialogism of the title becomes evident. (It involves not just the "new apartment" but also the city, Minneapolis, with its name, a blend of Indian and Greek languages, and its identity as a conflict-ridden population center for urban Indians.) The speaker moves from reflecting on "Indian people here before me," to directly addressing the reader: "be warned . . . the roofs of this town are all red / and we are looking through the walls of houses / at people suspended in air": not only the elder hung from a meat hook but also "the businessmen who hit their wives / and the men who are tender fathers," the "women crying or making jokes," and "some Pawnee . . . singing 49s, drumming the table." Within the building's walls "world changes are planned, bosses overthrown," and "the woman in room twelve" speaks of revolution. The poem shifts again: "Beyond walls are lakes and plains" and access to another kind of knowledge: "the stars are the key / turning in the lock of night. / Turn the deadbolt and I am home." With these words the speaker *is* home, "where there are no apartments, just drumming and singing" and restorative connections: "Hello aunt, hello brothers, hello trees / and deer walking quietly on the soft red earth." Though the poem might seem simply to retreat from its bleak urban realities, it demonstrates the possibility of recuperation and survival through spiritual contact with the traditional world. The reconnection with "soft red earth" substantiates the earlier warning that "the roofs . . . are all red." Life and blood are alive "in this town," in memory and in vision, and will not always be appeased with "coffee, / cigarettes, or liquor."

The potential signalled in "The New Apartment: Minneapolis" is realized in "Those Who Thunder" (71–72), which has the same urban setting, the same relocated and economically marginalized people, the same kind of shift from description to direct warning, the same drumming that we heard in "The New Apartment." But the proportions and the emphases differ. Roughly two-thirds of this poem are a warning to the audience, and the drumming is more insistent, reinforced by dancing, "thundering on wooden floors," and by pounding fists. Indeed, this poem's language virtually enacts the revolution that was still only a wish in "The New Apartment."

> You could say the sky is having a collapse,
> you could say it's our thunder.
> Explain to the president
> why I am beating on the floor
> and my name has been changed to
> Those Who Thunder.
> . . . .
> Those meek who were blessed
> are nothing
> but hungry . . .
> . . . .
> and those poor who will inherit the earth
> already work it
> so take shelter
> . . . .
> because we are thundering and beating on floors
> and this is how walls have fallen in other cities.

"Map" (*Medicines* 37–38), a poem grounded in history, makes no direct call for political struggle. What it offers is visionary faith, which may in turn become the grounds for action. The poem begins under the power of alienated colonizers: this world is now "vast and lonely," its "mountains / named for men / who brought hunger . . . and fear." Intuiting the world's resistance to their purposes, "knowing the fire dreamed of swallowing them / and spoke an older tongue," the invaders imposed their own language. They called the world "ice, wolf, forest of sticks," as a means of separation, control, and entry, "as if words would make it something / they could hold in gloved hands." The poem, then, is about the power of history and language.

But as Hogan turns toward the possibility of restorative vision, she imaginatively frees the world from the colonizers' maps and offers the hope of a new beginning. "This is what I know from science . . . This is what I know from blood." At first glance these lines might seem to promise only contradiction, especially if readers take dualism for granted, and associate science entirely with the Europeans' "gloved hands." But this is not what Hogan's poem tells us. For both science and blood show her the integrity of the living world: "wolves live inside a circle / of their own beginning . . . the first language is not our own." The poem thus moves from the invaders' rejection of relationship, to dialogic engagement; the lessons converge in renewed recognition of the world's "words" and visionary knowledge of "the other order," "never spoken / but in dreams of darkest creation," as Hogan says in the book's first poem ("History of Red" 9). The energy and continuity of life itself is the visionary promise of the poem's ending: "It is burning. / It is dreaming. / It is waking up." With lines that recall the conviction of "Those Who Thunder" Hogan implies that in the world's survival there is hope for new recognitions of relationship—and hence, ultimately, for restorative action. Rejecting the divisions drawn on maps, she finds hope in continuity and change. The final poem of *A Book of Medicines*, "The Origins of Corn" (87), makes even stronger the certainty that true knowledge of the world—nature and spirit—will bring us eventually into positive interaction, "so that . . . the plants who climb into this world / will find it green and alive."

Hogan's spiritual and political convictions and her healing purposes converge in the drumming that sounds like a heartbeat through her poetry. Across North American Native cultures, the drum voices the pulse of the natural world and the cultural and historical continuity of the people. It speaks of both faith and action. It "takes the side of the amazing and fragile life on our life-giving earth," like the healing language Hogan calls for (*Dwellings* 59). The healer drums and sings, "moving between the worlds . . . feeling, hearing, knowing . . . that which is around us daily but too often unacknowledged, a life larger than our own." He goes "into the drum . . . into the center" (*Dwellings* 38). In her poetry Hogan hears and joins in the drumming. It is in the "crickets . . . pulsing in the wrist of night," in "the great seas traveling / underground," carrying the stories "coming to light" (*Seeing* 20, 35); in "the earth's drum," the "earth . . . breathing / through the streets," and the "gone elk . . . drumming / back the woodland" (*Savings* 5, 19, 30); in the "stretched and beating wings" of the geese and "the blue drum of skin . . . the skin of water" (*Medicines* 46, 69). It is the accompaniment and means of vision in "The New Apartment: Minneapolis" and of action in "Those Who Thunder" (*Savings* 10 and 71–72). Beating through all of life, the drum unifies and its resonances deepen the poet's and readers' possibilities of growth and vision. Thus, as it heals, the drum voices a dialogics of nature, spirit and culture into which the individual and the community may enter, through which they may grow and struggle and survive. As it does so, it also opens a space in which Hogan's poetry and the drumming remembered, dreamed, and danced to in Young Bear's poems beat together, different voices joined in the purposes of healing and survival.

Whereas Hogan's is predominantly a poetry of vision, the poems by Ray Young Bear to which I now turn are moved primarily by dream. James Ruppert draws a helpful distinction: while "visions are messages from the story reality and those who inhabit [it]," and "always imply implementation in the present," dreams "put us in the experiential framework of the old culture." Ruppert's definitions are geared to his focus on Young Bear's uses of oral tradition; even so, the difference between being *in* a dream and *seeing* or *receiving* a vision may help distinguish the modes of spirituality in some of Hogan's and Young Bear's poems. More important than the distinction, though, is what unites them: "Underneath it all lies spirit and the possibilities of transformation and power" (101).

Young Bear describes the sources of his poetry as including myth, history, and especially dreams; he illuminates the places where dreams and other realities meet and the delicate negotiations involved in evoking those meetings within contested spaces, when he discusses his writing process.[8] His comments on the constraints he knows, as a Mesquakie writing in English, recall the question engendered by the gaps between traditional communities and outside audiences: "What is ethical to tell?" We have already seen how this question might complicate his allusive appeals to Algonquin relatives and representatives of non-Native culture, in "Emily Dickinson, Bismarck and the Roadrunner's Inquiry." His afterword to *Black Eagle Child* is similarly suggestive about what might be involved in exploring the interpenetrations of waking and dreamed experience, a central impulse of the narrative poems I discuss below.

"In the delicate ritual of weighing what can and cannot be shared," Young Bear tells us in the afterword, a "greater portion of my work is not based on spontaneity." Declining spontaneity in favor of "an exercise in creative detachment," his colloquially grounded and cryptically allusive narrative poems heighten the disjunction between the esoteric and the public, even as they enact the potent continuity of dreamed and waking experience, and "the artistic interlacing of ethereality, past and present." As he says, "the divisions between dream and myth are never clear cut" (254). For a tribal person like Young Bear the divisions between myth and contemporary actuality are always potentially permeable.

By Young Bear's account his Mesquakie community offers compelling disincentives to revealing privileged knowledge: this is strikingly evident in his grandmother's cautionary reference to William Jones, a Mesquakie protégé of Franz Boas. After collecting and publishing a considerable body of myth and other materials from the Mesquakie, Jones was killed in the Philippines, as he attempted to pursue further anthropological studies.[9] The poet reminds himself of another reason for reticence, the respect intrinsically due to relations, as to the spiritual, in "The Reason Why I Am Afraid Even Though I Am a Fisherman"; further, this poem tells us, "answers have nothing / to do with cause and occurrence" (*Invisible Musician* 9). Dreams by their nature defeat illusions of possession, even as they invite interpretation; they seem to offer Young Bear an oblique, protective way of approaching traditional material. Dream is thus a way of both telling and not telling. And Young Bear's cultural location and commitments thus create the conditions for a rich, distinctively nuanced heteroglossia. By evoking dreams, the poet inevitably tells about his culture, for self, culture, and dream are inextricably connected. Doing so cryptically, suggestively, mixing the apparently traditional (and note that an outsider must say "apparently") with the contemporary, the poet may both keep the traditional alive and protect its integrity, by refusing to concede to the desires or impositions of outsiders. Thus he is able to deal with the question of ethical telling in a way that is both creative and respectful of his community.[10]

He illuminates his approach when he likens himself to "an artist who didn't believe in endings," whose "sweeping visions . . . were constant and forever changing"; thus his "essential" commitment "to keep these enigmatic stories afloat in the dark until dust-filled veils of light inadvertently reveal . . . their luminescent shapes" (*Black Eagle Child* 255). The fluid suggestiveness of his narrative poems is evoked here, as are both

their resistance to closure and their sense of expectancy, of creative wait-
ing, for something like an illuminating veil that may allow a kind of
access to both poet/speaker and reader/audience without offering to ei-
ther the illusion of possession or complete resolution.

Toward the end of his afterword Young Bear suggests a link between
his awareness of borderland conditions and his poetry's combination of
openness and guardedness in words that recall Owens's "exquisite bal-
ancing act" (*Other Destinies* 15). As a writer, he says,

> I have attempted to maintain a delicate equilibrium with my tribal
> homeland's history and geographic surroundings and the world that
> changes its face along the borders. Represented in the whirlwind of
> mystical themes and modern symbols . . . the word-collecting pro-
> cess is an admixture of time present and past, of direction found and
> then lost, of actuality and dream. (260)

"The Handcuff Symbol," "Always Is He Criticized," and "The Black
Antelope Tine" (all in *The Invisible Musician*) interweave dreamed and wak-
ing realities in contexts at least partially defined by cultural dislocation.
Rather than providing clear resolutions to either contemporary narratives
or elusive threads of dream, they offer experiences that reverberate within
each poem and suggest continuities within and beyond the poems' con-
fines. Reading and rereading, we become aware of the proliferating possi-
bilities of internal cross-references and communal, perhaps mythic, conti-
nuities. And the poems' subtly offered possibilities seem to clarify, if not
the "meanings" of their allusions, then the dynamics of each poem's struc-
ture and its spiritual sensibility. At the same time, the layered possibilities
contribute to the poems' opacity: we see, when we do, through "dust-filled
veils of light." This effect is intensified by Young Bear's reliance on associa-
tive connections; even when he seems to explain, he does so in a context
pervaded by the juxtapositions and fluidity of dream, vision, and memory.
And yet the liberating paradox is that we can see. Though it is easy to
be aware of Young Bear's "veils," if we are receptive to the "light" it may, he
tells us, "inadvertently reveal" the stories' "luminescent shapes," and the
poems may bring us closer to the world of dream and myth than we expect
or can grasp.

"The Handcuff Symbol" (84–87) makes most explicit the dynamics
that move all three poems: the interplay of dreamed and other realities in
a context of cultural disruption that foregrounds the need for healing.

The poem begins with what appears to be a waking memory from the recent past:

> We were struggling over a small pearl-
> handled Saturday Night Special.
> Like three angry adolescents,
> so many thousands of miles
> from Black Eagle Child,
> we were turning an afternoon
> college kegger at the Greek Theatre
> into a perilous scene

Their displacement is evident in their physical distance from Black Eagle Child (Young Bear's fictional name for his Iowa Mesquakie Red Earth Settlement) and in the reference to the Greek Theatre (the culturally powerful name given a natural amphitheater on the campus of Pomona College, which Young Bear attended); their alcohol-fueled anger, directly related to that double distance, seems to impel them toward destruction: "the one who held / the pistol either wanted to shoot / himself or another." Heteroglossia and dialogism are foregrounded as the others plead "first in our language," hoping to remind their companion "of the acquiescent but *living* grandfathers":

> "*Ba ki se na no tta qwi ba*
> *e ya bi me ko ye be te na wa tti.*
> Let go of the pistol before you
> accidentally shoot a bystander."

But this appeal to traditional authority is ineffective. And the meaning of their cultural dislocation deepens: as the three struggle over the gun, their posture explicitly parodies the "famous war photograph of American soldiers raising a flag / over Iwo Jima." One of those soldiers was the Pima Ira Hayes; the American government's exploitation of his heroism led to his alcoholism, alienation from home, and death.[11] Young Bear's adolescents, symbolic heirs of Hayes, lose control of the gun, which fires, as it were, of its own accord. Besides indicating some causes and a historical context for the youths' anger, this first section suggests the dangers of spontaneity and thus may reinforce Young Bear's disavowal of that quality

in the *Black Eagle Child* afterword. Their anger, and the danger in which the
protagonists, in part, have put themselves, signal an important theme of
the whole poem, one that Young Bear develops at length in *Black Eagle
Child:* the "long uncomfortable adjustment to being an Indian, *E no no te wi
ya ni,* in the world of the white man" (167).

The poem's second section appears to continue recounting literal,
waking experience; in fact, until the speaker indicates that he has awak-
ened in "the log cabin [he] . . . was born in," it could be a direct sequel to
the first section, with the loudspeaker and helicopter's spotlight repre-
senting a police response to the shooting in the Greek Theatre. Though
subsequent details undercut this reading, the situations are closely re-
lated: now we see not only the threat but the actuality of physical injury—
the speaker's pillow is stained with "dried blood," and he "touche[s his]
face for wounds." Again, there is an appeal to traditional authority. First
another person "mouth[s] the Spectre's command: 'Surrender / yourself
to piety.' " Then "a tribal committee member . . . acting . . . on behalf of
the authorities," announces that " 'The family of the injured party is out
there also. So there's / witnesses.' " This statement makes the role of
authority and the outcome of an evidently threatening situation discon-
certingly ambiguous—and sets up the expectation that the third section
will continue the story Young Bear seems to be telling.

However, the third section turns back to the Greek Theatre before
offering not a continuation but commentary that applies to both the first
and second parts and identifies the anguish at the core of this poem. The
speaker recalls only

> . . . the final humiliating moment
> in being where we were, what we were about
> to do. There's nothing more disgraceful
> than Indians in serious trouble—
> in faraway places . . .
> . . . .
>   . . . Truth aside, we often react
> like beached whales, and this culture
> keeps throwing us back into the black,
> chaotic sea. Although we thrash about
> for our lives, however demented and painful
> it has been, we drown others in the process.

Young Bear sustains ambiguity with his "Truth aside"—a rhetorical reminder, perhaps, that we see obliquely, through "dust-filled veils of light." The illusion of explanation continues as the fourth (and final) section begins: "I am *simply* relating *this dream* / as preface to my belief they often / reoccur in reality. Sometimes in reverse" (emph. added). Young Bear proceeds to offer an explanation implying that the log cabin section was both a dream and, "in reverse," "reality":

> The handcuffs, for instance, were positive.
> . . . .
> *Point is,* the next night after this dream
> a police officer *actually* wrapped
> my bleeding palms and wrist with gauze,
> and he radioed an ambulance for me.
> And the gunshots? They *turned out*
> *to be* my palms busting through
> the hot windows of a burning
> but empty house . . .
>   . . . Small caliber
> gunfire *can sound like* glass
> being broken . . .
>   (Emphasis added)

While he uses the language of rational explanation to make the experience ordinary, in effect he heightens the vividness of the dream and undermines the assumption that dream and reality are fundamentally different. This dream did happen, even if "in reverse." Thus Young Bear leaves us with the sense of mysteriously intermingling realities. After the literalist, rational explanations quoted above, he further demonstrates the dream's reality, heightening the effect by ambiguously refusing to answer a question:

> But the drunk who I thought
> was in the burning house asked me
> for no apparent reason if I still
> possessed the pistol. Instead
> of being stunned by yet another
> correlation, I lied and purposely

implanted a continuing vision
of this evil piece in his mind.
I could have bled to death
were it not for the gauze cuffs.

"The Handcuff Symbol" blurs the meaning of *symbol* by drawing attention to the interpretive act while disrupting the expected identities of the symbol and the symbolized. But these are not the only disrupted identities. Having established the protagonist's real physical and cultural displacement, Young Bear disorients the reader when he defines another apparently literal reality as a dream; finally, he offers explanations that imply the mirroring identity of dreaming and waking realities. The reader's disorientation, however, is only a reflection of the protagonist's. For the speaker, an Indian "in serious trouble— / in faraway places," dislocation has disrupted identity: when someone defined by his cultural and geographic location is displaced, who is he, and how can he continue to be? The speaker's dreaming/waking experiences reinforce each other, drawing attention to his vulnerability as he "thrash[es] about" for his life. His struggle is evidence of the need for healing, and healing is the focus of the poems to which I now turn: it is the end explicitly sought in "Always Is He Criticized," and its possibility is realized almost as if by surprise in "The Black Antelope Tine." In both, the impulse toward healing is related to an intensified focus on the interpenetration of dreaming and waking experience.

When Young Bear turns to ritual to restore and heal, the protective veil becomes visible in maneuvers that allow him to describe without disclosing the ritual itself and the spiritual experience it enables. The first three sections of "Always Is He Criticized" (81–83) recount a dance procession that involves a mountain climb and ends with an attack by a bear. But, although the narrative is continuous, it is not completely straightforward, especially in the first section. Blending colloquial speech with evidently esoteric allusions, telling the story and commenting on it, the speaker demonstrates heteroglossia's competing intentions. He seems to caution us against excessive awe. This may be a strategy to deflect excessive curiosity, for he is evidently deeply serious in his effort to participate in tradition in the midst of a disorienting flux that is both climatological and cultural. The poem begins casually—"There was this dance procession / I was a part of"—but casualness does not imply a readiness to divulge anything that shouldn't be told. Nor will the formally constructed lines of the song, which close the first section, expose any of the implications beneath the words: " 'Always / is he criticized, always is he / criticized—in the manner of a pig / I dance.' "

After stating that the dancing men are "demonstrating / our place in Black Eagle Child society," the speaker complicates their position by introducing the "cultural paradox" of their dependency on women's earnings. Offered as a parenthetical afterthought, this aside actually identifies the men's need for healing from the effects of cultural upheaval: "We are still / warlike but perennially unemployed."[12] Their need is the source of both energy and reverence:

> We were singing an energetic, non-
> religious song, but we gave it
> reverence as if it were one,
> admonishing anyone who forgot
> such compositions could not
> have been made by humans.

These lines are crucial, for they introduce spiritual, nonrational, and potentially healing energy into the dance procession and the poem itself and admonish us to remember. The first section thus moves from literal exposition and commentary to a reminder of spiritual presence.

In the second section the narrative continues as the song and the dreams it evokes enable the dancers to "crawl . . . up the difficult mountainside. / Sometimes we depended on the heart's blissful / intonation for dreams when powdery / snow incapacitated our bodies." The heart becomes a drum; song and dream bring the speaker to vision. In *Black Eagle Child* Young Bear similarly evokes the compelling power of music, as song and drumbeat revitalize the participants in ritual:

> The music lifted above the crowd of dancers and stayed in place before lifting further, flying away, and then coming back to encircle us like an eagle whose powerful black and golden wingtips brushed our faces, waking us, telling us to see this dance through for my grandfather. (155)

Such passages remind us that Young Bear himself is a drummer, while they also recall the healing power of the drum in Hogan's poems.

The dancers move through dream and snow, and the speaker again alludes to esoteric knowledge: "As the blizzard left for earth, / we saw the still, inflated corpses / of those who succumbed to His domain." Young Bear seems to evoke the same power that he refers to when he tells us, in *Black Eagle Child*, that "the snow-covered ground symbolized [the Creator's] . . . return" (164).[13] But all that uninitiated readers can infer with certainty, as the poem proceeds, is that other-than-human power is at work in this fusion of material and spiritual realities.

As the narrator struggles to continue dancing in the falling darkness, accompanied by the ongoing beat of the song, a "large, lumbering shadow" appears in the distance.

> And here, whether it was part of the dance
> or actual fear, we cringed at the sight
> of our cousin who was outfitted in a loose,
> oversized bear suit. He snarled and moved
> about in anger. What he didn't realize
> was that a grizzly bear was standing
> beside him, foaming at the mouth.

Twice in this passage the speaker distinguishes between the "actual" or "real," on the one hand, and the dance, its paraphernalia, and the powers that vitalize them, on the other. Again, what we know is that through song, dream, and dance, realities have merged. This second section ends with another powerfully suggestive statement: with the bear's arrow driven between his ribs, "Fred Bloodclot Red / was suspended on the wooden suit support like / a crucifix." A painful instance of cultural heteroglossia and dialogism, these lines imply one source of the men's need to "demonstrat[e their] place in Black Eagle Child society" and the terrible difficulty of doing so.

Those final lines of the second section are disorienting on several counts. The ones that immediately follow, at the start of the third section, are equally so:

> In half-delirium and half-sleep
> I thought I heard new cowboy boots
> being test-walked over the thin
> floor boards of our trailer.
> "For New England," Fred had joked
> before his demise . . .

The sound of the boots being "test-walked" may echo "the loud / repetitive verse" of the dance song or anticipate it—we do not know whether this memory precedes or follows the dance procession. In fact, the "half-delirium . . . half-sleep" returns us to a nonrational, dreamlike state, in which these events may be simultaneous. Reference to Fred's demise, if it implied that the bear killed him, would signal a continuation of the story but back into the past. Yet a few lines later the suggestion that he died in a plane crash requires a revised reading. By this time we've learned more about Fred:

> . . . As a lifetime
> resident of Carson Red Hat Reserve
> whose sole highlight would have been
> this one lecture on tribal prophecy
> at Cambridge, he was embarrassed
> for being dependent on his grandmother
> for footwear . . .

Fred's embarrassment recalls the dancers' need to confirm their place in Black Eagle Child society. His undelivered "lecture on tribal prophecy" remind us that dream and esoteric knowledge, the sources of spiritual healing, may never be wholly amenable to explanation.

The poem's last eight lines return to the state of "half-delirium and half-sleep," in which the speaker knows "no way to reverse Fred's impermanence." Thematically, these lines signal conclusion. Yet repetition that reinforces the dreamlike condition may also imply continuity. Apparent references to ritual and oral tradition again create opacity:

> Certain bones affixed to my limbs
> will not transport me to bring him
> back. An attempt at The Contrary
> would only interfere with a shadow
> that continually relives
> its preparation for death.

This final paradoxical image may refer to the power that moves the whole poem, dance, and song; for the shadow, in its unending movement between life and death, different and yet inseparable conditions, seems to evoke the knowledge conveyed by dream and vision, the presence of "the Creator."[14]

These final lines suggest that healing has occurred, albeit painfully, in the recognition of almost unbearable paradox. The cold that pervades the poem's first half seems to be an image for this difficult healing. If this is the speaker's experience, Fred's healing may have come in the encounter with the bear: he is crucified but apparently not killed. Rather, he becomes one with the bear, receiving its power and thereby his "place in Black Eagle Child society," as, evidently, an initiate into "tribal prophecy."[15] How such effects come to pass is not revealed. That they arise from the mergings of dream or spirit with literal realities is what we are enabled to see. The fusing or intermingling of realities, then, is both part of the healing process and part of the "veil" that keeps us at a respectful distance.

Like "The Handcuff Symbol," "Always Is He Criticized" contains numerous examples of dialogism that draw attention to the realities among which Young Bear and his speakers work to maintain integrity. The "cultural paradox" in the first section prepares for the "crucifix" of the second; the grandmother's Mesquakie words remind us of the unanswerable questions and the multiple meanings that pervade the whole poem. Young Bear's affirmation of a vital continuity between dream and outer reality keeps open the possibility of mythic, visionary knowledge and of healing. That is one of the promises of "The Black Antelope Tine."

Several things in "The Black Antelope Tine" (74–76) seem to allude to overlapping personal, cultural, and historical pasts: the character Lucretia Rude Youth's name and her childhood mementos, the speaker's memory of his own childhood illness, possible allusions to cultural and cosmic beginnings (the flood, the "supernatural hunters"), apparent allusions to invasion and colonization.[16] These references, mostly unelaborated, suggest that a key issue for this poem is how to respond to the past, how to evoke its perhaps esoteric meanings—how to know what to tell. That Young Bear envisions spiritual experience as a source of connection between present and past links this poem to "Always Is He Criticized" and "The Handcuff Symbol." At the same time, in "The Black Antelope Tine" he is able to suggest less tenuously the possibility of healing, in part because, rather than structuring the poem basically as a movement from an apparently literal narration to its disruption by dream, memory, and overt questioning, here he weaves a more complex structure, in which threads of literal narrative, dream, memory, and vision are continuously intermeshed.

The poem's first two sections blend an apparently straightforward narrative—of a night when the speaker sought shelter from the flooding river in Lucretia's home—with hints of a supernatural presence that are incorporated into the matter-of-fact narration. Most notably, the air becomes cooler (recalling the cold of "Always Is He Criticized") as Lucretia brings out her childhood mementos, and the change seems to cause anxiety. The end of the second section confirms that this is not a simple story: "something was amiss." The third section consists of a series of three questions, increasingly complex and never directly answered:

> Was it the night? Or was it the finely-
> clothed figurines whose plaid material
> resembled shirts we used to wear?
> Did our frightened eyes reflect like
> marble stars in the searchlights
> of supernatural hunters?

As the speaker grasps at possible explanations, his questioning evokes culturally mixed images, and suggests susceptibility to the supernatural.

His memory is evidently jarred by these questions, for the following (fourth) section recalls a dream of many-layered vulnerability and complicity: six "doll-sized / human beings . . . intoxicated dwarfs . . . asked to be rolled together in a towel" and "put . . . in a trash can" to avoid being arrested. Eventually, though, they "suffocated because [the speaker] . . . forgot to pick them up. / And now here they were in the form of antique / toys. An alcohol-related tragedy." Like the youths in "The Handcuff Symbol," the dwarfs were vulnerable to forces from outside (the law) and within (their alcohol consumption, a likely sign of cultural upheaval); also, significantly, they were vulnerable to the speaker's forgetfulness. (Young Bear refers to dwarfs a number of times in his first book, *The Winter of the Salamander,* where they tend to be associated with mystical powers. If they recall such associations here, then we might read this dream episode as an instance of cultural forgetfulness, loss, or dislocation.)[17]

As the fifth section begins, Lucretia tries to keep the speaker's attention, with her "Philippine / coins, old wax seals and war photographs." Her effort suggests that she wants to protect the speaker and that the flooding creates or accentuates some spiritual vulnerability. In any case the situation does ultimately remind the speaker of a past experience of vulnerability. Meanwhile, Lucretia's efforts are successful for no more than two lines; then the speaker becomes "conscious of

another strength—cool and invisible—emanating from a cast iron / toy
kettle." This pivotal awareness both recalls the cool air he sensed in the
first section and is the powerful center of the concentricity he recognizes
in the next (sixth) section. Most immediately, this awareness coincides
with the pounding rain that makes Lucretia's storytelling "inaudible"
and directly evokes, through dreamlike association, a memory out of a
perhaps distant past:

> . . . *There was this kind*
> *of power once: tribal celebration dancers*
> *flashed their sequins under the nightlights*
> *and the ground bloated beneath their feet*
> *until we all stood on what seemed a little*
> *earth . . .*

This memory echoes "Always Is He Criticized," with its cryptically de-
scribed ritual. Here the memory and image imply continuity and the line
that concludes it, "*Roots to combat sorcery*," may offer the possibility of
release from the complicity dreamed in the episode of the "suffocated"
dwarfs.

From this memory the speaker returns, in the sixth section, to Lucre-
tia's kitchen, but his awareness of his surroundings is transformed by the
mysterious quality of this night: in a startling and surreal vision, every-
thing is "concentric," a slice of bread "levitate[s]," and "the odious mass
of a Spanish galleon / [breaks] . . . through the toy kettle and hover[s]"
above. The "Spanish galleon" may be a model ship, or an image from one
of the Philippine coins, but it is revealed here as something else too. It
returns the speaker to an experience of childhood illness which perhaps
he can only now recognize as culturally caused, a malady of the border-
lands: "It was the same ship / whose ochre clouds held me down as a
child / near death."[18]

In the seventh and final section, the speaker remembers the child-
hood experience to which the galleon has recalled him:

> I found myself in the arms of my elderly father.
> He was taking me to Well-Off Man's gathering
> where I would soon be spoon-fed with *amanita* tea
> to subdue my seizures. I knew all of this
> and I wanted to say so. When we entered

the canvas and tin-covered lodge,
Calvin Star, the appointed drum-maker,
was winding a thin rope around the tripod
legs of an overturned kettle. In his delicate
but rapid hands, the black antelope tine
which would be used to tighten and tune
the drum sparkled in the kerosene lamp's
bronze light.

If the child was unable to say what he knew at the time, the remembering speaker can now at least suggest his knowledge of healing power. Perhaps the poem, like the drum, has been tuned from the start by his memory of the black antelope tine. Integral to the continuing vitality of healing power, the memory circles back from the childhood scene to the cool air of the present, via the images of the kettle and the antelope-tine tuning device. In doing so, memory doesn't erase the initial mystery or ominousness of the coolness, but it does suggest that the cool air may be a portent of healing power. By so circling back and by its ritual content, the poem's final section integrates the literal (there is probably a kerosene lamp in Lucretia's kitchen too) and the dreamed—or blurs the distinction, depending on the reader's perspective. This circling back and illumination, "in the kerosene lamp's / bronze light," thus partially answers a question implied in the poem's first section (whence, and why, this coolness?), while leaving unanswered (unanswerable?) questions about the deeper mysteries of continuity, healing, and dream.

What Hogan celebrated in "Drum" (*Medicines* 69), Young Bear intimates here, as he in effect retunes the ceremonial drum: a continuous process of transformation in which recognizing the fluidity of the boundaries between past and present, dream and waking, the spiritual and the material, enables us to recover, if not fully to grasp, the connections that keep us alive. The difference between intimating and celebrating suggests other differences generated in part by Young Bear's position as a member of a conservative community for whom the tension between disclosure and preservation of tradition is always present. It also recalls his statement that his work is "not based on spontaneity." Hogan's, in contrast, especially the poems in *Seeing through the Sun* and *Savings*, can be characterized as transparent in some measure because of the impression of spontaneity she creates. Likewise, Young Bear's commitment to his community must contribute to the often oblique and cryptic qualities of his style, qualities that also suggest a different sense of poetry's orientation. While Hogan conceives of poetry as both spiritual and political action, the poems of *The Invisible Musician* seem generally chary of direct political engagement. This is a matter not just of thematic emphasis; Young Bear's apparently necessary obliqueness implies a different conception of what poetry can do. (Young Bear's poems are certainly not without political content, but they do not give the impression of being calls to action, as some of Hogan's do.) While such differences distinguish the poets and their work, they also illuminate their shared engagement with paradox, with the mythic, and with spiritual or nonrational realities.

Joy Harjo's contexts, emphases, and stylistic choices create distinctively nuanced poems that also reveal strong threads of continuity with those of Hogan and Young Bear. All three undertake, as Harjo puts it, to "make that spiritual realm more manifest" (*Spiral of Memory* 79). For all three history and myth are sources of knowledge and commitment. While Young Bear speaks primarily from within his Mesquakie culture, and Hogan's vision reflects her responses to the natural world, Harjo's orientation is often distinctively urban. (These are only intended as general characterizations; all three respond to diverse situations.) All recognize the vitality of myth in the mundane. Young Bear evokes mythic power strikingly but cryptically—the bear, in "Always Is He Criticized," the dancers on the "little earth," in "The Black Antelope Tine." In Hogan's poetry, mythic experiences are both understated and more transparent: the mutual recognition with the mountain lion, turning the starkey to go home, in "The New Apartment: Minneapolis." Harjo tends to create mythic experiences more directly and to elaborate on them more expansively. She combines grittiness like that we see in "The Handcuff Symbol," with something akin to the transforming joy that shines through "Morning: The World in the Lake," and ends, often, with qualified resolution.

Harjo's work resonates with a border consciousness shaped by her awareness of ongoing history and her own experience as an urban Indian of mixed origins. Like Hogan's, hers is a political project, in keeping with her hope "that bitter experience can be used to move the world" and her belief that "if we, as Indian people, Indian women, keep silent, then we will disappear."[19] Her vision of a world in motion, with its layered landscapes and permeable boundaries, its multiplicity, is thoroughly heteroglossic and dialogic.

Harjo speaks often of her profound sense of interrelatedness and continuity, her "understanding of the world in which the spiritual realm and the physical realm are not separate but actually the same thing" (*Spiral of Memory* 79). Her images sometimes suggest "the fusion of categories," the "bringing together [of] presences from wholly different realms," that marks "the characteristic, juxtaposed Surrealist image."[20] The probability that Harjo would question the existence of "wholly different realms," even while delighting in disparate images, implies the limit of her affinity for Surrealism. She suggests the indigenous affinities of her practice in a statement that links her art as a poet and as a saxophonist to tribal perceptions: "for me, the art of poetry is not separate from the art of music. There is not such a separation in tribal cultures." Moreover, "there is not just *this* world, there's also a layering of others. Time is not divided by minutes and hours, and everything has presence and meaning within this landscape of time-lessness." Particularly in America, she says, "There is no past, present, and future. The present is of massacres; the present is of ceremonial events, and so on. We walk in and out of them all the time."[21]

Such perceptions inform the healing impulse of poems conceived in the sense of relationship that grounds language's traditional functions and its power—poems conceived as "alive forms of dynamic energy" that aim "to be useful in a native context," to be a "bridge over the sea of paradox." Such a poetry will "adapt" the changes facing Indian cultures and "claim the past," because, "when you are able to articulate something that is terrible that is inside you, that lives in you, and you no longer deny it, you are able to bring regeneration."[22]

Harjo's healing intent is clear in "Call It Fear" and "I Give You Back," the first and last poems in *She Had Some Horses*. The first, like "The Woman Hanging from the Thirteenth Floor Window," locates us on an "edge," "an ocean of fear of the dark" (13); in the second the poet releases her fear to reclaim herself (73–74). "Grace," the first poem of *In Mad Love and War*, describes "the epic search for grace," which was briefly success-ful in a moment when "we once again understood the talk of animals, and spring was lean and hungry with the hope of children and corn." Even though this moment of knowledge was only a moment, its promise remains: "I know there is something larger than the memory of a dispos-sessed people. We have seen it" (1). In situation and movement "Grace" recalls Hogan's "The New Apartment: Minneapolis." But Harjo's poem is more provisional, the unexpected finding of grace in the "dingy light" of a truck stop contrasting with the purposeful return home in Hogan's.

Setting the two poems together, then, foregrounds the desire, and modu-
lates the sense of accomplishment, in "The New Apartment." Harjo's
"Transformations," however, shares with "The New Apartment" its belief
in the power of language and the healing reality of visionary re-creation:

> I know you can turn a poem into something else. This poem could be
> a bear . . . Or a piece of seaweed . . . What I mean is that hatred can
> be turned into something else, if you have the right words, the right
> meanings, buried in that tender place in your heart. (*Mad Love* 59)[23]

One of Harjo's best-known poems, "She Had Some Horses," em-
bodies the self-recognition fundamental to healing and empowerment:

> She had horses who were bodies of sand.
> She had horses who were maps drawn in blood.
> . . . .
> She had horses who were clay and would break.
> She had horses who were splintered red cliff.
> . . . .
> She had horses who waltzed nightly on the moon.
> She had horses who were much too shy . . .
> . . . .
> She had horses who liked Creek Stomp Dance songs.
> She had horses who cried in their beer.
> She had horses who spit at male queens who made
> them afraid of themselves.
> She had horses who said they weren't afraid.
> . . . .
> She had horses who had no names.
> She had horses who had books of names.
>
> . . . .
> She had some horses she loved.
> She had some horses she hated.
>
> These were the same horses.
>
> (*Horses* 63–64)

The poem foregrounds the kinds of internal collisions that can result
from borderland polarizations. But its rhythms recall the healing poten-

tial of drumming in Young Bear's "The Black Antelope Tine" and in Hogan's poetry, and, in her interview with Bill Moyers, Harjo identifies the poem's healing knowledge: "I see the horses as different aspects of a personality . . . We *all* have herds of horses, so to speak, and they can be contradictory" (*Spiral of Memory* 48–49). Harjo also spoke with Moyers of her desire for resolution; her terms suggest how the last lines (quoted above) of "She Had Some Horses" might offer the possibility of reconciliation and thus of healing. Whatever a poem's topic, she says, "I somehow always want it to resolve, and in some manner I want the resolution to be love. I *do* have to be open for the poem to go its own way, but I think the natural movement of love is an opening, a place that makes connections" (47).

The theme of regeneration is clarified in "Explosion." This poem shares the somewhat surrealistic cast of lines like "She had horses who waltzed nightly on the moon," and it fuses the ordinary—the "explosion" occurs "near Okemah, Oklahoma"—with the mythic: "Maybe there is a new people, coming forth / being born from the center of the earth, / like us, but another tribe." Or "maybe the explosion was horses . . . a violent birth." The horses immediately take over the poem, traveling through literal and dream landscapes. Though "some will not see them," the poem promises self-knowledge for others, who "will see the horses with their hearts of sleeping volcanoes / and will be rocked awake / past their bodies / to see who they have become" (*Horses* 68–69). In these last lines, too, the rhythm of heart- and hoof-beats, and imagination, drums a restorative energy.

The merging of the mundane and the mythic in poems like "Explosion" reflects Harjo's understanding of myth's continuity with the ordinary and its power. In words that recall "The Black Antelope Tine" she says, "I . . . see memory as not just associated with past history . . . past stories, but nonlinear, as in future and ongoing history, events, and stories. And it changes." Similarly, "myth is an alive, interactive event that is present in the everyday . . . It's the shimmering framework for all else to occur." And memory itself is mythic. It is

the nucleus of every cell; it's what runs, it's the gravity . . . of the Earth. In a way, it's like the stories themselves, the origin of the stories, and the continuance of all the stories. It's this great pool, this mythic pool of knowledge and history that we live inside.[24]

Harjo articulates the painful but life-giving necessity of dream and memory, and hence of myth, in "Autobiography," a poem moved by her knowledge of the insidious destructiveness of borderland history and ongoing grief. Here here characterization of dreams recalls Hogan's "Mountain Lion," even as she proceeds to a different kind of "translation" and transformation:

> . . . Dreams aren't glass and steel but made from the hearts of deer, the blazing eye of a circling panther. Translating them was to understand the death count from Alabama, the destruction of grandchildren, famine of stories. I didn't think I could stand it. My father couldn't . . .

> I have since outlived . . . my father and that ragged self I chased through precarious years. But I carry them with me the same as this body carries the heart as a drum. Yesterday there was rain traveling east to home. A hummingbird spoke. She was a shining piece of invisible memory, inside the raw cortex of songs. I knew then this was the Muscogee season of forgiveness, time of new corn, the spiraling dance. (*Mad Love* 14–15)

It follows, then, that not only does "the act of writing, of witnessing mean . . . taking part in the healing of the people" but also that "the resolution is through reassertion of tribal self." Thus Harjo's disagreement with an interviewer's attribution of "ambivalence about tribal culture" to some of her poetic personae and her own resolve "not [to] allow the duality of blood and cultures to destroy me."[25]

The need for and reality of "forgiveness . . . new corn, the spiraling dance," the healing powers of tradition, memory, and myth, in the gritty world of "broken survivors," is the burden and hope of three deer poems from *In Mad Love and War*. In "Deer Dancer" (5–6) a raggedy dancer brings the possibility of transformation to her audience of "hardcore" drinkers in "the bar of misfits." The mythic recollection she offers is all the more powerfully promising for its unexpectedness. The promise is intimated in the prose poem's first paragraph:

> . . . We were Indian ruins. She was the end of beauty. No one knew her, the stranger whose tribe we recognized, her family related to

deer, if that's who she was, a people accustomed to hearing songs in pine trees and making them hearts.

The barroom crowd responds variously, with a "miracle," a jealous rage, and a couple of unsuccessful efforts at betrayal, while the speaker acknowledges that "this language" cannot say "how the real world collapses," and the poem proceeds to show us that the "collapse" may be a visionary infusion of healing memory and energy. The turning point comes midway, in the juxtaposition of two questions, the first from a braggart trying to flirt with the dancer, "the proverbial dream girl": "*What's a girl like you doing in a place like this?* / That's what I'd like to know, what are we all doing in a place like this?" The second question foregrounds the heteroglossia of the first, drawing attention, retrospectively, to the dialogism of "dream girl," and transforming a self-interested cliché with the possibility of communal resistance; it thereby opens the poem to life-saving questioning, risk, and vision, the knowledge that "the way back is deer breath on icy windows."

The next dance none of us predicted. She borrowed a chair for the stairway to heaven and stood on a table of names. And danced in the room of children without shoes.

She danced to a blues song, "and then she took off her clothes . . . shook loose memory, waltzed with the empty lover we'd all become." As she was transformed, so was her audience: "She was the myth slipped down through dream-time. The promise of feast we all knew was coming. The deer who crossed through knots of curse to find us. She was no slouch, and neither were we, watching."

The final paragraph confirms that the vision has proceeded from the healing powers of imagination fed by memory: "I imagined her like this . . . the deer who entered our dream in white dawn, breathed mist into pine trees, her fawn a blessing of meat, our ancestors who never left." In this ending Harjo affirms continuity and relatedness, the myth- and memory-sustained reality that enables survival.

In "Deer Ghost" (*Mad Love* 29) the deer's "glass voice of the invisible," its myth-grounded healing power, allows the speaker to reaffirm her relationship to home and people:

> . . . I am lighting the fire that crawls from my spine
> to the gods with a coal from my sister's flame. This is what names
> me in the ways of my people, who have called me back.
> The deer knows what it is doing wandering the streets of this
> city; it has never forgotten the songs.

The wonderful vitality of song is affirmed in "Song for the Deer and Myself to Return On" (*Mad Love* 30); "overwhelmed" by the beauty of the predawn sky, the poet sings "a song to call the deer in Creek, when hunting," a song taught her by Muscogee elder poet Louis Oliver. The song's success both confirms language's efficacy and the power of memory's connections and brings a trace of healing humor: the "deer came into this room / and wondered at finding themselves / in a house near downtown Denver." Now what is required is a creative collaboration: "Now the deer and I are trying to figure out a song / to get them back, to get us all back, / because if it works I'm going with them."

"The Woman Who Fell from the Sky" (*Woman* 5–9) offers a multi-layered collaboration with and within the mythic, demonstrating the creative possibilities of memory's continuity and the nonlinear simultaneity of past, present, and future: "Everyone turns together though we may not see each other stacked in the invisible dimensions" (7). The hope for healing here is that the prose poem's main characters, Lila and Johnny, *do* see each other. The first paragraph establishes the creative interpenetration of myth and the mundane: "Once a woman fell from the sky . . . She was rather ordinary, though beautiful in her walk . . . When I see her I think of an antelope grazing the alpine meadows in mountains whose names are as ancient as the sound that created the first world" (5). Shifting perspectives also suggest the poem's mythic implications: the first-person speaker, Saint Coincidence/Johnny, Lila, and even an abandoned cat, represent the story's continuity and its openness to variation and creative interpretation.

Harjo grounds the story's meanings partly in Johnny's and Lila's experiences of cultural oppression. Saint Coincidence, now panhandling in a Safeway parking lot, sees the falling woman and remembers Lila, with whom, "at Indian boarding school," he "stood witness . . . to strange acts of cruelty by strangers" (5, 6). The meaning of their witnessing deepens when we recognize their openness to mythic truth. Lila has knowledge that enables her to participate actively in myth: "The woman who was to fall from the sky was the girl with skinned knees whose spirit knew how to climb to the stars. Once she told [Johnny] . . . the stars spoke a language akin to the plains of her home, a language like rocks" (6).

Lila's knowledge includes "the story told before she'd grown ears to hear," a story of women who, out of anger, boredom, frustration, or the desire for "travel and enlightenment," went away with stars who had come "to the earth to find mates." Years later one of these women "dared to look back," fell to earth, "took up where she had left off, with her children from the stars," and "was remembered" (8). Not only is this story "Lila's refuge . . . in the school dorms"; later she chooses to enter the story, to leave "on the arms of one of the stars," in search of love and then, in response to a song (perhaps Johnny's), she leaps, with her children, back into this world (9). More specifically, she leaps into "the place her [star] husband had warned her was too sacred for women," a "forbidden place" (9), and her mythic action thus becomes a continuation of her and Johnny's childhood acts of resistance.

The poem ends with paradox and convergence, both of them promising:

> She fell and was still falling when Saint Coincidence caught her in his arms in front of the Safeway as he made a turn from borrowing spare change from strangers.

> The children crawled safely from their mother. The cat stalked a bit of flying trash set in motion by the wave of falling—

> or the converse wave of gathering together. (9)

"The Woman Who Fell from the Sky" shows us that participation in myth constitutes a potentially restorative struggle against the indignities Native people suffer in the borderlands and more specifically in Owens's "territory"; thus the poem can anticipate healing. The myth's ongoing power also contributes to the poem's dialogism. The most obvious instance of dialogism is in the setting, the icy *Safeway* parking lot. Other examples are Johnny's chosen name, "Saint Coincidence," the nuns' condemnation of "blasphemy," Lila's need for "refuge" from prayers, and, in the context of the Catholic boarding school, the idea of falling itself. As the poem alerts us to such words' multiple intentions, it reminds us of the struggles enacted in the "dialogics of the oppressed."

This poem recalls elements of the "Star Husband" stories told in many

American Indian cultures. Generally, in these stories women take the initiative in ascending to the sky world; they also tend to initiate their returns to this world. Sometimes a woman returns with a child, who may then become the hero of his own stories. Often, though, the women die in the process of returning, usually due to their sky husbands' jealousy.[26] Given some of the details Harjo includes—the mythical women's motives and Lila's star husband's prohibitions—we might read her poem as in part an empowering revision of the traditional stories' active female characters.[27]

The poem also recalls the Iroquois origin story, in which a woman falls from the sky world, pregnant and bearing cultural gifts; her fall instigates the creation of the earth. This woman's daughter becomes the mother of twins (a history perhaps condensed when Harjo's woman falls with "the twins in her arms and her daughter" clinging to her skirt with "her small fists" [9]). In some versions the falling woman becomes an evil grandmother; always the twins embody good and bad. Still, this is a story that establishes how people came to live on the earth, a story that, in a mythical sense, continues to make life on earth possible. Thus it is a story of promise, as is Harjo's.[28] Beyond its resonances with traditional narratives the poem itself establishes its story's mythic reality, as the characters cross the boundaries of the natural and supernatural and interact creatively with humans and others.

"The Woman Who Fell from the Sky" gains further power and mythic resonance from its mutually illuminating relationship with other poems of Harjo's. Noni Daylight, who moves through *What Moon Drove Me to This* and *She Had Some Horses*, could be a predecessor, even an older cousin, of Lila's. Like Lila, Noni is economically and politically marginalized yet travels readily between the mythic and the mundane. At once trapped and visionary, she is saved from suicidal impulses by her insistence upon choosing her own life and relationships, her sense of connectedness, and her anger, "a fierce anger / that will free her" ("Heartbeat," *Horses* 37). Noni is never far from the edge. "The air . . . tempts / Noni to violence . . . But she needs / the feel of danger, for life" ("She Remembers the Future," *Horses* 46). *But* reminds us that she is *on* the edge, she hasn't stepped over it; at the poem's end she suggests that we should

> ". . . ride colored horses
> into the cutting edge of the sky
> to know

that we're alive
we are alive."

Noni embodies the proximity to desperation, and the need constantly to
recover and affirm one's grounding in life, that Lila's story underplays
but that is evident in that of her schoolmate, Johnny/Saint Coincidence.[29]
In "The Woman Hanging from the Thirteenth Floor Window" we see
someone who lacks Noni's saving anger (or at least hasn't yet admitted it)
and who has almost let go of the edge. Without anger or vision she may
dangle until she falls from exhaustion. While the poem's ambigious end-
ing may offer hope that the dangling woman will grasp her possibilities
for recovering, Lila embodies hope and healing even as she falls, pre-
cisely because she has never lost sight of her traditional sources of em-
powerment. A participant in interactive mythic reality, she is herself em-
powered and may contribute to Johnny's healing, as well as to her own,
and to cultural continuity.

Harjo implies a vital affinity between myth and music when she says
that "playing saxophone is like honoring a succession of myths . . . here
comes Billie Holiday and there's Coltrane . . . When you play you're part
of that." She finds in music, especially in the rough edges of jazz, images
for struggle, healing, and power that contribute to her project of cross-
cultural transgressions of borders.[30] "Music," after all, "doesn't have the
added boundary of words." We have seen this in "Song for the Deer and
Myself to Return On," where a traditional song brings the deer into urban
Denver. She describes her writing, too, in terms that confirm the impor-
tance of crossing and blurring boundaries: "My writing technique is a
fusion, much the way jazz is a fusion . . . I've had to make poetry some-
thing that fused the various systems of communication."[31]

In "Healing Animal" (*Mad Love* 38–39) music offers healing connec-
tion, as Harjo recalls how

Josiah's uncle brought . . . [Coltrane's] music
        to the Papago center of the world
                and music climbed out of his trombone
into the collected heartbeat of his tribe.

(38)

And in "We Encounter Nat King Cole as We Invent the Future" (*Mad Love*
51) music and dreams, myth and the mundane, the real and the surreal,

merge in a revelation of energy, order, and beauty. What seems to insti-
gate this moment of wonderful convergence is relationship charged with
multivalenced desire, the intimate but elusive and reticent reunion of two
women. Driving home, the speaker sees

> . . . a double rainbow
> two-stepping across the valley. Suddenly,
> there were twin gods bending over to plant something like
> themselves in the wet earth, a song
> . . . .
> whipping everything back
> into the geometry of dreams: became Nat King Cole
> became the sultry blue moon became all
> perfumed romantic strangers became Camme and me
> became love
> suddenly[32]

Numerous elements, but especially the music, the homeward journey,
the event that is beyond prediction, and the vision of another "myth
slipped down through dreamtime" (*Mad Love* 6), suggest that "We En-
counter Nat King Cole" represents another version of the promise of
continuance with which Harjo ends "Deer Dancer."

In "The Place the Musician Became a Bear" (*Woman* 51–53), a tribute
to Creek saxophonist Jim Pepper, Harjo again grounds myth and music in
the mundane. Beyond reiterating the healing power of music, this poem
with its coda (52–53) opens a pathway to creative survival in the border-
lands and beyond. In the coda Harjo tells us that Jim Pepper

> *was a fine jazz saxophonist, constructing a music that included the tribal
> musics he heard as a boy taken by his father on the powwow circuit through
> Oklahoma as well as the more traditional elements of jazz . . .*
>
> *I've always believed us Creeks . . . had something to do with the origins of
> jazz. After all, when the African peoples were forced here for slavery they
> were brought to the traditional lands of the Muscogee peoples. Of course
> there was interaction between Africans and Muscogees!* (52)

The poem itself begins with "the lush stillness of the end of a world,
sung into place by singers and the rattle of turtles in the dark morning."

But the serenity of cyclic and cultural continuity is disrupted, as she admits that "it's the how that baffles. A saxophone can complicate things." As she suggested the visionary good of the real world's collapse, in "Deer Dancer," she now lets us see the necessity of this complication, a complication integral to the dynamic interactions and multilayered realities of the gritty and wondrous world. "I'm talking about an early morning in Brooklyn, the streets the color of ashes, do you see the connection? It's not as if the stars forsake us. We forget about them." However, music and the universe embrace each other, as living cycles accommodate the new: the "wings of the Milky Way lead back to the singers. And there's the saxophone again." And the instrument's presence is

> . . . about rearranging the song to include the subway
> hiss under your feet in Brooklyn.
>
> And the laugh of the bear who thought he was a human.
>
> As he plays that tune again, the one about the wobble of the earth
> spinning so damned hard it hurts.

As the poem ends on this note, its initial serenity has been recomposed into a different, less comfortable, and equally real kind of certainty. Still, the "bear," Pepper, *is* "play[ing] that tune again" even from the Milky Way, the spirits' road to the world above, where Harjo tells us she knows he's gone.[33]

The cross-cultural improvisations and creative dialogism that Harjo hears in jazz, and that she writes into her poetry, challenge the divisiveness of borderland history and politics and any illusions of cultural survival in stasis. In this light we can read "The Woman Who Fell from the Sky," with its echoes of stories from different Native cultures and its vision of myth's efficacy in a hostile world, as a poem that both crosses boundaries among Native American cultures and resists territorial impositions. In "Hieroglyphic" (*Mad Love* 53–54), a poem dedicated to African American poet June Jordan, Harjo alludes to the transformative effects of cross-cultural openness: "I met myself in the Egyptian Room . . . my heart had become a phoenix of / swallowed myths." And she credits another African American writer, Audre Lorde, with helping her to affirm that "when the body-spirit-mind-emotions-soul are an integrated whole, then a true relationship is experienced in both the inside and outside worlds."[34] Like the intimate cross-cultural project Wendy Rose accomplishes in "Margaret Neumann" (*Going to War* 65–69), the crossings and fusions in Harjo's poetry represent a perception and practice that promise healing, continuity, and power.

Harjo's, Young Bear's, and Hogan's poems suggest that people may be empowered to resist internal and external dislocations and oppressions, through a vision of the world in which the boundaries between past and present, dream and waking, the mythic and the mundane dissolve or become permeable. To connect with such knowledge of wholeness is to be strengthened to (re)negotiate painful and destructive divisions. The fact that they often write from places "between"—between this world and others, between dream and waking, sometimes between cultures, while it enables them to deal creatively with the tensions experienced in contested spaces, also seems to make special demands of language. "Each time I write," Harjo says, "I am in a different and wild place, and travel toward something I don't know the name of" ("Ordinary Spirit" 265). Young Bear makes language an issue with his surprising juxtapositions and his resistance to spontaneity, his "veils of light"; Hogan seeks a "language that knows the corn." As they reach for language adequate to the realities they inhabit and envision, they remind us that language itself, in traditional perspectives, is infused with spirit. Thus, though borderland conditions may aggravate its potential as a site for conflict, language can also be a source of creative connection and power, of healing and survival.

In storytelling, too, we find language's diverse potentials realized, whether in transparent affirmation or in the kind of suggestive ambiguity that perhaps throws into sharpest relief the need for an engaged audience. Whether directly or indirectly, the poems I discuss in chapter 6 suggest storytelling's power for survival. As Chrystos puts it, "I stalk any story that will let me see / another spring" (*Not Vanishing* 54).

CHAPTER 6

Telling Stories

And it is through my own story and stories of my family and my
circle of people that I become whole . . . At gatherings . . .
stories would roll out and encircle the group. From each telling
we would become strengthened, released from a sense of
isolation. We fed ourselves with these stories.
—Elizabeth Woody, *Seven Hands, Seven Hearts*

The thing I remember mostly about stories . . . the thing that I
remember most vividly is the idea of being set free.
—Gerald Vizenor, qtd. in *Gerald Vizenor*

Storytelling, like language a mode of both connection and liberation,
is vital for modern Indian writers, as it has been vital to the survival of
Native cultures. Poems as varied as "Reaching Yellow River," "The Black
Antelope Tine," "Deer Dancer," and "Near Crater Lake" show that con-
temporary poets tell stories in styles ranging from the cryptic and mini-
malist, to highly descriptive and figurative modes rich in imagery. Their
stylistic choices can often be linked to practices from oral tradition and
read as reflecting, emulating, or modifying oral storytelling and song
styles.[1] The desire for an active, participating audience cuts across all
variations in story style or emphasis and unites contemporary Native
poets in an inspiriting and empowering bond with communal, oral tradi-
tion. The cultivation of dialogic relationships with the audience is, in fact,
the most consistently evident sign of these contemporaries' affinities with
oral tradition and with traditional understandings of language's depen-
dence on a responsive audience's participation in creating meaning.
Whether through direct address to the reader or inclusion of multiple
voices, or through the openness and ambiguity that Vizenor considers
" 'like the oral tradition' " because it " 'leaves open the possibility of dis-
course,' "[2] storytelling poets invite or challenge their readers to respond,
for, in so doing, readers may enter the storytelling process and, in ways
that may vary according to their cultural/historical locations, affirm the
community that stories sustain.

Simon Ortiz, in particular, has dedicated himself to creating a written poetic style from oral tradition. In the preface to his second collection of poems, *A Good Journey,* Ortiz explains that he "wanted to show that the narrative style and technique of oral tradition could be expressed as written narrative and that it would have the same participatory force and validity as words spoken and listened to." Simultaneously, he wanted "the poetry [to] show the energy that language is, the way that the energy is . . . transformed into vision, and the way this vision becomes knowledge which engenders and affirms the substance and motion of one's life" (151).[3]

Among the traits of traditional oral literature identified by Walter J. Ong and Paul Zumthor, many are especially strong in Ortiz's first three books. These include an "additive rather than subordinative" style (Ong 37), "the predominance of speech acts over descriptions" (Zumthor 98), and a quality of being "close to the human lifeworld," "empathetic and participatory," and "situational rather than abstract" (Ong 42, 45, 49). As Ortiz says, the stories "weren't just stories . . . they were views on . . . the way we—the community of Acoma Pueblo, the larger Native American world, the world in general, lived" ("Always the Stories" 57). Perhaps the most prominent stylistic quality of oral stories and poems is repetition; central to the necessary reciprocity of story/poem, speaker/poet, and listener/reader, repetition, "whatever its form . . . constitutes the most efficacious means to . . . make the listener participate" (Zumthor 111–12).

How stories come into being and meaning is suggested in several poems from Ortiz's *A Good Journey.* In "When It Was Taking Place" (267–70) an old man tells his grandson of something that happened long ago. Context and place are crucial to the story's origin, its present telling, its meaning, and, most important, its reception by the boy, who can see what his grandfather remembers. Seeing, the boy may become in his imagination and memory a participant and thus a guarantor of the story's continuity. "Hesperus Camp, July 13, Indian 1971" (162–63) suggests a similar relationship between place, story, and meaning. As two Anglo visitors reveal their inability to appreciate the Southwestern landscape, the poet-speaker reflects on how knowing the story of a place enables him to recognize its beauty. If the landscape is one source of stories, another is implied in the small talk between the narrator and his visitors. These two unelaborated lines from "Hesperus Camp" are richly suggestive: " 'Flower was up, says he's working.' / 'Unbelievable.' " If we recognize the unspoken presence of stories known but not detailed by these speakers, we also recognize the continuing dialogic creation of stories, out of people's day-to-day lives.

Ortiz's commentary in the second part of "Two Coyote Ones" (230–32) shows more directly how an ordinary contemporary encounter has the potential for becoming a traditional story. "One night in summer in southern Colorado," he begins, "I was sitting by my campfire."

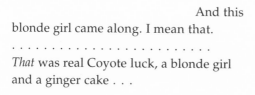

>   And this
> blonde girl came along. I mean that.
> . . . .
> *That* was real Coyote luck, a blonde girl
> and a ginger cake . . .

The speaker thinks about Coyote, as they talk about "the goats [the girl's family was raising] and what I was doing / which was living at the foot of the La Plata / Mountains and writing." Story possibilities occur to him: "I think I could have / done something with that gimmicky-sounding / line, which was true besides, but I didn't." After the girl drives away, however, he begins, again:

> There's this story Coyote was telling
> about the time he was sitting at his campfire
> and a pretty blonde girl came driving along
> in a pickup truck and she . . . And so on.
>   (Ortiz's ellipsis)

As the speaker transforms experience into story, we see the "closer narrative relationship with Coyote" that Patricia Clark Smith discerns in Ortiz's poetry and prose (197), and recognize what Ortiz himself states to Bruchac: "Coyote has, for me, been the creative act . . . It is something that never dies . . . a symbol . . . of continuation" (*Survival* 228). Thus we may expect to encounter Coyote's spirit at work even in poems where he is not obviously present. Two other poems about Coyote exemplify Ortiz's integration of stylistic qualities and an ethics of storymaking drawn from oral tradition.

"Telling About Coyote" (157–60) begins and ends by reminding us of the tradition's continuity; this pair of stories is introduced by the conclusion of another story and ends with the promise that "he'll be back." The

poem is marked by repetition, often involving direct address to the audi-
ence, and an additive structure (the ellipsis is Ortiz's):

> He was sitting at one side of the fire.
> And the fire was being fed large pine logs,
> and Crow was sitting downwind
> from the fire, and the wind was blowing
> that way . . .
>   and Coyote was there.

Not only does Ortiz invite us to respond, but the presence of several
different voices demonstrates the reality of communal creation and the
vitality of a communal dialogics: each voice adds to and contextualizes
the jointly known story, in a harmony of unified intentions.[4] This mul-
tiple voicing, the manifestation of a communally created intention, al-
lows the poet to acknowledge that the story's telling and reception are
inevitably touched by different languages and expectations—and to in-
corporate non-Pueblo elements humorously.

> "Yet, he came so close
> to having it easy.
>   But he said,
> "Things are just too easy . . ."
> Of course he was mainly bragging,
> Shooting his mouth.
> The existential Man.
> Dostoevsky Coyote.
>   (Ortiz's ellipsis)

Though virtually every reference to Coyote is potentially a moral ex-
ample, Ortiz instead emphasizes Coyote's persistence, his indefatigable
"trucking along," and the reassuring certainty of his continuance. Coy-
ote's identity, for Ortiz, as symbol of the creative spirit, gives this reassur-
ance added importance.

"Like myself, the source of these narratives is my home. Sometimes
my father tells them, sometimes my mother, sometimes even the story-
teller himself tells them." This title, of another poem that tells two stories
about Coyote (168–71), announces the contributions of multiple speakers
and the possibility of change within continuity. Language is a major

theme in both stories. The first, told by the poet's father, highlights the relationships and the differences between the Acoma and Laguna people, as they are revealed by language:

> the Kawaikamehtitra—the Laguna people—
> were having a rabbit hunt.
> Tchaiyawahni ih—as they say in Laguna.
> But in Acoma, it means
> "hunting and killing each other."

The poem thus indicates that cultural boundaries exist within the indigenous world. But, at least in this first story, tensions can be mitigated: Coyote comes back to life to stop the Laguna Coyote People from chasing the Acoma who has "killed" him.

In the second story, however, there is no reconciliation; this time the different voices are those of Coyote-Pehrru and the "troop of sandahlrrutitra–soldiers" who want his apparently magical kettle. And in the colonized borderland one or the other must finally win. Ortiz uses language to draw attention to the border situation, pointedly not translating Pehrru's longest and perhaps most important Acoma statement and thereby putting his non-Acoma readers into a position even closer to that of the soldiers. Further, though he uses both languages to introduce the outsiders, through most of the poem he refers to them simply as "soldiers," perhaps reflecting the position of dominance that, whether Spanish or American, they've historically taken for themselves. But in the end, when Pehrru has duped them into paying a high price for "the plain old smoke-blackened kettle," they are again "sandahl-rrutitra." Rather than reconciliation, then, this story shows how Pehrru uses language, and the interlopers' overly eager gullibility, to win an understated victory.[5] While the story of the rabbit hunt turns on Coyote's ability to survive "killing," this one humorously emphasizes the survival power of his wit and his understanding of his adversaries. Both stories thus sustain the promise of "Telling About Coyote": "He'll be back."

Fight Back: For the Sake of the People, For the Sake of the Land, "written in commemoration of the Pueblo Revolt of 1680," is centrally about survival (Ortiz, "Always the Stories" 66). This book both remembers and assures: "The songs, stories, poems and advice will always remember / my father, mother, and my people" (287).

> Standing again
> with all things
> . . . .
> we acknowledge ourselves
> to be in a relationship that is responsible
> and proper, that is loving and compassionate
>   (289)

From this position of memory and relationship Ortiz can affirm that "we shall have victory" (287). It will be a victory marked, and in part accomplished, by the telling of stories.

The story poems of *Fight Back* generally share the stylistic and structural attributes evident in the *Good Journey* stories. The language is colloquial, the emphasis concrete and situational, and the structure of the stories is largely additive. There is less direct dialogue, yet the mode is predominantly narrative, with relatively little description; there is repetition, but it is less emphatic. These are, after all, new stories written in an orally grounded voice, rather than stories whose characters and situations are historically rooted in memory-dependent oral culture. Though we generally hear directly only one speaking voice, Ortiz implies communal voices by incorporating words, phrases, and sentences, often not directly translated, in the Acoma language. And, though we see little direct evidence of a listening audience, as Andrew Wiget observes, "his passing on of the story, his informing of us, implicates the reader in what and how Ortiz knows"—and thus, I would add, implies a communal audience as well.[6] Far more than any of the *Good Journey* story poems, those in *Fight Back* focus on borderland experience; in many of them Ortiz speaks, as it were, directly across the border to those of us on "the other side," to challenge and inform us, even as he affirms and encourages his own people. Thus even a "single" voice speaks at once in different registers and dialogically. Though there are no Coyote stories, per se, in *Fight Back,* nonetheless, Coyote's spirit is present—in the creative power of the stories, in Ortiz's manifest awareness and exploitation of language's dialogic potential for arousing political awareness and struggle, and in the determination to go on, to survive, that moves the entire collection.

This spirit is present, in an understated way, in the first poem in *Fight Back.* "It Was That Indian" (295–96) reports two Anglo versions of the discovery of uranium by "that Indian," the Navajo Martinez; doing so, the poem establishes concretely and succinctly what Native people are up against and subtly insinuates, with Coyote-like skill, an exposé and critique of the Anglos' stories and their motives. The first version of Martinez's discovery, we're told, glorified him. "Tourist magazines did a couple spreads / on him, photographed him in kodak color," and "the city fathers named / a city park after him." In this version Martinez is the hero of the uranium boom, and he is celebrated as long as the Anglos succeed in enriching themselves without facing the consequences of exploitation. Eventually, however, the Anglos' story changed. Confronted with complaints about the socially and environmentally destructive effects of the mining boom, "they—the Chamber of Commerce—pointed out / that it was Martinez / . . . it was that Indian who started the boom."

Both Anglo versions of discovery and responsibility served to co-opt language, story, and the earth itself, with the further aim of alienating "that Indian" (and all of "those Indians") from those same sources of life. Indeed, both versions show the Anglos imposing territorial conditions, in Owens's sense, on the people and the land: "mapp[ing] . . . a place of containment . . . to control and subdue . . . Native peoples" (" 'The Song Is Very Short' " 59). Both the weakness of the Anglo versions and the people's hope for survival are conveyed as Ortiz's speaker distances himself from the Anglos' assertions: "That's what they said," he tells us, reminding us of the heteroglossia that inevitably threatens to disrupt their self-assured and self-serving, publicity-oriented adulation of "that Indian," whose name they haven't bothered to remember. The rift between the exploiters' vision and the Native population's experience becomes more obvious as we learn that the Chamber members "forgot for the time being / that the brothers / from Aacqu . . . had killed that state patrolman . . . and . . . that the city had a jail full of Indians." Coyote-like, the speaker reveals his own recognition of language's susceptibility both to manipulation and to reinterpretation; the poem demonstrates the need for a resistant dialogism.

The need for dialogic struggle is differently presented in "The First Hard Core" (306–8), a story about language and silence in the borderlands. The Indian speaker, "just a teenager" at the time, tells how he put up with a seemingly endless catalog of stereotyping remarks from Herb, a white coworker; his response to each of Herb's questions and challenges was the same: "I didn't know how to answer him / so he'd believe me if he could. / I just said I don't know." These lines show us a breakdown in oral communication itself: the boy, as Herb's audience, couldn't respond adequately; Herb, as the boy's potential audience, couldn't have heard—or understood—any substantial response. This poem starkly implies the need for a third sensibility, the reader's, to listen and respond, and thereby change the story's outcome, its final stymied silence. As in "It Was That Indian," "The First Hard Core" must engage the reader in a dialogic exchange, against the racists and exploiters who otherwise will monopolize language and the story. (Chrystos and Rose, we've seen, act on a similarly urgent necessity as they incite readers to respond to injustice.)

"To Change in a Good Way" (308–17) offers a hopeful, even redemptive, story of dialogue across cultures, grounded in family, relationship to the land, and the similarity of white and Indian mineworkers' experiences. Embedded in this story is an account of a white workingman's halting new awareness of the fragility of patriotic rhetoric and official history. At the funeral of his brother, killed in Vietnam, Bill hears his relatives declaring "that someone had to make the sacrifice / for freedom," that his brother had "done his duty for America." We see how these abstractions begin to dissolve as Bill "trie[s] to say . . . that the mine"

> that Slick had stepped on was American
> and that the fact he was in a dangerous place
> was because he was in an Army
> that was American, and it didn't seem
> to be the same thing as what they were saying
> about past folks fighting
> Indians for democracy
> and it didn't seem right somehow.

Bill is still far from recognizing that history as a story of heroes "fighting off Indians to build homes" is utterly at odds with his own experience of working with Indians in the mine. Even so, and despite the fact that none of his relatives "really heard him," he is beginning to develop an understanding similar to that which moves the speaker in "It was That Indian." Thus the story of his and his wife's friendship with a Laguna couple offers substance to the hope for solidarity that moves the union organizer-protagonist and the speaker in "What I Mean" (326–29). As a promise of continuity, change, and relationship, "To Change in a Good Way" is also thematically in tune with the origins and the survival impetus of traditional oral stories and may function at least provisionally as a counterweight to exploitation, danger, and grief.

While hope for solidarity may be grounded in commonality, it also depends upon knowledge of our true histories, if people like Bill are to be empowered to forge bonds across the borders created by racism and exploitation. In "Final Solution: Jobs, Leaving" (318–20) Ortiz continues this effort of memory and empowerment for his people. The history recalled in "Final Solution" actually predates the mining boom that brought white and Native workers together in "The First Hard Core" and "To Change in a Good Way." In fact, "Final Solution" refers to a major reason why Indian mineworkers were reluctant to complain out loud or to unionize: as the speaker of "What I Mean" says, "We were just glad for the jobs we had, / union or no union" (328). The history told in "Final Solution: Jobs, Leaving," then, is necessary to successfully negotiating the difficulties of solidarity in the more recent past and in the present.

"Final Solution: Jobs, Leaving" (318–20) is one of *Fight Back*'s most structurally innovative story poems. Its collage-like narrative tells how, "surrounded by the United States," forced into a cash economy, the adult men of Acoma (and other Native communities) "would leave / on Sundays from the depot in Grants," in search of jobs away from home. This personal and communal history is told in the intertwined voices of adults and children, the men who took to the road, and the poet—whose own father was one of these men, and who, in remembering, fights back. These, then, are voices of the participants, making and telling their own story. We hear the children's grief: "Good bye. Good bye Daddy. Daddy, / please come back. Please don't go . . . O Daddy. Please train." And that of the men: "The children would cry. / The women would be so angry. / So angry. / Silent, we left." We read one father's letter to his family and hear another man grieving the loss of a friend on the road: " 'He step off / the train. That was the last time / I saw him. My friend.' " And the poet catalogs the men's destinations, reminds us of the meanings of their work:

> They kept the railroad repaired,
> and the trains raced through
> their land. Hearts. Blood. Bones
> and skin. Wrenched muscles.

Ortiz creates not only a powerful example of communal dialogism in struggle but also a direct challenge to the reader—both through the power of the feelings he evokes and in his foregrounding of heteroglossia: the poem's title, recurring references to trains, and variations on the phrase *never again* recall the Nazi holocaust and thereby force us to recognize the disastrous history of North America. As it does for Jews, "Never again" signifies for the Indian people in Ortiz's poem both grief and the determination to survive.

In the poem's story we can see quiet resistance even in the desolation of distance and separation. On the one hand, the men (and the poet) recognize that, in the face of economic need, "the solution was to change, / to leave, to go to jobs"—thereby becoming ever more vulnerable to the United States's ongoing policy of separating Indians from land. Yet writing to his family from his temporary exile, one father refuses that separation, as he continues to teach his children the truths that will sustain them:

> . . . Children, help your mother
> and take care of each others
> and around our home. Remember
> that you must always love
> your mothers. Think of the prayers
> for the land . . .

As the poet does in "Mid-America Prayer" (289–90), one of the prefatory pieces to *Fight Back*, this father stands "with all things" as he teaches his family "to be in a relationship that is responsible." This resistance continues in the prose passage with which Ortiz concludes the poem:

> Yes, we would wait again. Weeks, weeks, months, but not those years again. O Daddy, never those years. Never again those years. Our own solution will be strength: hearts, blood, bones, skin, hope and love. The woman anger and courage risen as the People's voice again.

The poet's voice merges with and arises from the children's voices, tracing the growth from a child's grief to an adult's determination. Bringing together once more images and motifs that run through the poem (their repetition, too, recalling the processes by which experience enters oral tradition as story, to sustain the community), Ortiz promises renewed resistance, grounded in knowledge of continuance.

Like the Indian railroad workers in "Final Solution: Jobs, Leaving,"

Ortiz himself is away from home in *After and Before the Lightning.* Being away, indeed, is the impetus for the poems; in the preface he tells us that writing these poems was "like . . . putting together a map of where I was in the cosmos" (xiv). This book differs from Ortiz's earlier accounts of travel in that it does not trace his return to his home; rather, it shows how, by being attentive to the people, land, and weather around him, and their stories, he survives winter and finds himself spiritually at home on the South Dakota plains.

Like Ortiz's earlier collections, *After and Before the Lightning* weaves together varied genres—stories, prayers, notes, songs, meditations, impressions—in both poetic and prose forms. The book's structure is both linear (its pieces are dated from November 18 through March 21) and cyclical. The stories reveal the shape, human reference points, and meanings of a landscape and season that, at the outset, seem dauntingly unfamiliar. Sometimes narratives are repeated, revised, or continued at intervals; sometimes Ortiz simply hints at the presence or the possibility of stories (as he did through the small talk in "Hesperus Camp").

Many of these stories, like those in *Fight Back,* foreground border conditions. They may differ stylistically from those in Ortiz's earlier collections—with narrative now muted by description or reflection, fewer signs of multiple voicing or communal telling, and less overt evidence of a participant audience. Yet the language is generally colloquial, an additive structure appears occasionally, and the stories, like the entire book, are deeply grounded in place. Further, by including multiple versions of some stories or incidents Ortiz suggests the retelling and revising that make an oral tradition.

The stories with the strongest oral stylistic elements are those from Ortiz's home. The three Acoma stories help give an emotional grounding that enables the poet to hear and tell stories of the northern plain and its people and thereby make it through the rigorous winter. For example, the two-part story of his father and the Snow Shiwana (4, 44–45) reminds him that, as an Acoma person, he has known winter and offers humor, along with memory, as one way to deal with the season.

The second Acoma story (19–20) strongly emphasizes the communal nature of stories and the importance of a responsive audience. As Ortiz tells (and revises) a story from home, he demonstrates and comments on the storytelling process itself and reflects on the importance of stories. Doing so, he speaks to several overlapping audiences, and he implies these audiences' roles in creating and continuing the story.

Stories are as basic as good bread and a warm fire, no more than that . . . Yes, they say winter is the time for stories . . . Eh heh, that's what you say to show that you're listening . . . So gather the children around.

In this first paragraph he gradually goes from commenting to directly engaging his audience. He continues: " 'Let's see . . . I remember. We had our cattle up the canyon toward Tsuuschcki Tsaigaiyamihshru. Why is it called that? Well, you know, it's because of Tsuuschcki. That coyote, you know.' " After responding to listeners' questions, Ortiz eventually ends this passage with ellipsis points that suggest the completion of a typical Coyote story. Then, reminding us that "winter is the time," he begins a story of early winter:

"In those days, people would go on top of Horace Mesa to gather piñon nuts. Once, in October, they went for two days. On the second day it started to snow . . ." No, it's not that way. The story goes its own way . . . the basic story plus the imagination and memory . . . my mother's and father's words . . . and my own mind's knowledge.

. . . .

"They gathered dyaiyaahnih for two days and then an old man said, 'We better start homeward. It's going to snow very heavily.' . . . And just as they turned onto the road toward their home, my father— your grandfather—looked northward . . . And there were thick clouds above Horace Mesa, and it was snowing, just like the old man said it would."

As he begins this story, details evidently come back to him, and he suspends his storytelling voice for a reflective passage that may or may not be addressed to a listening audience. When he returns to the narrative it includes the multiple voicing, both direct and implied, that gives the story its communal meaning. An old man speaks and thus brings the story into being; then, by referring to "my father—your grandfather," Ortiz acknowledges an earlier teller and anticipates future tellings by the next generation. He concludes this intricately dialogic passage with the hopeful assurance of survival through multiply textured language:

Snow that October, the language of experience, sensation, history, imagination are all in the story and how it carries forth. Story has its own life, its very own, and we are the voice carried with it.

The story of Aliyosho, the third Acoma story, is told and retold in three segments (33–34, 82–84, 95–96). Clearly influenced by Mexican/ Spanish culture, it tells of Aliyosho, a poor young boy who sets out across the desert to a town where the "rey," the king, has offered a "prize." On his way he encounters a sick horse, for whom he has compassion and who, transformed, then assists him.[7]

The first telling simply summarizes the story; in the fifty pages that follow, Ortiz recounts a vast range of human experiences, intensified by the harsh prairie winter: desperation, wrath, battles with cold and drought, the promise of morning light, suicide. The second telling of the Aliyosho story (82–84) seems to respond directly to the experiences of struggle, grief, and hope evoked in the pages that precede it. Now we see the young boy's encounter with the sick old horse, his fear of its "terrible-looking running sores" and "the smell of death" all around it. We hear him address the horse respectfully and see him bring water for the horse to drink and to bathe the animal's "hot painful sores." Then we hear the horse thank Aliyosho and offer to help him. When the boy replies, " 'I'm sorry but I don't think you can help me,' " the horse directs him to bring more water to bathe his sores; when Aliyosho, despite his hurry, does so, "the sores wash . . . away and in their place [are] white spots. The old horse [becomes] Caballo Pinto."

In this second version of the story its oral qualities (thus its communal grounding) are richly evident. Not only does it have the additive structure noticeable in the summary, but it is full of narrative detail, repetition, and dialogue, all serving to engage the audience. Further, we see the story repeated and revised on the page in front of us: under the title heading "No, The Story Is This Way" Ortiz switches to poetry and completes the second telling by revising it. Now we learn that the horse spoke "quietly, crying," that Aliyosho "gently washed" its sores, and that as he did so, he spoke: " 'Beloved Horse, may you get well.' " Now, too, we hear Caballo Pinto thank him for his compassion and show how he will reciprocate: " 'Now / get on my back for I am a young horse again, / and I'm quite fast enough. I can help you.' " Through the mutual love and aid of its two characters and through its communal, collaborative essence as part of oral tradition, the story reminds us of the necessity and power of the compassion and respect so grievously missing in many of the book's other stories and memories.

After additional evocations of promise, grief, fear, and anger, as the book moves toward spring, the final segment of the Aliyosho story (95–96) concludes with a moral lesson; interestingly Ortiz does not repeat the narrative conclusion (Aliyosho's winning the reward) with which the first telling ended. This omission reminds us of oral storytelling: when the story is continued and retold the second and third times, the reader already knows its outcome, just as would the oral teller's community of listeners—yet the combination of history, memory, and imagination is still compelling. Aliyosho's story, which may be about winter, is also a valuable story *for* winter: it tells of a sojourn through a difficult landscape, which ends with a view of "a little green valley through which a gentle river flowed" (95). And while, as the horse, Caballo Pinto, tells Aliyosho, the story is about compassion, we can see that it is also about attentiveness and about the proper response to what one sees and hears—habits vital both to surviving winter in a harsh climate and to the survival of oral story tradition.

Among the book's many South Dakota stories one of the most powerful exposes the absence of compassion and responsiveness. I give it here in full:

> I've forgotten part of the story, but I remember she said, "The girl and the other children were standing at the door, their hands held out, ice in their hair." She spoke in the voice of her mother. "Her husband, my father, said, 'Close the door. It's just the Indians. They are used to the cold.' " She spoke in the voice of her father, the voice she heard her mother speak.

> When the woman looked at her husband, he was glaring at her. All around them, the walls were solid with winter. Silently, the children of the frozen woods stood there, ice in their hair. Would they always be there? And the woman, her husband, their daughter, their future? And again the children with ice clinging to their black hair, would they always be there?

> "This is the quilt made from that story," she said.

> (8–9)

The image of the freezing children confronts us with the ultimately lethal effects of being "control[led] and subdue[d]" under territorial conditions.[8] In retrospect we can see that this story establishes the need for the Aliyosho story. The fact that this one is told by the daughter of the white man who closed his door on the freezing Indians draws attention to the question of implication, a question always, I think, implicit in storytelling: where is the storyteller, in relation to the story, its contexts and meanings? The question is doubly complicated here by the story's complex voicing and its silences. We can imagine dialogism as a contest within the white family; we can also hear the dialogism that comes into play as an Indian hears and retells the story, repeating the white daughter's and father's words, and the mother's silence, in his own voice, his words echoing the story's impact on him. Drawing the daughter's telling into his own (communal) purposes, Ortiz refuses to allow the displaced children to disappear as he reminds us again that storytelling is a process of both continuity and revision. The present meaning of the daughter's telling is not developed (nor is that of "the quilt made from that story") and thus remains open to reimagining and retelling by engaged readers or listeners, also involved in questions of implication, who through this process may revise their own understandings of history and of obligation.

In *After and Before the Lightning* Ortiz tells stories of struggle and sometimes survival. There are a rancher's battles with the winter weather; stories of murder and suicide; one farmer's "courageous story" of quitting after "no rain / for five years" (59–60); and a supermarket holdup, just before Christmas, by a man wearing "a green coat and a gorilla mask" (39–41). Some stories are simply suggested, perhaps too painful to be told: "what could we say? / Friend, sister, poet, warrior, human. / When grief finds us, we learn of loss" (88–89). Yet as Ortiz acknowledges that "loss and loss will stalk us," he resolves to continue: "But we will hold and hold."

Rather like "To Change in a Good Way," the story of Charley's housebuilding (85–87), another cooperative effort involving Indians and whites, serves as a hopeful counterpoint to ongoing grief and destruction: "Charley . . . carefully puts moist sage into the joint. / There. It fits now, the people, land, / the sacredness, sky, and walls joined" (87). But though the house will stand and winter is followed by spring, the book resists simple comfort. The housebuilding is shortly followed by a conversation about congressional cutbacks, "Indian people faced with decisions that should never be made" (90). Soon, as the book moves toward spring, we hear Caballo Pinto tell Aliyosho, " 'Just remember to always be kind and be humble, and you will be successful in your endeavors" (96). But "Hungry Questions" begins, "What does the cosmos / have to do with money?" and ends with "no answer, / still hungry" (98). What seems clearest in the proximity of such apparent contradictions is the immediacy of both despair and the desire for a community of sacred relationship; the immediacy and the desire speak in the book's unresolved, internal dialogics. They speak, too, in the alternatives offered in the fragment of story recounted in "This or This":

> Telling the story, Wahpepah says,
> " 'We need unity,' Leonard said.
> 'Peace and brotherhood.[']
> . . . .
> And then Leonard said, 'This.'
>
> > Holding the Pipe aloft,
>
> looking at all of us,
> Indian and White,
> and then he turns it around
> and over, and puts it
> to his shoulder, and sights
> along it, and aims it.
>
> And then he said, 'Or this.' "
>
> > > (110)

Such multiply voiced stories (here the poet, the storyteller Wahpepah, and Leonard all speak) remind us again that in the borderlands, continuance and survival require struggle. What we can be sure of, Ortiz tells us, is that storytelling will continue as part of the struggle, as the hope for survival.

Ortiz may be the most prolific teller of stories among contemporary poets and perhaps the one who has worked most intently to develop a poetic style reflecting oral tradition. Indian poets, however, take diverse approaches to storytelling; some contemporaries have developed styles that are visual, image based, figurative, and descriptive, highly evocative and sometimes ambiguous. Narration, which may be merely suggested, does not necessarily move directly from beginning to end, and may not dominate the poem. Yet these poems do tell stories, as does

Ortiz's "Final Solution: Jobs, Leaving," which, in its evocative power and its de-emphasis on direct narration, bears an affinity to some of the poems I will discuss in the rest of this chapter.[9] It bears repeating that a visual, evocative style also has analogues in indigenous oral poetics. Blaeser reminds us, for example, of the vivid imagery of Ojibway dream songs and of the importance of " 'visual thinking' " in oral tradition.[10] As approaches to storytelling vary, so do subject matter and emphasis. As a source of history, an affirmation of spirit, and an impulse toward the communal, toward continuity, storytelling may be especially valuable in contested spaces, but the stories Native poets tell are not limited to explicit borderland themes. Even so, marked contrasts among these po- ets' storytelling styles—and subjects—are complemented by continuity, in their various affinities with oral poetics. And this continuity is espe- cially evident in their shared commitment to involving readers or hearers in the story process.

In "Crazy Dogholkoda" (*The Light on the Tent Wall* 50–51) Athabascan Mary TallMountain uses a series of condensed narratives to validate a communal oral tradition. A question-and-answer format directly engages the reader; the central question is "Why are [the weatherbeaten caches] here?" Niguudzaagha, a medicine man, first challenges the questioner— " 'You think we should pull them down?' "—and then answers the ques- tion with brief narrative memories:

> "That one," he rumbled, "one time
> we put in biggest bunch of *k'odimaaya*
> anybody ever trap.
> Those ones over there. We stay in there
> that winter our *yah* burn down.
> This one, *eeta bitoa'* die in here.["]

While at the poem's outset the caches were presented figuratively, "hud- dled in rows like sad old men, / their faces silver grey," by the end the suggestions of decay have been countered by the implied stories of their actual importance to the people. Story has thus functioned to recall the past and link it to the present and to maintain continuity.

Whereas TallMountain involves readers by raising questions we might ask but then only sparingly implies the story-answers, Jim Barnes's "Wolf Watch: Winding Stair Mountain, 1923" (*Sawdust War* 36–43) re- quires that we enter into the storytelling process; indeed, Barnes requires that we construct the story itself. Like Ortiz's "Final Solution: Jobs, Leaving," this poem, a series of thematically linked monologues, is made up of the voices of its participants. Also like "Final Solution," the sequence outwardly provides only a skeletal narrative: a cattle herder, "the last of his breed," sets out on some undefined quest; he is found dead, evidently of heart failure, far from herd, cabin, and horse, his "eyes . . . fixed west." The motives, beliefs, and emotions conveyed in their distinctive voices by the herder, his wife, a preacher, and one of the searchers who find his body invite readers to interpret and thus to create a fuller and more complex story. The first and last segments, "Prelude" and "What Waits," are spoken by another voice, that of the poet, who sets the cyclical context for the sequence. Thus the "Prelude" begins, "Green turning yellow, the oaks / acknowledge first frosts" (36), and the sequence ends with the assurance that "all things abide awhile in time. / What waits, poised for spring, walks in cadence with the night" (43). By framing the other monologues with this voice, Barnes draws attention to the constructed nature of the piece and makes the artist's process of composition a subtle but undeniable presence throughout. We are aware, for example, that the composer has arranged the monologues and that he speaks a different idiom, less colloquial and more grounded in imagery than that of the other speakers. The colloquial monologues bring oral storytelling most clearly into play.

Each monologue implies awareness of an audience: the herder speaks to justify his position; the preacher tries to persuade him to leave his herd and testify at Sunday services; the herder's abandoned wife addresses the "Lord" in anger and pleading; the searcher explains the circumstances in which the dead herder was found. These speakers implicitly assume that their language can affect an audience; at least two of them, the preacher and the searcher, speak to communal purposes, while the wife is moved in part by communal experience ("This has got to end. Neighbors talk behind / my back. I have no friends"). Their voices remind us of the shared process of telling and revising in oral traditions and suggest that they are participants in the creation of what will become local oral lore: the story of the last herder. Further, as each voice speaks from a different perception of the herder's position, and to some extent contests the others, the sequence represents the language of storytelling as dialogic. And, finally, as happens in many of Ortiz's poems, by inviting us to participate in this dialogic process, Barnes's sequence makes us aware of our own role, as responsive readers, in creating the story.

Roberta Hill Whiteman's "Steps" (44–45) stretches the meaning of storytelling. It comes close to the center of a collection whose poems trace both personal, relational, and cyclical growth, and experiences of profound loss and mourning. Such a complex counterpointing seems to surface within "Steps" as part of the ambiguity that invites the reader to enter into the poem's process even while it undermines any illusions of closure that we might harbor. Through vivid imagery the poem evokes a series of moments, sensations, and emotions that suggest a narrative of a woman's development from childhood through adolescence and into adulthood. Social contexts are suggested: "in green schoolrooms, chalk bit blackboards," and, later, "men stroked her thighs, tried to make her sleep." Other poems in the collection, along with the poem's cryptic statement that "her father sat, muttering, 'She's dead,' " seem to imply the loss of a mother. But the poem does not delve into social or familial circumstances. Rather, using imagery drawn from nature, it movingly conveys the woman's vulnerability, emotional responsiveness, and vitality; Whiteman declines, however, clearly to define the outcome toward which her "steps" have led. The poem's final stanza is richly textured with ambiguity:

> Pretend these mountains are not hungry.
> I've heard a young voice
> muttering at wind, like straw on fire.
> She moves drunk toward the lightning,
> letting her arms stiffen, wanting to be fog,
> the smell of ripe fruit. I've covered her tracks
> with a difficult river, and like a plover,
> wade from water to rock and back. It foams beryl green
> in the sunset, and at every bend, leaves something behind.

The ambiguity is complicated by the introduction of the first-person pronoun. Previously, the speaker has maintained an apparently objective distance, but now a question arises about the possible relationship between the speaker and the woman whose "steps" are described—together with what seems the unresolvable question of the outcome: have these moments and images led to survival or defeat? Is this a story of recovery and continuance? Loss and remembrance? These possibilities may not be mutually exclusive, but, by inciting the questions and leaving us only multiply evocative images on which to base answers, Whiteman focuses our attention on the individual's emotions and keeps the ambiguity intact. At the same time, she compels our presence as active readers, bringing us into awareness of the communal dynamics of storytelling.

TallMountain's and Barnes's story poems, like Ortiz's, are moved by communal awareness and communally oriented purposes. Even the iconoclastic individualism of Barnes's herder resonates in the communal context established by the other monologues of "Wolf Watch." In "Steps" Whiteman alludes only sparingly to social contexts, though her intensely suggestive imagery deepens the possibilities inherent in the allusions. The absence of an overtly communal purpose, however, should not be assumed to define the poem's orientation as primarily individualistic. The question in this poem, I believe, is about survival, about what one must confront, and what nurture and protect, in order to survive spiritually and emotionally. Whiteman's language evokes a strong responsiveness, and sense of relationship, to the natural world, undoubtedly an element vital to the poem's concern with this question. Further, as Whiteman's implicit invitation to the reader, to enter into the interpretive, storytelling process might suggest, each person's survival depends on and is essential to communal continuity. (This necessity may be implied by the entry of the first-person voice in Whiteman's last stanza, as it is by the grandfather's presence in her "Reaching Yellow River.")

The ambiguity of a poem like "Steps" most readily recalls Vizenor's belief that stories are liberating in part because of their openness to multiple possibilities. In liberation and, as Elizabeth Woody affirms, in connection stories can make people whole. Freedom, relationship, wholeness, and, in Ortiz's terms, the visionary knowledge that "affirms . . . one's life" (*Woven Stone* 151)—these are some of the values inherent in communally responsive stories and storytelling. These terms also identify the communal purposes that move poets like Maurice Kenny, Louise Erdrich, and Paula Gunn Allen to engage in the reclamation and retelling of written history.

CHAPTER 7

Claiming History

It tells the story of a people's capture
It tells the story of a people's struggle to survive
    —Kimberly M. Blaeser, *Trailing You*

In poems like "The State's Claim" and "Final Solution: Jobs, Leaving"
Simon Ortiz writes a new history. So do Wendy Rose, in "Margaret Neu-
mann," and Carter Revard, in "Wazhazhe Grandmother." By "new his-
tory" I mean not that such histories have never been told. Though they
may be traceable through written accounts, they have been kept alive in
oral culture and as such they have largely been omitted from the familiar,
documentary American history favored in officially sanctioned textbooks.
If available in archives or in publications of limited circulation, these
histories have generally been reserved for specialists. In writing poems
such as "The State's Claim" and "Margaret Neumann," Native poets are
adding to the body of history available to their readers as well as asserting
Indians' authority to tell their stories.

    The poems I discuss in this chapter undertake a different project,
though the poets are surely moved by similar aims: to complicate received
history, to move readers to reconsider and respond, and thereby to con-
tribute to the survival of Native peoples. Blaeser reminds us that survival
is what is at stake, when she says that "the creation and interpretations of
histories have . . . functioned directly as the justifications for possession
or dispossession" (*Gerald Vizenor* 84). In "Captivity," "The One Who Skins
Cats" and "Pocahontas to Her English Husband, John Rolfe," and *Black-
robe: Isaac Jogues*, respectively, Louise Erdrich, Paula Gunn Allen, and
Maurice Kenny turn directly to history as recorded by colonizers and their
descendants, to question and revise it. Their revisionary agendas neces-
sarily foreground borderland experience and draw attention to cultural
and linguistic dialogism.

    In "Pocahontas" and "The One Who Skins Cats" Paula Gunn Allen gives
voice to Indian women who served as intermediaries between indige-
nous and colonizing cultures and who consequently have sometimes

been criticized by Native people, even as their lives have been distorted or diminished by accounts that use them to promote colonial or modern European American agendas.[1] As Allen imagines them, they tell their own stories, reclaiming power for themselves, redefining the contexts of their actions, and enunciating distinctively female experiences of colonization and cultural appropriation. In her monologue each woman further complicates our responses to her already contested life, her intentions, understanding, and roles, as she claims language for her own purposes instead of offering her powers once again in the service of (alien) others.

Pocahontas (c. 1595–1617), daughter of Powhatan, the most powerful Native American leader of eastern Virginia, is famous as the rescuer of Captain John Smith, a role she may never have played. She is known to have visited the English settlement of Jamestown as a girl, to have been married in her early teens to one of her father's supporters, and, in late 1612 or early 1613, to have been abducted to Jamestown, where she spent over a year. There she learned English, was baptized (as "Rebecca"), and married John Rolfe. "The good relations between the English and Indians that followed the marriage allowed Rolfe to learn about tobacco planting" (Champagne 1333–34). With Rolfe and their son she traveled to London, where she was received in Court and also contracted the disease of which she died in 1617, after being removed from her homebound ship as too weak to travel.[2]

Sacagawea (c. 1788–1812? 1884?), a Shoshoni from Idaho, was taken captive at about the age of eleven by the Hidatsa, who sold her to a French Canadian fur trader, Touissaint Charbonneau. She was living with Charbonneau in the Mandan village where the Lewis and Clark expedition spent the winter of 1804–5. Charbonneau was hired by Lewis and Clark in 1805, and Sacagawea and their infant son accompanied him. Though made famous a hundred years later (by white women's suffrage activists) as the "guide" of the expedition, Sacagawea appears, rather, to have been an interpreter and intermediary, especially with her Shoshoni people; she was also valued for her ability to identify edible plants. And, as a woman with a child, she provided an image to verify the expedition's peaceful intents. After the expedition Sacagawea went with Charbonneau to St. Louis and may have remained there after he departed—or she may have separated from him there before he left, due to his abuse. Confusion about her life from this point on is partly due to the fact that Charbonneau had three Indian wives, whose names aren't always provided in the records. One theory has Sacagawea dying at about twenty-five of a fever while with Charbonneau on a trading expedition for William Clark. The other has her leaving Charbonneau, making her way to Oklahoma, marrying a Comanche, and eventually moving to the Wind River (Shoshoni) Reservation, where she died an old woman, in 1884.[3]

Allen has Pocahontas speaking directly to her English husband, chiding the ethnocentric ignorance of this "foolish child" who presumed to use (and condescend to) her. She begins, "Had I not cradled you in my arms / oh beloved perfidious one, / you would have died" (8). She deflates Rolfe's presumptions, asserting that only her teaching enabled him to succeed in growing tobacco and pleasing his "masters," the English investors. Reversing his Eurocentric categories, she describes him as "chattering nonsense about a God" he "had not wit to name" and wondering at the silence of the "simple wanton . . . savage maid" who was ignorant of "the ways of grace" (8–9). By thus redefining her husband, Allen's Pocahontas turns the tables of linguistic appropriation. She also claims a perception beyond Rolfe's understanding, a recognition of irony and of "other / powers" that take part in the ongoing history of his descendants.

Speaking directly to contemporary readers, Sacagawea adamantly resists others' appropriations of her story or her self. The debate over Sacagawea's life span is in part a contest between oral and written history, with the claim that she died early relying on written records and the case for her survival into the 1880s drawing heavily on testimony gathered by the Sioux physician Charles Eastman from Indians and others said to have known her.[4] By accepting the second theory and letting Sacagawea speak of experiences long after the Lewis and Clark expedition, Allen chooses the oral over the literate—a choice reflected in Sacagawea's language—and the Native over the white. This choice enables her to imagine Sacagawea as an old woman, an independent agent who is no longer defined as mother, "maid," or wife, someone who can, with the knowledge gained from long experience, finally speak for herself. Doing so, Sacagawea revels in her multiple identities and roles ("I am the one who wanders, the one who / speaks, the one who watches"), her knowledge, and her freedom: "I come / and go as I please . . . I am free" (15).

Sacagawea acknowledges that she has been accused of betrayal: "so many of my own kind / call me names. Say / I betrayed the Indians / into the whiteman's hand." In response, she both concedes and argues with her accusers. "They have a point, / but only one" (17). Her own points include several kinds of contextualization. She has already stressed her varied roles and quoted the proverb that gives her poem its title:

"There's more than one way to skin a cat." She has also referred to the role of white suffragists in idealizing and inflating her part: they "decided I alone / guided the whiteman's expedition across / the world. What did they know?" (15). Thus some of the Indians' accusations, as she later states, are prompted by the self-serving falsifications of white women. What she does admit, "Oh, I probably betrayed some Indians," she contextualizes in yet another way: "But I took care of my own Shoshonis" (18). Allen is giving us a person (not a statue) who understands her life in terms of the complex realities of gender, race, culture and history, one who is empowered by such understanding to claim her own identities and to dismiss the illusion that would make one Indian woman answerable for the colonization of the American west.

Both women, in the monologues, play intentionally on the multiple names or epithets assigned them by others. Each name can be heard as representing a different version of the woman herself. Though Pocahontas doesn't repeat the "Indian princess" tag so often attached to her, surely it is present for many readers, along with the labels she does ironically recite: "simple wanton . . . savage maid" and "dusky daughter of heathen sires" (9). Sacagawea wrests the power of naming from those who would control her (including the white women who simultaneously put her on a pedestal and exposed her to blame) and flaunts her many names: "Slave Woman, Lost Woman, Grass Woman . . . Chief Woman . . . Bird Woman. Snake / Woman. Among other things" (15).

Each speaks of and against the words that have been used against her; their self-consciousness as speakers and awareness of the duplicitous and creative potential of language draw attention to the politics that underlies heteroglossia and the liberating energy of dialogic discourse. Their double awareness—of self and of language—is evident or implied in every line. Sacagawea simply and clearly draws attention to language, and to heteroglossia's inherent politics, in her first line: "Bird Woman they call me." And she plays with meaning as she draws attention to competing intentions in the language the suffragists used to re-create her:

> Indian maid, they said.
> Maid. That's me.
> But I did pretty good for a maid.
> I went wherever I pleased, and
> the whiteman paid the way.
>   (15–16)

Irony, evident in these lines, is used by Pocahontas, too. Just as she ironically repeats the epithets used against her, Pocahontas turns a word of praise into an ironic epithet when she addresses Rolfe as "my fair husband." And she draws attention to the ironies of situation and history when, having claimed credit for the success of Rolfe's tobacco growing efforts, she continues, "It is not without irony that by this crop / your descendants die" (8). The irony becomes terrible when she later refers to "my son," implicitly complicating, as she does so, the connection between her "son" (and hence her motherhood) and Rolfe's "descendants." The terms may be virtually synonymous, but myriad implications of colonialist appropriations are foregrounded as she splits them.

If Pocahontas thus implies that her son and his descendants (who are also hers) embody heteroglossia, Sacagawea claims that she herself embodies language. She announces, "I am legend. I am history" (14), and proceeds to demonstrate that legend and history are multiple, not unitary, and that she is a capable maker of them. Her assertion seems wholly affirmative; having acknowledged the pain potential in language, she does not fear it—she has, after all, as Allen imagines her, lived a long life, which has confirmed her own power to use language to invent and recreate. It is easy to understand why Mary TallMountain saw Sacagawea as exemplifying the "spiritedness" and "the true motives of [Native] women who comprehended and aided destiny": "she kept faith with herself and her obligation to the task that was hers."[5]

These monologues offer both possibility and uncertainty. On the one hand, the contested histories of Pocahontas and Sacagawea, and their silences, persist. On the other, Allen imagines for each speaker a sense of her own prerogative. Each poem addresses the present, by referring directly or otherwise to the ongoing consequences of colonialism and by suggesting the possibility of retelling other stories, renaming other historical figures. In these ways Allen's poems imply that the retelling of history can be empowering for contemporary descendants of her speakers— indigenous peoples and especially indigenous women.

Allen might be criticized for presuming to speak in the voices of historical women whose own voices are not recorded. Certainly, the uses made of Pocahontas over centuries demonstrate the insidious effects that are possible when a historically silenced figure is appropriated.[6] Yet Allen is writing against the colonialist appropriations of these women (even though she doesn't address the full implications of such appropriations). She opts for speculative imagination, informed by what usable historical traces are available, as an alternative to the imposed silences—which are, after all, not really silent, but filled with the words of others: Disney's screenwriters, romance novelists, the writers of elementary textbooks.

Allen's position as the writer of these monologues contrasts to Erdrich's, in writing "Captivity," while Maurice Kenny, as the writer of *Blackrobe: Isaac Jogues*, shares some common ground with each of the others. That is, Mary Rowlandson, the inspiration for Erdrich's "Captivity," and the Jesuit Isaac Jogues wrote accounts of their experiences: their own records exist. Kenny, however, also imagines voices for people whose stories have only been recorded by others. The problem of writing "for" those whose voices are lost can be read in these instances as not so simply highlighting the fact that written American history still belongs almost entirely to non-Natives. (Even recorded oratory and as-told-to autobiographies are contested: we can never be completely sure whose voices we hear.)

It is surely in part because of this near-monopoly of the powerful that Erdrich searches out alternative possibilities in Rowlandson's church-sanctioned language, rather than silently accepting an unalterable conflict of "savages" and "saints" as the only possible construction of New England colonial experience. If Allen's monologues draw attention to the absence or questionable reliability of historical records, Erdrich's poem, too, raises questions about the meanings of documentation.

Like Allen, Erdrich begins with a story that is virtually a cornerstone of popular American history. While Allen wrests some space for imagined Native voices, and in the process exposes European versions of Native lives as not disinterested constructions, Erdrich turns the tables yet again: by imagining alternative implications for a specific, white-authored historical document, she explores a potentially subversive perspective for her European American protagonist. Just as "the story of Sacagawea, Indian maid, / can be told a lot of different ways" (19), so, Erdrich demonstrates, can the story of Mary Rowlandson, Puritan minister's wife. Rowlandson was captured in the Narragansett attack on Lancaster, Massachusetts, on February 1, 1675/76, in what became known as King Philip's War, after the English name of its Wampanoag leader, Metacomet. She traveled with her captors for almost twelve weeks, until she was ransomed and returned to Boston. Her account of her ordeal, first published in 1682, went through numerous editions into the middle of the nineteenth century (and has been republished several times in the twentieth).

Its full title conveys Rowlandson's intent and some of the impact her story must have had on early readers: *The Sovereignty and Goodness of God Together, with the Faithfulness of His Promises Displayed; Being a Narrative of the Captivity and Restoration of Mrs. Mary Rowlandson.* Later American editions (and the 1682 London edition) modified the title to de-emphasize the "sovereignty . . . of God" and foreground the dangers encountered by the captive; thus several editions from the late eighteenth century are entitled *A Narrative of the Captivity, Sufferings and Removes of Mrs. Mary Rowlandson, Who Was Taken Prisoner by the Indians with Several Others; and Treated in the Most Barbarous and Cruel Manner by Those Vile Savages: With Many Other Remarkable Events during Her Travels.*[7]

Not only, as its titles suggest, did Mrs. Rowlandson's narrative serve important cultural purposes for generations of European Americans, but it was the first publication in English of what was to become an enormously popular genre of American writing, right up to and beyond the "closing of the frontier" in the 1890s, and which, besides producing numerous true accounts, contributed to the fascination with "Indian captivity" that has marked American fiction since its beginnings.[8]

In her poem "Captivity" (*Jacklight* 26–27) Louise Erdrich draws on Rowlandson's language to reinterpret not just this narrative—it is not absolutely necessary to read the poem's voice as that of Rowlandson herself—but possibilities perhaps inherent in many such experiences and accounts. While retaining the point of view of a white woman, Erdrich creates an alternative version of the captivity narrative, a version that, among other differences, contrasts to Rowlandson's as it replaces assertions of moral and theological certainty (Rowlandson's bulwark against the nearly total physical uncertainty she faced—and perhaps also against skeptics in the New England community) with a pervasive, destabilizing uncertainty. The poem makes transparently clear a contemporary Indian writer's dialogue with diverse traditions and heightens the reader's awareness of the generally suppressed dialogic potential of Rowlandson's account; these effects simultaneously multiply the layers of meaning in Erdrich's own text.

Erdrich's poem begins with an epigraph attributed to Mary Rowlandson: " '*He [my captor] gave me a bisquit, which I put in my pocket, and not daring to eat it, buried it under a log, fearing he had put something in it to make me love him.*' " This sentence refers to one of Rowlandson's most constant concerns—food—and introduces a theme that surfaces only rarely in the *Narrative*, sexual fear. She twice expresses wonder and gratitude that she was never imposed upon sexually. In the ninth Remove,[9] a little less than halfway through the account, she remarks upon "the goodness of God to me, in that, though I was gone from home, and met with all sorts of Indians, and those I had no knowledge of, and there being no Christian soul near me, yet not one of them offered the least imaginable miscarriage to me" (33). And again, in the twentieth Remove, near her book's end:

> I have been in the midst of those roaring lions and savage bears that feared neither God nor man nor the devil, by night and day, alone and in company, sleeping all sorts together, and yet not one of them ever offered me the least abuse of unchastity to me in word or action. Though some are ready to say, I speak it for my own credit; But I speak it in the presence of God, and to his Glory. (70–71)

In short, the epigraph does not appear in Rowlandson's *Narrative*.[10] Even the epigraph, then, raises questions about history, truth, and their uses. Of course, it is possible that this sentence is attributed to Mary Rowlandson in some source other than the *Narrative*. It seems more likely that Erdrich, who plays freely in the poem itself with incidents and language from the *Narrative*, is beginning with an intentionally ironic invention: ironic in that, if we accept the epigraph at face value (as most readers must), then we have begun our reading by replicating earlier readers' likely acceptance of Rowlandson's assumptions. Further, our subsequent recognition of ironic complexity in the poem itself must be shadowed by our having granted credence to a questionable text. The questions thus raised by the epigraph parallel questions that the poem differently raises about Rowlandson's and Erdrich's accounts; the epigraph itself becomes part of the poem's project of destabilizing received history.

From the beginning to the end Mary Rowlandson maintains that her ordeal was a punishment and a test sent to her by God and thus a sign of God's goodness and concern for "his people," who, so chastised, might be moved to accept divine grace. In this scheme of things the Indians become agents of the devil, and, even though she describes many individual kindnesses to her, her account never really breaks free of this conviction. Even her many references to Quannopin, her master, "the best friend that I had of an Indian, both in cold and hunger" (37), are always in tension with all-encompassing references to "the heathen," "pagans," and "our enemies." Thus a major change in Erdrich's rendition is to focus the captive's attention on one particular individual and to trace the devel-

oping complexity of her response to him. The poem's first incident estab-
lishes this focus as it revises one from the *Narrative*. In Rowlandson's text
the sixteenth Remove begins as follows: "We began this remove with
wading over Baquag river. The water was . . . very swift and so cold I
thought it would have cut me in sunder . . . The Indians stood laughing
to see me staggering, but in my distress the Lord gave me experience of
the truth and goodness of [His] promise" (49). In contrast Erdrich's poem
begins with the recollection of being rescued from the icy stream by an
Indian man.

The poem's second verse paragraph illustrates the frightening disori-
entation that the captive experiences. It first displays the dichotomous
thinking fundamental to the Puritans' theology and their animosity to-
ward the indigenous peoples: the speaker characterizes the unknown
pursuers of the Indians and their captives as either "God's agents" (colo-
nial troops) or "pitch devils" (another party of Indians). The contrast is
then slightly eroded as she tells that her child was fed by an Indian
woman. That this action has at least jostled her assumptions is implied in
the section's final line: "the forest closed, the light deepened." This ambi-
guity forecasts the pained ambivalence of the poem's ending.

The sexual theme introduced in the epigraph culminates in the mid-
dle of the poem. The speaker recalls that although she intended to starve
rather than accept food from him, when her captor killed a pregnant doe,
he shared the meat of the fawn with her, and she ate:

It was so tender,
the bones like the stems of flowers,
that I followed where he took me.

. . . .

After that the birds mocked.

. . . .

He did not notice God's wrath.

In the empty white space between verse paragraphs, something unspeak-
able happens. In the *Narrative* Rowlandson, always hungry, does not re-
solve to starve; she does fear God's wrath, but for her own earlier failings.
The *Narrative* does include, in the fourteenth Remove, this passage: "As we
went along they killed a deer with a young one in her. They gave me a piece
of the fawn and it was so young and tender that one might eat the bones as

well as the flesh, and yet I thought it was very good" (47). Within the poem revision proceeds as the captive realizes that sin has failed to produce its expected consequences and that what she sees as an obvious sign of divine wrath has no effect on the Indian. The certainties on which she has relied for emotional and spiritual survival are crumbling (the same certainties that were used to justify the expansion of the English colonies and later of the United States). And this, not the implied sexual transgression, is what is most devastating.

The captive is rescued, but, unlike the historical Rowlandson, she does not claim to find in Scripture the assurance that would sanctify her experience and reinforce her belief. She prays, but her prayer is to no orthodox avail: rather than being reassured of her place within the Puritan community, at night she recalls her exclusion from the Indians' "circle." Here is the worst of this captive's experience: she has been rescued into the knowledge of unremitting loneliness. (Perhaps this depiction of loneliness implies, too, something of what led a considerable number of white captives to remain by choice with the Indians, even when offered "redemption."[11]) She continues, remembering how "he led his company in the noise / until I could no longer bear / the thought of how I was." Beating with a stick on the earth, she "begg[ed] it to open / to admit me / . . . and feed me honey from the rock." These, the poem's final lines, reveal a terrible ambivalence. Twice the words seem to invite one reading then imply another, and this seeming invitation reveals the heteroglossia and dialogism of the poem: what the speaker can "no longer bear" is not the "noise" but her isolation; she begs the earth not to swallow her (and her presumed sin) but to unite her with "him"—and to "feed [her] honey from the rock."

The allusion to Psalm 81 echoes Rowlandson's reflection on her experience, near the end of her *Narrative:* "I remember in the night season how the other day I was in the midst of thousands of enemies and nothing but death before me. It was hard work to persuade myself that ever I should be satisfied with bread again. But now we are fed with the finest of the wheat, and (as I may say) with *honey out of the rock*" (78). In Rowlandson's account, the allusion implies that God has rewarded her submission to his ways. In the poem it is virtually blasphemous.

Having lived with the "enemy" and returned to Christian civilization, Erdrich's captive knows herself to be effectively excluded from both worlds, her former certainties undone, the possibility of a new way of seeing and being decisively cut off. Perhaps a similar intimation stirs below the surface of the *Narrative,* as Rowlandson continues, after the passage just quoted, "O the wonderful power of God that mine eyes have seen, affording matter enough for my thoughs to run in, that when others are sleeping mine eyes are weeping" (78). Both Susan Howe and Mitchell Breitwieser suggest that such lines adumbrate an estrangement similar to that imagined in "Captivity," though not grounded in sexual experience, as Erdrich implies.

Howe emphasizes Rowlandson's status as a Puritan woman and implies that she might have told a different story had she not been subject to the requirements of the New England theocracy. On the day of the Narragansetts' attack she finds Rowlandson "look[ing] out at the absence of Authority and see[ing] that we are all alone" (94); "abducted from the structure of experience[,] Rowlandson wraps herself in separateness for warmth" and to defend herself against "limitlessness, where all illusion of volition, all individual identity may be transformed—assimilated" (96). Back in the English colony "perhaps she told her story to assure herself and her community that she was a woman who feared God and eschewed evil" (123). Such persuasion would have been necessary if, in her memory, "captives and captors . . . [were] walking together beyond . . . Western culture" (124).

In a similar vein Breitwieser finds Rowlandson's *Narrative* an "intense and unremitting representation . . . of experience as a collision between cultural ideology and the real," a "narrative . . . which fails to annul the powers of anomaly" (4). For Rowlandson, he argues, "experience came to mean disconnection from enclosing contexts, not only from the life she enjoyed before the war and the Algonquian life amidst which she survived, but also from the social reality constructed in the aftermath of the war, a labor of construction to which her narrative was supposed to be an important contribution" (6). He argues that, "despite her best intentions," in the course of her writing "things get loose or come forward that . . . signal the vitality of a distinctly non-Puritan view of her experience," and thus her text "allows various anomalous glimpses, not only of her own emotions, but also of her captors" (8–9). Rowlandson's narrative thus becomes "an account of experience that breaks through or outdistances her own and her culture's dominant means of representation" (10).[12]

Arguing that Rowlandson's text reveals traces of suppressed doubt and a disruptive vision, Howe and Breitwieser offer readings that complement Erdrich's poem. As Erdrich, Howe, and Breitwieser look through the surface of Puritan didacticism, they illuminate the dialogism hidden in the *Narrative*: prompted by their insights, we can recognize that even the biblical quotations expose heteroglossia and dialogic potential, as Rowlandson struggles to bring her experiences into line with her culture's most authoritative language.[13]

Erdrich cannot have read the *Narrative* without noting Rowlandson's unending search for food and for shelter against the cold and dark; her poem depicts the captive as engaged in a parallel search, for spiritual and emotional shelter. One of the poem's most powerful dialogic reversals is its suggestion that she might have been able to find such shelter in the alien world of the Indians. Further, Erdrich recognizes that the need for shelter is the need for inclusion, for community. The historic Mary Rowlandson sought inclusion by reading the Bible she'd been given by an Indian, searching out opportunities to see her children and other English captives, and anticipating her eventual rescue. Perhaps prompted in part by passages in Rowlandson's text that record changes in attitude—toward food, tobacco, herself—Erdrich envisions for the captive an elusive opportunity for integration with a Native community (perhaps prompted too, as Breitwieser suggests, by evidence of Rowlandson's economic integration, as she knits and sews, and is paid for her work).

The history Erdrich constructs, in dialogic response to Rowlandson's *Narrative*, is one not of rescue and return, however problematical it might have been, to the colonists' community; rather, she tells of a lost opportunity for a new vision of relationship and community. One might ask whether Erdrich's history is too easy—what about the terrible suffering that Rowlandson and other captives endured? But Erdrich does not deny them. Once Rowlandson's name appears in the epigraph, the story she told is unavoidably part of the poem's dialogical struggle, even the focus of that struggle, grounded as it is in the question whether the history might reveal more truths than those Rowlandson could see or acknowledge.

In *Blackrobe: Isaac Jogues* Mohawk poet Maurice Kenny, too, exposes the contested nature of history and vision. Like Erdrich's and Allen's poems, Kenny's poetic sequence engages multidimensional language in dialogic discourse that recreates borderland experience. Kenny complicates the project and its effects further by recounting his history through the diverse voices of French and Dutch colonists in North America, the Jesuit missionary Isaac Jogues, and Mohawks who encountered him. The history thus becomes a web of stories in dialogue across cultural, geographic, and temporal borders, as Kenny shows us how diverse voices created meanings and realities in the past and continue to do so now as well.

Isaac Jogues's story may not be as widely known as those of Pocahontas, Sacagawea, and Mary Rowlandson. However, it is evidently quite familiar to Mohawk people. "For generations now," Joseph Bruchac says, "the Mohawk people have been told they must feel guilty about killing this holy man and approaching that story is like cauterizing an old wound for Kenny" ("New Voices" 158). Like Rowlandson's story (and like those invented by whites for Pocahontas and Sacagawea), Jogues's represents major themes in European American versions of the history of North America: most saliently, here, the colonizers' dedication to a transcendent mission and their sufferings at the hands of indigenous aliens.

Jogues arrived in New France in 1636 and joined a mission to the Hurons in southern Ontario. In June of 1642 he was sent to Quebec to obtain supplies, and in August, on their return trip, he and his party of forty, mostly Hurons, were attacked by a larger force of Mohawks. Jogues's account of his subsequent captivity graphically details the tortures he witnessed and endured, while it reveals his dedication to his priestly work of instructing, baptizing, absolving, and comforting both the Huron and the French captives, and his readiness for martyrdom. In the course of this captivity he may have been adopted into the Wolf clan; in any case he was sheltered by an older woman of that clan who had recently lost a son and whom he called "aunt."[14] Brought eventually into the vicinity of the Dutch colony at Renselaerwyck (Albany, New York), he became the object of unsuccessful Dutch efforts to ransom him; finally, after Jogues had persuaded himself that by fleeing he could better serve God, the Dutch helped him to escape. He returned to France but only to recover his strength and secure permission to return to Canada, which he did in the spring of 1644.

Back in Montreal, he accepted an assignment to establish a mission among the Mohawks, with whom a tenuous peace agreement had recently been made. He set out in May of 1646 as an ambassador from the French. The Mohawks "welcomed [him] as a friend"; he dispatched his ambassadorial duties by exchanging greetings and gifts, then "turned to his spiritual avocations" (Jogues 10), but the Indians pressed him to leave, and he turned back to Canada in mid-June. Eager to return to the Mohawks, he was delayed until September by rumors that the peace had failed. On this final journey Jogues, his assistant, Jean de La Lande, and Otrihoure, a Huron envoy, were captured by a Mohawk war party and taken to Ossernenon, the town where Jogues had previously been a captive. As had happened before, he was told that he would die. Though the Turtle and Wolf clans were opposed, members of the Bear clan were determined to kill the missionaries. (Kenny describes the Bear clan as "holding a strong religious persuasion" [68], perhaps suggesting an additional motive.) On October 18, 1646, while a council of Mohawk leaders was meeting in another town to determine the prisoners' fate, he was summoned to eat in a lodge of the Bear clan and was killed on the way. De La Lande was killed within a day. A letter from the Dutch governor indicates that some of the Mohawks believed religious paraphernalia left behind by Jogues in June had blighted their corn (Jogues 68). Jogues was canonized in 1930.

Kenny's *Blackrobe* tells not only of Jogues's life and death but also of the French in North America and the Mohawk people—and of the rifts among the Mohawks perhaps occasioned, or at least aggravated, by European colonization, trade, and proselytizing. The sequence is framed with history and prophecy. Two poems, titled "Peacemaker" (3, 5) and "Aiionwatha" (6), tell of the establishment of the Iroquois confederacy, for peace and protection. An ominous note is sounded, however, by the first "Wolf" poem (4), in which "heavy footsteps" intrude in the forest. "Little People" (7) seems to identify the intruder as a Christian priest who enters the woods and fails to acknowledge the presence of the little people, protectors and benefactors of the Iroquois. The poem that follows, also titled "Wolf" (8), intensifies the sense of foreboding as it alludes to "the Mohawk Prophecy" of two devouring snakes, Canada and the United States (67). These first poems, then, both establish the context of traditional values and ways of life and foreshadow the impending cultural disruptions.

In the body of the work Kenny creates direct speech, journal entries, letters, commentaries, and accounts by Jogues, individual Mohawks, and observers of or participants in the French colonial effort. Thus we read statements by Cardinal Richelieu, the explorer La Salle, and the Jesuit Father Superior of New France, Vimont, as well as letters from Jogues to his mother, and an assessment of the missionary by a Dutch official, Arendt Van Corlear; there are also recollections from Jean de La Lande and Hoantteniate, "Jogues' Adopted 'Wolf Brother.' " Kenny follows a basically chronological order, from Jogues's eager but somewhat fearful first voyage to Canada to his death. However, he condenses and somewhat conflates Jogues's several sojourns and two captivities so that the sequence not only tells the French priest's story but also explores the meanings of Jogues's entry into the Native world. A number of poems dramatize a difference in views and feelings between "Bear" and "Wolf 'Aunt' "; far from simply illuminating the Jesuit's impact, these poems deepen the depiction of the Mohawk people, whom he wished to convert.

The sequence concludes as Kenny completes the frame of history and prophecy: first, two later historical Mohawk converts speak, in poems that bear their names. "Tekakwitha (Kateri)" (57) combines full commitment to the new faith with alienation from the earth, the Mohawk community, and the flesh; "Aroniateka" (58), who also speaks in "Hendrik" (59), using his European name, suggests a return, perhaps after death, to older ways. Then "Turtle" (60) offers a prophecy about the colonizers' descendants. This poem is somewhat ambivalent, yet it represents, I think, an effort to be hopeful: "Someday they will come / to learn . . . not to teach" (Kenny's ellipsis). However, it is followed by "Rokwaho" (61), dated 1978, which returns to history and grief:[15]

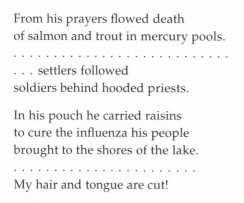

> From his prayers flowed death
> of salmon and trout in mercury pools.
> . . . .
> . . . settlers followed
> soldiers behind hooded priests.
>
> In his pouch he carried raisins
> to cure the influenza his people
> brought to the shores of the lake.
> . . . .
> My hair and tongue are cut!

Only after so painfully testifying to the ongoing consequences of colonialism can Kenny bring his book to end with serenity and unambiguous hope. He does so in a poem dated 1979 (62), in which Rokwaho speaks directly to him, reminding him that, though "we do not speak [the Peacemaker's] name / in an act of respect," still "his thought moves among us / through the pine / and his power."[16] This final poem reveals most clearly Kenny's commitment not only to historical reclamation but also to continuity and survival.

The struggle for survival is embodied in language, in the dialogic contests of the poems that make up the book's core, particularly those that juxtapose French and Indian voices and the differing perspectives of Wolf 'Aunt' and Bear. A number of poems tellingly counterpoint Jogues's voice to those of Indians with whom he came into contact. In "First Meeting with Kiotsaeton" Jogues responds (inwardly) to the Mohawk chief sent both to welcome the Jesuits as visitors and persuade them not to stay (67). The poem begins in the vein of exoticism with which Kenny has already had Jogues, in his journal, describe the Hurons ("Les Hures" [14]). "Like some marvelous bird," Kiotsaeton "stood on the river bank in plummage [*sic*] . . . in rainbow colors" (19). The Natives' physical presence is powerful: Kiotsaeton's "air of royalty stunned my sensibilities," and Jogues fears the motives of his warriors, "whose faces—on which I can discern / paint!—margin the woods."[17] Jogues "exchange[s] gifts of food" with Kiotsaeton, but he resists recognizing Native prerogative: "I / represent the French crown! / and shall not be . . . denied my route"; secure in his knowledge that he is "son of God and priest / of Christ's blood," he comes away from this meeting determined to prevail. The following poem, "Kiotsaeton," gives us the Mohawk's speech to Jogues (20). He counters European claims with indigenous authority, when he begins, "through my lips / the Nation speaks." He offers Jogues reassurance and hospitality but also defines his people's terms: they "will respect your customs / and invite you into the lodge / if you maintain respect for ours." Placing this poem after the preceding one throws into relief Jogues's failure to accept the requirement of mutual respect. These two poems together highlight his (and the Church's) breach of the rules of the traditional culture and prepare us for his part in the fulfillment of the prophecy of "Wolf" (8), when he becomes in effect an accessory to the devouring snake.

Jogues's perspective is next voiced in "Approaching the Mohawk Village," presented as an excerpt from his "Journal" (24). Defying advice, he carries a cross before him.[18] The rest of this "journal" entry demonstrates that converting the Indians would in essence mean possessing them:

> Iroquois, give me your children,
> . . . .
> Iroquois, give me your chieftains.
> Give me your pride and arrogance.
> Give me your wildness.
> Give me your souls for God
> and your sins for hell.

Further, a "Marginal Note" implies material wealth to be had, if not by Jogues then by others, for he comments on the "Richly furred / beaver pelts" at the lodge entrances.

Using the church's language in such a compromised circumstance, Kenny has already drawn attention to its heteroglossia and conveyed his own dialogic intention. In "Bear" (25), the poem that immediately follows (and the first of five so titled), he draws attention to the dialogic struggle between Jogues and the Indians. Bear begins angrily, "What do I want with his raisins!" His challenge continues as he claims that "there is blood on that cross he wears" and that Jogues's rosary "beads are / the spittle of a snake." That the Mohawk's objection is political, too, is apparent: "Didn't he come / from Huron country[?]" Bear seems to demonstrate a limitation analogous to Jogues's, when he questions the humanity of one who doesn't conform to his own cultural expectations: "What kind / of human is this who does not hunt for his own food[?]" Then he voices his primary concern, one certainly not limited to his own culture: "If he would leave / the children alone . . . children make men . . . / I would not interfere" (Kenny's ellipses). In fact, Jogues's *Narrative* indicates that another French captive, Rene Goupil, was killed precisely because, "taking off the cap of a child in the hut where he lived, he made him make the sign of the cross on his breast and forehead" (30–31). An act of piety and love to a devout young European Catholic, this gesture evidently conveyed dreadful possibilities to the child's Mohawk grandfather; Goupil might be said to have died of cultural heteroglossia.

Bear, I think, can be read as one member of the Bear clan or as several, speaking in succession; he might perhaps be read as speaking for his clan. The five "Bear" poems give this voice an importance almost matching that of Jogues. Bear speaks next in two consecutive pairs of poems that juxtapose his words to those of Wolf 'Aunt.' In the first pair the speakers justify their actions: Wolf 'Aunt,' her "adoption" of "Blackrobe" ("I had the right to choose. / It is customary" [37]), and Bear, his anticipated killing of Jogues ("Our corn withers! . . . We will starve / if this Blackrobe remains" [38]).

In the second pair each tells the story of Jogues's death. Wolf 'Aunt' speaks from inside her lodge (39–41). She describes her efforts to persuade the priest to leave the village, and to instruct him in propriety and respect, his obstinacy, her hope that "he would learn our ways," and finally the moment when "they came to the door, / called him by name," he stepped out of the lodge, and she "heard a thump and . . . knew / his body

crumpled under the club." Bear (43–45) recounts Jogues's offenses, focus-
ing on "his preaching, / his determined wish to change . . . his power to
strike out a past / that has taken centuries to build"; he also admits his
own dislike of "the hook of his nose," an ironic echo of Jogues's "journal"
description of the Hurons (14) and further evidence that Kenny sees these
figures as complex and flawed—there are no paragons in *Blackrobe*. After
affirming that the Mohawks had "carr[ied] out the law" by offering "sanctu-
ary" and "hospitality . . . to satisfy the demands / of the Seneca," Bear
recalls the night of Jogues's death: his own preparations, how he and two
friends summoned Jogues and heard "his aunt's . . . arguments," her last
effort to protect the priest. "Then the clubs rained upon his head." After-
ward, Bear "returned to [his] lodge," where "the doctors purged [his]
flesh / with burning cedar smoke," and he "awaited the Seneca runners."
Mentioning the Senecas again, Bear alludes to the dissension not only
among the three Mohawk clans but also among the peoples of the Iroquois
League, over how to deal with the French; Kenny thus silently reminds us
that, by killing Jogues, the Bear clan members preempted the right of the
council to decide on an appropriate, communal resolution. These paired
poems spoken by Wolf 'Aunt' and Bear powerfully demonstrate the dia-
logism of history. Both accounts are true, and both speakers justify their
attitudes and actions in terms of their culture's traditional expectations, yet
obviously their emphases and implications differ, even while each leads to
the same conclusion, Jogues's death.

While Wolf 'Aunt' and Bear reveal conflict within Mohawk culture,
an analogous tension is evident within European culture, for Kenny gives
us not only poems from Jogues's perspective but others in the voices of
more secularly oriented Europeans. "The French Informal Report" (51) is
representative. It shares the Natives' assessment of Jogues as a fool; it
also shares with the fourth "Bear" poem (50), which precedes it, a view of
the commercial-political agenda as primary for the French in North Amer-
ica. Bear states that "the French . . . demand retribution, / but will settle
for beaver pelts . . . and an opened gate to the Mohawk / Valley." And
the "Informal Report" rages that Jogues "foiled our plans. The Dutch
laugh / in our face, and the English frigates / approach New Amsterdam
harbor." (Ironically, Bear is the speaker who most unambiguously honors
the courage of La Lande and Jogues. In the fifth "Bear" poem (52), his last
words, he acknowledges that "it is that very courage, bravery / in men
that I fear most.")

In *Blackrobe: Isaac Jogues* Maurice Kenny revises the documentary record in a number of significant ways, each of which foregrounds the inherent heteroglossia and intensifies the border-inflected dialogism of the history, or histories, and the telling. He does so, perhaps most importantly, by giving voice to Native speakers who've been "heard," if at all, in records written by the French and their successors; in so doing, like Allen with Sacagawea, he implicitly counterpoints the oral and the written. Conversely, he barely alludes to a major theme of Jogues's *Narrative*, the excruciating tortures suffered by the Mohawks' Indian and French prisoners. This may have been a choice he felt necessary if he was to lead his audience to think beyond stereotypes; it may also be appropriate to his focus on his Mohawk characters' (and predecessors') motives.

Kenny also complicates the position and characterization of Isaac Jogues, to suggest his implication in worldly motives and expand our sense of his religious commitments. First, there is the suggestion that Jogues may not have escaped complicity in the French pursuit of wealth. His "journal" note (24) on the "richly furred / beaver pelts" in the Mohawk village and his statement in a "letter" to his mother, that "the pelts / will make handsome chapeaux for our French / gentlemen and the grandees of China" (29) might imply such complicity. That he was expected not to interfere with commercial interests and, if only by deferring, to promote them, is implied in the "French Informal Report." And that he in effect served the larger European agenda of conquest foretold in "Wolf" (8) is the claim of the sequence's penultimate poem: "Out of his black robe came Kraft, / feedmills, blight, Benson Mines" (61). Ironically, perhaps tragically (and even if unwittingly), the man who would be a tool of God became a tool of commerce and worse.[19]

More difficult to assess are the passages in which Kenny attributes sexual interests to him. Sexual fear is evident in the first such passage, from Jogues's "letter" to the Jesuit Father Superior in France:

> . . . I hardly dare
> speak of the danger there is
> . . . amongst
> the improprieties of these
> savages. I understand adultery
> flourishes throughout their country.
> (11)

This passage might echo one from near the end of Jogues's account of his first captivity: "Purity is not, indeed, endangered here by delights, but is tried, amid this promiscuous and intimate intercourse of both sexes, by the perfect liberty of all in hearing and doing what they please; and, most of all, in their constant nakedness" (Jogues 45).[20] Kenny gives Jogues himself only one other expression of sexual interest. It comes in the "journal" passage entitled "Les Hures" (14), which focuses on the exotic physicality of "naked, reddish-brown bodies," and concludes (the ellipsis is Kenny's),

> It is exciting to be
> here among these fetching
> people . . . rogues which we Jesuits
> will change into angels and saints.

This poem's evident fascination with the Indians' bodies and its language (exciting, fetching, rogues) make the more directly stated suspicions of Bear and Wolf 'Aunt,' that Jogues is unusually interested in boys, seem not implausible. Bear objects that "his eye / is always either on pelts or dis- / tracted by the boys" (25); after Jogues's death Bear elaborates:

> he could not bear the sight
> of naked flesh, nor two people
> coupling in the shadows of the lodge.
> Chastity, he called, chastity!
> . . . .
>   . . . Yet, he stared
> at the young boys swimming nude
> in the river. And flew to make signs
> over their heads.
>
>   (43)

Wolf 'Aunt,' concerned for Jogues's safety, fears that "one day . . . some boy would resent his stares" (41). And in "Hoantteniate" (53) "Jogues' Adopted 'Wolf Brother'" remembers "trembl[ing] / when his warm hand touched / my bare shoulder"; Hoantteniate says that he

> . . . will miss the touch of his fingers
> and his whispering through the corn fields

while reading his book, and the sweet
raisins he offered the boys and myself . . .

These passages don't lend themselves to a clear, singular conclusion
about the meanings of the characters' (including Jogues's) statements,
suspicions, and memories. Each is entangled in her or his own needs and
commitments. Would Bear, for example, condemn a homoerotic interest
as such? Another passage might suggest that he would (44). Is he, rather,
objecting to the possibility of an adult's exploiting the young? His earlier
statement that if Jogues "would leave / the children alone" he, Bear,
would "not interfere" might suggest that interpretation. Could these ob-
jections of Bear's actually be ironic, revealing his own intolerance? And is
Hoantteniate remembering Jogues's seduction or the seductiveness of
unfamiliar sensory experiences? These questions, I think, are unanswer-
able. Two things do seem clear. First, by inviting such questions Kenny
again undercuts the image of Jogues as a purely religious person, one
who transcended worldly needs and desires. Second, he may be respond-
ing critically and ironically to the Europeans' sexualization of the Ameri-
can landscape and of Native peoples as "parts of" the landscape, which
converted land and people into objects to be enjoyed and exploited by
outsiders.[21] (Allen and Erdrich also respond to the implications of such a
practice.)

Another possibility is that implying Jogues's perhaps homoerotic
interests might be a way for Kenny, a gay poet, obliquely to complicate the
issue of sympathy. Walter Williams includes the Iroquois among "aborigi-
nal American cultures [that] did not recognize berdaches [men who do not
conform to standard men's roles, usually blending men's and women's
work and roles] as a respected status" (39). Kenny himself, in his essay
"Tinselled Bucks: A Historical Study in Indian Homosexuality," does not
refer specifically to Mohawk or Iroquois attitudes, though he maintains
that "homosexuality was found in all American Indian tribes" (18). A
young man, he says, who had "forfeit[ed] his right to masculine privilege"
by choosing not to take the warrior's path, "possibly exposed himself to
insulting ridicule and abuse though rarely would he have been castigated,
ostracized, or expelled" (20). His poem "Winkte" (*Between Two Rivers* 61–
62) emphasizes the respect accorded *berdaches* in Sioux, Cheyenne, Crow,
and Ponca cultures, contrasting such acceptance with the intolerance
that, it implies, gay Indians and berdaches meet elsewhere—and perhaps
met, even in some traditional communities. Bear's words about Jogues,

then, could anticipate and echo scornful words that gay and lesbian Indians have heard even from within Native communities. (Recall, too, Chrystos's essay "Askenet, Meaning 'Raw' in My Language" and some of her poems.) If so, Bear's remarks might veil Kenny's own engagement in dialogic discourse with tribal forebears and contemporaries.

Jogues has his last word in "His Visions" (47–48), which follows the accounts of his death. Here Kenny alludes to visions that may allow us more directly to sympathize with Jogues. In the poem itself Kenny only implies the import of these visions, but their significance becomes clear if we read this poem's tone and language in the context of words earlier attributed to Jogues. The most important element of the vision is contained in these lines (emphasis added):

> What greater sacrifice can I
> make for God and the salvation
> of these *brothers* who I shall
> and must lead to God.
> . . . .
> I will example my life for Jean
> and for these *innocents*
> who are in need of God's love.

No longer do we hear him speaking of "lost souls," "savages," "rogues," or the "wildness" of exotic and dangerous warriors, for he has had a vision of the Natives' humanity. Kenny makes this clear when he responds to Bruchac's observation that his picture of Isaac Jogues is "almost sympathetic." He reveals his own ambivalence when he responds at first, "No, it's not really sympathetic at all . . . I try to show him in the round as much as possible." As he speaks of the visions, however, Kenny seems to modify his position:

> But what did happen with Isaac was that he had two visions when he came to this land . . . totally believing the bilge that Indian people were just plain wild savages . . . he had his first vision in which was told, and he came to understand and accept, that the Indian people . . . were his brothers and sisters . . . And his second vision told him that because he had finally accepted the people as his brothers and sisters that he must remain with them and die. (*Survival* 153–54)[22]

As Kenny describes them here, the visions offer a way of imagining a sympathetic potential in Jogues. The Jogues of "His Visions" has already moved beyond the insistent preacher who "openly refute[d the Indians'] foolish tales / that the world was built on a turtle's back" (36). But Kenny sees in these visions the potential for further growth, foreclosed though it was by Jogues's death: in accepting the need to remain with his "brothers and sisters," Kenny believes, Jogues

> was throwing The Crown away. He would eventually, I am sure, have fought against The Crown . . . it would have been a different story. But because of Isaac Jogues the state of New York . . . and . . . the United States of America is a different place . . . He was the first missionary to come to this area and survive for any length of time . . . So it is directly upon his head. So you see where I might favor him a little bit . . . had he lived longer, it might have been different. (154)

"What should we make of this man-priest[?]" Kenny has the Dutch official Arendt Van Corlear ask (31). In the poems of *Blackrobe* and his comments to Bruchac he demonstrates his knowledge that we do *make* something of Jogues, and of history, and that history is susceptible to revision. Each of the successive monologues, speeches, journal entries, letters, and recollections of *Blackrobe* illuminates the others, complicating and deepening the meanings of the parts and the whole. In doing so, they demonstrate the vitality of history and show that true history, or history that approaches being adequate to lived experience, must be polyvocal and dialogic. Early on Kenny allows the explorer La Salle to assert confidently that "we have all plotted our places in history" (9), but he proceeds to show that the stability La Salle takes for granted is illusory. Every voice, every piece, in *Blackrobe* implies dialogic struggle in some sense, even if only (as is probably so for La Salle) in the relationship between a voice or a poem and its contexts. With Erdrich and Allen, then, Kenny shows us that the still-contested histories and interpretations of colonization demand, even create, dialogic discourse. Directly confronting and reimagining the victors' accounts, their poems draw attention to the historical project they share—in part, and in countless permutations—with other Native contemporaries.

Kimberly Blaeser's poem "Certificate of Live Birth: Escape from the Third Dimension" (*Trailing You* 84–86) represents at once a beginning, an end, and an assurance of continuity. It thus also can represent a recognition intrinsic to most (if not all) of the poems that participate in this project: the recognition of the vital interconnectedness of past and present, and the importance of understanding and reinterpreting the possibilities inherent in that interconnectedness. Blaeser's poem offers immediate, personal testimony to the complex circumstances that create documentary history and the need for re-vision: a daughter, the poet-speaker, recognizes that her birth certificate documents her Indian mother's "capture"; she imagines the emotional torment that compelled her mother to check the box identifying herself as "caucasian." Blaeser allows the document to stand, as an "accurate" representation of "the history of Indian people in this country" and

of her own heritage. But she simultaneously revises it, for the poem itself is "the certificate of our live birth," her mother's and her own, and of their "escape" from the "prison" that crumbles with the affirmations of the poem's final lines: "Father, caucasian. / Mother, American Indian. / Daughter, mixedblood." In these lines is confirmed the redemptive power, the power for survival, in contesting and reclaiming history.

CHAPTER 8

Toward a Native Poetics of Contested Spaces

Is there an American Indian borderland poetics? Continuities among the writings of Indian poets and the fact that, as we have seen, many define aspects of their ethics and aesthetics in terms of the influences and intersections of Native and other cultures, history, and politics, all suggest that there is. In this chapter I identify some of the characteristics of such a poetics as I find them implied by the poetry I have discussed. The chapter's title is meant to suggest a process, an inquiry moving *toward* understanding a poetics, rather than arrival at a definitive formulation. The title also acknowledges that I am identifying aspects of *a* poetics, one that may be modified or contested, according to others' readings.

A borderland is an area, geographic or not (sometimes both), of uncertainty and contention; these conditions are aggravated, if not created, by divisions that are often imposed or intensified by the powerful, to marginalize and control the disenfranchised. Borderlands can be dangerous for Indian people and cultures, especially when they become, in Louis Owens's sense, territorial; despair is among the greatest dangers. Yet those who are enabled to see that such conditions are not necessarily immutable may be moved to creative resistance, for resilient survival. Native poets working in the borderlands are engaged at once in the work of continuance and of confrontation: they reweave connections among Indian people, with the land, and with ancestral cultures, and confront the powers that would control, subdue, or deny Native stories, relationships, and voices. We can honor their work by attending to the particulars of language and circumstance that give life to their poetic projects, as I have aimed to do in the preceding chapters, and by remaining responsive, even as we generalize, to the variety of those particulars.

Both traditional understandings of language and the practices of these poets imply the inseparability of ethics and aesthetics in contemporary Indian poetry. This inseparability is nowhere clearer than in the communal orientation reflected (and created) by the poetry. Such an orientation implies commitment to the integrity and survival of Indian people, a commitment that may in turn imply intentions ranging from preservation to criticism. For some poets this commitment leads to advocacy on behalf of all indigenous, colonized peoples. The communal orientation encompasses relationship to the earth and to a particular geographic place or places, which may be urban as well as ancestral. Relationship to the land itself, especially ancestral land, can encompass any of the aspects— ecological, familial, linguistic, historical, mythological—that give identity and meaning to place. A communal orientation extends as well to relationships across time, to the past and future, and to the worlds of spirit.

Such a complex sense of communal relationship is at the core of Elizabeth Woody's "Waterways Endeavor to Translate Silence from Currents" (*Luminaries* 97–98). This poem begins in mourning, with the "desolate synthesis of weeping, rain, / into dry creek beds," a consequence of the destruction of Celilo Falls, Wyam, "the heart of our homeland" (*Seven Hands* 67), by the 1957 completion of the Dalles Dam on the Columbia River.[1] Woody recalls the traditional unity of language, place, and community; she alludes to the fishing culture that flourished at the falls, and the disruption of sustaining relationships:

> In our genesis, the beginning of words
> meant that we would not be without land or relationships.
>
> Vacuity, the lack of emotion etches into destruction
> the scaffolds of abundance, rapids, falls, spawning beds,
> the echo of falling water. The nascent place of all
>
> the songs lingers amongst the multitude of ancestors,
> commonly wedged into bone hills, vandalized and catalogued.
>
> Dislocated from one another, we are now flooded
> . . . .
> The river elegantly marks swirls on its surface,
> a spiral that tells of a place
> that remains undisturbed.

The poem functions not only as exposé and lament but also, I think, as part of a process of communal, relational reclamation. Woody's preface to *Luminaries of the Humble* suggests the special importance of Celilo Falls in such a project:

My concern in this volume is to give voice to those who are not often heard from, like the salmon, forest trees, our little relatives that nourish us, the edible roots, berries, deer. All that may die from our neglect. I still believe in the lessons in nature, especially in the tenacious will in salmon to return to their source. . . .

My conceptual return is to imagine the "echo of falling water," Celilo Falls, inundated in a dam's backwaters in 1957, and the collective voice of the many people who struggle to make small gains in renewal . . . of our heritage . . . (xiv–xv)

In "That Place Where Ghosts of Salmon Jump" (19) Sherman Alexie has written what we might read as a companion piece to Woody's "Waterways Endeavor to Translate Silence from Currents." Alexie grieves the disappearance of the salmon from Spokane Falls, also caused by damming, and the consequent disruption of relationships involving place, history, salmon, and family. Whereas Woody's tone is reflective and meditative, perhaps suggesting a turning inward for recollection, Alexie begins with storytelling that becomes a series of challenges to Coyote, implicitly to his audience, and to himself:

Coyote, you're a liar and I don't trust you. I never have

but I do trust all the stories the grandmothers told me.
They said the Falls were built because of your unrequited love
· ·
but look at the Falls now and tell me what you see. Look

at the Falls now if you can see beyond all of the concrete
the white man has built here. Look at all of this

and tell me that concrete ever equals love . . .
· ·
· · · · · · These Falls are that place

where ghosts of salmon jump, where ghosts of women mourn
their children who will never find their way back home,

where I stand now and search for any kind of love,
where I sing softly, under my breath, alone and angry.

Although different elements of relationship tend, ultimately, to be interwoven—as they are in Woody's and Alexie's poems—communal orientation creates varying emphases in contemporary American Indian poetry. The sense of geographical place, people, and language, as constitutive of community, may be virtually seamless, as in Simon Ortiz's writings; Ray Young Bear's poetry suggests a somewhat conflicted, yet still powerful, conviction of a similar unity; Woody's and Alexie's poems yearn toward recovery of such communal conviction. (That these four are among the most strongly land-based of the poets I've discussed throws into relief the diversity among all of the writers.) In Chrystos's poetry the aspiration toward a (spiritually empowered) human community often predominates. Yet though that community may not be imagined in terms of a particular place, Chrystos lets us know that it cannot be realized apart from an interdependent relationship with the natural world. And, differently, for Jim Barnes and Linda Hogan, reflections on specific places, or responses to particular natural phenomena, can imply the potential for human and spiritual connectedness. Barnes's poetry, like Wendy Rose's, reminds us, too, that an orientation toward relationship can be evident not only in a sense of belonging but also in exclusion, desire, or ambivalence.

For contemporary Native poets an ethics and aesthetics of relatedness is likely to be responsive to the oral and to suggest the poet's participation, on some level, in the continuance of oral tradition. Evident when a writer uses a tribal language or draws directly on oral stories or songs, this orientation can be embodied in other ways as well. Perhaps more important than the immediate presence of an indigenous language or tribal lore is an ethics of involvement, of engaging the audience in creative, responsive relationships with story, history, mythology, language, and hence with community. From this perspective structural and stylistic approaches that reach out to engage the audience may be read as literary traces of the ethics and aesthetics of oral traditional practices. Thus presenting multiple voices, drawing attention to language's malleability through wordplay, integrating indigenous languages and different levels or kinds of diction, directly invoking or addressing multiple speakers or listeners (whose responses are thus implied as they're invited)—all of these can draw a poem, and readers, into an orally inflected communal dynamics. (Paradoxically, perhaps, such devices may also be used to draw attention to linguistic conflict.) Conversely, veiling strategies, in the sense of Young Bear's "dust-filled veils of light," may recall the exclusivity of some aspects of traditional cultures and the different necessities both of transmitting and of protecting communal cultural knowledge.

Then readers may be at once drawn to interpret and reminded of the limits of interpretation.

Traces of oral tradition are so pronounced in the poetry of many Indian writers, and have been so frequently discussed by critics and poets alike, that an oral presence has become virtually a criterion for Native American poetry. Yet expectations about the presence of traditional oral elements may become somewhat problematical when questions arise about contemporary writers' access to tradition and about the ethical implications of translating or adapting a community's sacred stories for the purposes of contemporary literature.[2] I draw attention to such complications not to diminish the importance of the oral elements, but because such questions, compelled as they are by postcontact history, reinforce the value of caution, in the matter of defining a poetics.

In the poetry of the borderlands oral traces and traditional elements often coexist with, and may be less salient than, evidence of influence from other sources. If indigenous cultures never were static and "pure," the cultures as they have evolved certainly have not been unaffected by the languages, technology, politics, and history of those that now surround them. Alexie's "Defending Walt Whitman" (14–15) illustrates wonderfully the hybridization that integrates continuity and change; the poem combines an element of oral tradition with allusion to non-Native "mainstream" American culture in a single poetic feature, repetition:

> Basketball is like this for Walt Whitman. He watches these Indian
> boys
> as if they were the last bodies on earth. Every body is brown!
> . . . .
> Walt Whitman dreams of the Indian boy who will defend him,
> trapping him in the corner, all flailing arms and legs
> and legendary stomach muscles. Walt Whitman shakes
> because he believes in God. Walt Whitman dreams
> of the first jump shot he will take, the ball arcing clumsily
> from his fingers, striking the rim so hard that it sparks.
> Walt Whitman shakes because he believes in God.
> Walt Whitman closes his eyes. He is a small man and his beard
> is ludicrous on the reservation, absolutely insane.
>
> . . . .
> There is no place like this. Walt Whitman smiles.
> Walt Whitman shakes. This game belongs to him.

The poem both challenges and accommodates Walt Whitman, and with him the influence and language of the dominant U.S. culture. The counter-pointed repetitions of "Walt Whitman . . ." and "Every body is brown" (which is repeated several times) highlight the dialogism that pervades the poem; it is especially apparent in the title and in the interplay between the title and the poem's last sentence: "This game belongs to him." Such features and the tensions they create give the poem an energetic edginess that is partly generated by and partly responsive to its cross-cultural dynamics. This energetic edginess is evident, too, as the poem's relatively formal elements—repetition, parallelism—and its colloquial tone—"absolutely insane"—locate it within oral tradition and make audible a dialogics of both opposition and exchange.

A particularly intense engagement with history seems to be invited by the tensions aggravated, and the opportunities for creative redefinition offered, in the cultural, political, and geographic borderlands, where any illusion that history is singular or monovocal is destroyed as conflicting histories compete for influence and thus for continuance. Poems like Rose's "Excavation at Santa Barbara Mission" and "To Make History," Kenny's *Blackrobe: Isaac Jogues,* and Davis's "Saginaw Bay: I Keep Going Back" show that history is both powerful and *made*. With this recognition, history becomes not only reportorial and archival but imaginative, dialogic, and sometimes oppositional.

Another poem by Elizabeth Woody, "Translation of Blood Quantum" (*Luminaries* 103–4), exemplifies the making of multiply valenced, recuperative history. It exemplifies, too, a dialogic attentiveness to language and an activist, communal orientation characteristic of this poetry. I quote the poem in full, for it is truly an example of the fusion of ethics and aesthetics; extracting a few lines would divorce them from the poem's relational meanings.

31/32   Warm Springs–Wasco–Yakama–Pit River–Navajo
1/32   Other   Tribal roll number 1553

THIRTY-SECOND PARTS OF A HUMAN BEING
SUN MOON EVENING STAR AT DAWN CLOUDS RAINBOW CEDAR
LANGUAGE COLORS AND SACRIFICE LOVE THE GREAT FLOOD
THE TORTOISE CARRIES THE PARROT HUMMINGBIRD TRILLIUM
THE CROW RAVEN COYOTE THE CONDOR JAGUAR GRIZZLY
TIMBER WOLF SIDEWINDER THE BAT CORN TOBACCO SAGE

MUSIC DEATH CONSCIOUS OF THE SPIDERWEB RESURRECTED PROPHETS
RECURRENT POWER OF CREATION IS FUELED BY SONG

Like the lava, we have always been indomitable in flowing
purposes. A perpetuity of *Ne-shy-Chus* means we are rooted
in ancestral domain and are *Free*, with any other power
reserved in the truce of treaty, 1855, or any other time.
We kept peace. Preserved and existed through our *Songs,*
Dances, Longhouses, and the noninterruption of giving Thanks
and observances of the Natural laws of Creating by the Land
itself. The *Nusoox* are as inseparable from the flow of these
cycles. Our *Sovereignty* is permeated in its possession
of our individual rights, by acknowledgment of good
for the whole
and this includes the freedom of the *Creator* in these teachings
given to and practiced by *The People*. We are watched over
by the mountains, not Man, not Monarchy,
or any other manifestations
of intimidation by misguided delusions of supremacy
over the Land or beings animate or inanimate.[3]

While Blaeser, in "Certificate of Live Birth," emphasizes the immediate personal and familial consequences of white-imposed quantification and documentation of race-based identity, Woody elaborates upon the understanding (which she shares with Blaeser as with their other Native contemporaries) that with language we make and remake ourselves and our histories. For an Indian person who has been defined by the Federal government in terms of fractions and fragments, the recovery of communal, relational identity voiced in this poem must be particularly compelling and liberating.

American Indian poets confront the collisions of tribal and other histories; re-create the intersections of mythic histories with the daily world; bring to light suppressed histories; and search out the possibilities of weaving diverse histories into more complex fabrics. Their poems, and the poetics they imply, are moved by the need to make history more visible, more polyvocal, more complete, and thereby to revise the possibilities that history offers to the future. History is essential to survival; in the works of these poets the telling of history is part of a communal, dialogic ethics and aesthetics.

The poetry's responsiveness to the oral, foregrounding of complex relationships among indigenous influences and others, and communal orientation all imply that dialogism—variously inflected, and encompassing both creative exchange and oppositional challenge—is integral to the poetics I have been tracing. So embedded does it seem in indigenous conceptions of community and language that we might consider *dialogism* in some respects simply a non-Native, theoretical name for something that traditional Native peoples have long known: the relational, responsive nature of living language. This is certainly suggested by the centrality, in indigenous oral cultures, of the relationship between teller and listener: active engagement in creating meaning implies dialogic exchange. What Bakhtin most significantly contributes—and what is particularly important in contested borderland spaces—is the emphasis on language's inherent contest of meanings and intentions (heteroglossia) and on the oppositional dialogic intent that may follow from that knowledge. Also underlying dialogism is another concept integral to Native oral cultures—that of language's efficacy, its power to change the world. The poetry's dialogism demonstrates what the traditional concept assumes and many of the poets assert or imply: a poetics of action. The development of such a poetics becomes visible in Alexie's "Capital Punishment" (86–90). As the speaker "prepare[s] the last meal / for the Indian man to be executed" and then sits alone "in the dark kitchen / when they do it, meaning / when they kill him," the poem traces his progress toward communal commitment as he moves from insisting "I am not a witness" to asserting "I am a witness."

The English language is both an integral and a problematical element of contemporary Native poetry. English isolates indigenous languages, makes them exotic, changes the names (thus perhaps the impact) of traditional places and figures; it represents the powers that would impose territorial control, to dominate the borderlands. As such, in this poetry it is implicated in tension, and it incites creative dialogic resistance. English reminds us that borderland poetry is necessarily, however ambivalently or comfortably, bicultural or cross-cultural. This not only implies influence from non-Native sources but may also mean that the nature of a writer's or poem's relationship with Native culture(s) is at issue.[4] What does it mean to write and publish in English yet to be affiliated with a community for whom English and publication have been foreign, potentially alienating concepts—or to think or write in an indigenous language under circumstances largely determined to suit the powers represented by "the language / the presidents speak" (Hogan, *Seeing* 8)? In an important sense English confirms the poetry's location in contested space(s), its participation in borderland consciousness. In the sixth part of "Drum as Love, Fear, and Prayer" (68–72) Alexie throws these issues into sharp relief:

> These prayers have not been easy, how
> do we say Indian prayers in English
> and which God will answer? Is God red
> or white? Do these confused prayers mean
>
> we'll live on another reservation
> in that country called Heaven?

For many of the poets whose work I've considered, English is a reminder of loss. In some instances the loss is absolute: ancestral lands flooded or paved over, ancestral languages obliterated. That other losses might be reparable the writers dare to imagine or affirm. This at least tenuous hope is a major source of the poetry's ongoing vitality, not only for commemoration or accusation but also for promise and struggle. Knowledge of loss, in contemporary Native poetry, becomes an impetus for recovery and re-creation. English, for some a sign of complicity or bereavement, becomes also an instrument to be retuned, a power to be grasped and made "useful in a native context" (Harjo, *Spiral* 43). Doing so, Indian poets create new ways of honoring and continuing tradition, exposing and fighting oppression; they offer new possibilities for interaction among Indian peoples and between the tribal or pan-tribal and the dominant, non-Native cultures. Thus they give their poetry the life of relationship and resistance, as they turn it to the communal work of healing, liberation, and survival that is at the heart of a vibrant borderland poetics.

NOTES

Chapter 1

1. I use *Native American, Native, American Indian,* and *Indian* interchangeably, to acknowledge different Native people's practices and preferences and to draw attention to the political-cultural contests and the heteroglossia involved in self-naming and naming by others. I use specific tribal names when referring to particular communities, cultures, or individuals. When faced with a choice of names, I try to use the tribal name(s) that each writer seems to prefer. For Joy Harjo I use both *Creek* and *Muscogee,* as she does. For Gerald Vizenor I use both the name he accepts, as an enrolled member of the White Earth Chippewa, and the one he evidently prefers, *Anishinaabe.* See *The People Named the Chippewa* for Vizenor's most extended discussion of tribal names and naming.

I agree with Brian Swann that "the latest insult is" for non-Natives in particular "to measure blood" (intro., xx); therefore, in identifying the poets whose work I discuss, I initially indicate simply the tribe(s) with which each identifies. When a writer's mixed-blood identity is pertinent to works under discussion, that will be made clear.

2. In "The State's claim . . . ," for example, Simon Ortiz gives compelling testimony about his Acoma people's experience of encroachment and redefinition (*Woven Stone* 254–60).

3. Mary Louise Pratt's concept of the contact zone offers some parallels to border theory, especially in its reference to social and political spaces, and may also serve to illuminate those aspects of the poetry. Pratt defines the contact zone as "social space . . . where disparate cultures meet, clash, and grapple with each other, often in highly asymmetrical relations of domination and subordination" (4); it is the "space of colonial encounters . . . usually involving conditions of coercion, radical inequality, and intractable conflict" (6).

4. Compare Hertha D. Wong's definition of the "boundary culture" of late-nineteenth- and early-twentieth-century Native American autobiographies (89). Wong is discussing a kind of text whose production differs starkly from those of Anzaldúa and the poets I will discuss.

5. *Frontier* itself, not surprisingly, is a contested term, as Owens's effort to rehabilitate it suggests. The term's unavoidable baggage—and the difficulty more generally of finding a language suitable to this literature—is clearest in Krupat's ongoing use of it and his ongoing need to redefine it. (See *For Those Who Come After* 33–35; *The Voice in the Margin* 167; and *Ethnocriticism* 4–5.) For a critique of Krupat's usage—and, in effect, of the use of the term generally—see Moore, "Decolonizing Criticism" 28–30.

6. Blaeser mentions the work of Gordon Henry, Gerald Vizenor, Arnold Krupat, James Ruppert, Louis Owens, and Keith Basso as being notably based on dialogue or mediation.

7. Heteroglossia is the internal, inherent, and socially/historically conditioned stratification of language, continuously brought about by the fact that "every socially significant verbal performance has the ability . . . to infect with its own intention certain aspects of language" (290). Because of heteroglossia, language "represents the co-existence of socio-ideological contradictions between the present and the past . . . between different socio-ideological groups . . . between tendencies, schools, circles and so forth" (291). As a consequence, language "is populated—overpopulated—with the intentions of others" (294).

As Holquist and Emerson put it, "Dialogism is the characteristic epistemological mode of a world dominated by heteroglossia . . . There is a constant interaction between meanings, all of which have the potential of conditioning others" (426). But it is even more complex. Embodying the "centrifugal" forces of living language, Bakhtin says, dialogic language is "consciously opposed," "aimed sharply against the official languages of its given time" (272–73); dialogism, or dialogized heteroglossia, thus implies tension and struggle grounded in particular social contexts. "The living utterance . . . cannot fail to brush up against thousands of living dialogic threads, woven by socio-ideological consciousness . . . it cannot fail to become an active participant in social dialogue" (276). As Bakhtin uses his terms, heteroglossia and dialogism can seem almost to merge, so inevitably, in "living," nonunitary language, must dialogism arise. Again, intention is key: "With each literary-verbal performance, consciousness must actively orient itself amidst heteroglossia, it must move in and occupy a position for itself within . . . heteroglossia." In other words, "concrete socio-ideological language consciousness, as it becomes creative . . . discovers itself surrounded by heteroglossia" and must become dialogized (295). Language cannot be neutral. (All quotations from Bakhtin are from "Discourse in the Novel"; Holquist and Emerson are quoted from their glossary. All are in *Dialogic Imagination*.)

8. Hybridization is "a mixture of two social languages within the limits of a single utterance, an encounter within the arena of an utterance, between two different linguistic consciousnesses"; "an intentional [artistic] hybrid is precisely the perception of one language by another language, its illumination by another linguistic consciousness" (*Dialogic Imagination*, 358, 359).

9. For a detailed analysis of Vizenor's dialogic methods, see Blaeser, *Gerald Vizenor*, 164–97.

10. Hitchcock draws on *Marxism and the Philosophy of Language* as well as on the essays of *The Dialogic Imagination*. Regarding the question of authorship of such disputed works as *Marxism and the Philosophy of Language* (published under the name of V. N. Voloshinov), Hitchcock notes that he uses " 'Bakhtin' as a referent for the 'collective' author of the works of the Bakhtin Circle" (204n. 3).

11. All quotations from Moore in chapter 1 are from "Decolonizing Criticism." Moore's dialogism draws on Bakhtin's "Discourse in the Novel" and on James Clifford's "Identity at Mashpee."

12. Moore's virtual equation of dialogics and dialogue, similar to Blaeser's usage, would no doubt dismay Hitchcock but does not seem to be at odds with Bakhtin's own usage in "Discourse in the Novel," where more than once juxtaposition or syntax suggests virtual equivalence (e.g., *Dialogic Imagination*, 272–74, 278–79, 324–25).

13. *Other Destinies* 6. Owens draws on the work of Ashcroft, Griffiths, and Tiffin, who, he points out, omit any discussion of Native American writers.

Analogously, Krupat argues that "for any person who identifies himself or herself as an Indian, the writing of autobiography . . . generates a textual self that is in greater or lesser degree inevitably dialogic" (*Voice in the Margin* 133–34).

14. Bruchac, *Survival This Way* 246.

15. Making readers aware of our relationship to the story is, of course, a way of drawing us closer to the assumptions of oral culture. Louise Erdrich may be doing something similar in her novels when, as Catherine Rainwater argues, she "produces in the reader an experience of marginality" through the use of "conflicting codes" (406).

16. For example, "Language—like the living concrete environment in which the consciousness of the verbal artist lives—is never unitary," and "the orientation of discourse in the novel . . . is contested, contestable and contesting" ("Discourse in the Novel" 288, 332).

17. Smith points out "certain facts that argue strongly for Coyote's trustworthiness" in this poem (202).

18. In many American Indian cultures, including notably that of the Hopis, Rose's father's people, clowns are distinguished by their dramatic reversals of appropriate behavior, for purposes simultaneously spiritual and entertaining. See, for example, Emory Sekaquaptewa, "One More Smile for a Hopi Clown," in Dooling and Jordan-Smith 150–57; and Beck, Walters, and Francisco 291–317.

19. Both Ortiz's Coyote stories and Rose's "Trickster" draw on the trickster character's traditional identity as a transgressor of boundaries, an identity that no doubt prepares him to be a successful crosser of borders in the colonized world. See Babcock, Bright, and Ramsey, for further discussions of traditional trickster behavior.

20. Schöler, "A Heart Made Out of Crickets" 114.

21. Bruchac, *Survival This Way* 246.

22. These ironic ambiguities, and the clichés cited earlier ("they . . . put you . . . on your own two feet . . . pointed you in the right direction") demonstrate Bakhtin's "processes of centralization and decentralization, of unification and disunification," "the active participation of every utterance in living heteroglossia"; they also suggest a close variation on the "double-voiced discourse [that] . . . serves two speakers at the same time . . . expresses simultaneously two intentions [and] . . . is always internally dialogized." Bakhtin maintains that only a limited, sterile shadow of such discourse is possible in a language system like that of poetry, "hermetic, pure and unitary, . . . cut off from any process of linguistic stratification," but I read Davis's voice in these passages as at least triple ("Discourse in the Novel" 272, 324, 325).

23. "The only way to continue is to tell a story . . . Your children will not survive unless you tell something about them" (*Woven Stone* 153).

Chapter 2

1. Astrov 33; Gill 23; Ruoff 6. Also see Ong, chap. 3, on the concept of language in oral cultures.

2. See, for example, *The Way to Rainy Mountain* 46; "The Native Voice" 11–14; and Woodard, *Ancestral Voice* 115–18 and 197.

3. Blaeser shows how the story's details "clearly create a setting of border existence" (*Gerald Vizenor* 160).

4. Vizenor, in McCaffrey and Marshall 54.
Betty Louise Bell reads Almost as a deluded searcher for absolute truth, "a casualty of 'terminal creeds,' " hence the object of Vizenor's satire ("Almost the Whole Truth" 180). I think, though, that Vizenor's text disrupts such a conclusion. On the one hand, Almost does seem to privilege the "real" as he reiterates "that's the truth." On the other, he announces that "words are crossbloods" (surely indicating awareness of mutability and multidimensionality), rejects school as inimical to wildness, danger, and imagination, and mocks "men who rule words from behind double doors" (9). Altogether, such facts suggest that "Almost Browne" is a dialogic text that resists a single conclusion, and Almost a trickster-like character.

5. See "The Man Made of Words" 163, 166, and 167, and, for one of many other examples, Woodard 57. Similarly, in *Ancestral Voice* he says, "The imagination that informs these stories is really not mine, though it exists, I think, in the blood. It's an ancestral imagination" (57). Krupat assails the "racism" of such statements (*Voice in the Margin* 13–14), while other critics are at pains to explain them. David Murray, for example, cites Momaday's reference, in *The Names* (48), to his mother's imaginative choice of an "Indian" identity as evidence of his awareness that "there is no racial essence, or unified traditional sensibility" (*Forked Tongues* 81). H. David Brumble responds similarly (173–75); see also Wong 179.
Momaday seems most fundamentally concerned, in such statements, with cultural memory and the possible grounds of culturally specific responsiveness. These are issues of concern for other Indian writers, too. Vizenor has evidently worked to find an adequate language for naming such continuities; his at least provisional conclusion, at the time of Blaeser's interviews with him, leans toward "a larger collective unconscious . . . an intersection in the world." Blaeser says, "the issue for Vizenor is not race but established patterns of thinking" (*Gerald Vizenor* 218 n. 33; 127).

6. *Voice in the Margin* 177–78. Krupat refers only in passing to *House Made of Dawn*, the work of Momaday's that is most open to varied voices and discourses.

7. See Momaday, in Woodard: "One must not lose sight of the fact that

language is a very serious matter. It is to be controlled, because it is very powerful" (101). This is one of Ko-sahn's lessons, too: "Be careful of your pronouncements, grandson." Obviously, a writer who appreciates irony as Momaday does (see Woodard 22, 58, 90, 175) can't be simply characterized as averse to multiple meanings. But Momaday doesn't cultivate irony as Vizenor does multiplicity of all sorts, and I would argue that he tends to contain his ironies and multiplicities—as he does, for example, in *House Made of Dawn*, in which the ironic or disruptive impacts of Tosamah and Angela are contained within the novel's circular, ceremonial, unifying structure.

    8. "Bringing Home the Fact" 564.

    9. "Language We Know" 187; Coltelli 107.

    10. See Vizenor, in Bruchac, *Survival* 293.

    11. Bruchac, *Survival* 109–10, 124, 224–25.

    12. See Bruchac, *Survival* 320; for Momaday's comments on politics, see Woodard 41.

    13. *Defiant* is Bruchac's word; he recognizes this speaker as being "true to" himself, which enables us to characterize the speaker's position as one of resistance grounded in a sense of integrity (*Survival* 320).

    14. Vizenor describes "Wenebojo or Manabozho," the Anishinaabe proto-type for his tricksters, as "the compassionate trickster . . . the imaginative trickster, the one who cares to balance the world between terminal creeds and humor with unusual manners and ecstatic strategies" (*Earthdivers* xii).

    15. I am indebted to Robert Davis's comments, in conversation, for my reading of this poem, and especially for the statement that he sees the dance rattle functioning here as would a mask.

    16. Bakhtin's thought is in accord with these Native poets' understandings of the role of the audience: "every word is directed toward an *answer* and cannot escape the profound influence of the answering word that it antici-pates . . . every . . . sort of discourse . . . is oriented toward an understand-ing that is 'responsive' . . . Responsive understanding . . . participates in the formulation of discourse, and it is moreover an *active* understanding, one that discourse senses as resistance or support enriching the discourse" ("Dis-course in the Novel" 280–81).

    17. Owens, *Other Destinies* 4.

    18. Another insidious effect of linguistic colonialism is that, turning silence into a sign of weakness and defeat, it may also threaten to turn people from the power traditionally found in silence. See Astrov 39; Momaday, "The Na-tive Voice" 7; Woodard 109; and Walters 13–14.

    19. *Woven Stone* 4–6, 27; "Towards a National Indian Literature" 8, 10.

    20. "You . . . Who Have Removed Us: At What Cost?" 209.

Chapter 3

    1. Krupat notes that a "nearer approach to authenticity is likely to take us further from comprehensibility, while the privileging of comprehensibility

cannot help but sacrifice some of the strangeness and difference of other cultural production" (*Voice in the Margin* 218).

2. *Community* may signify a traditionally oriented group located on ancestral lands; however, the more general definition offered by Bonnie TuSmith (from Thomas Bender) is also appropriate to many Native contexts: community may be thought of as a " 'network of social relations marked by mutuality and emotional bonds' " (TuSmith 22; quoting Bender 7). Further, Tomás Rivera's suggestion that the Chicano writer wishes to create community as an act of decolonization also characterizes some of the work of contemporaries such as Chrystos and Rose (TuSmith 23; citing Rivera 17, 10).

Bakhtin discusses the centrality of the audience, the listener, in "The Problem of Speech Genres." See also "Discourse in the Novel" 280–84, on the internal dialogism of the word and the orientation of discourse toward the listener. Ortiz, in his preface to *A Good Journey*, makes a similar point: "without this sharing [by speaker and listener-reader] in the intellectual, emotional, physical, and spiritual activity, nothing much happens . . . the listener-reader has as much responsibility and commitment to poetic effect as the poet" (*Woven Stone* 151).

3. See TuSmith, especially chapter 1. TuSmith uses *ethnic* to refer to non-white, racially identified cultures and individuals, specifically to Asian American, African American, Native American, and Chicano/a writers.

4. Contemporary Native poets, too, assume the audience's active role. See, for example, comments by Maurice Kenny (148), Duane Niatum (200), and Gerald Vizenor (300–301, 307) in interviews with Bruchac (*Survival This Way*) and Simon J. Ortiz (*Woven Stone* 151).

5. Owens quotes "Discourse in Life and Discourse in Art" (408), originally published under the name of V. N. Volosinov but attributed by Robert Con Davis and Ronald Schleifer to Bakhtin.

6. Their desire to change the world, along with many of their emphases and strategies, relates both Rose and Chrystos to women's resistance poetry, as defined by DeShazer. See especially 47–48.

7. I had completed this study before I became aware of Helen Jaskoski's insightful work on Rose's dialogic poetry.

8. Owens argues that the "recovering or rearticulation of an identity, a process dependent upon a rediscovered sense of place as well as community . . . a truly enormous undertaking [in the face of "centuries of colonial and postcolonial displacement"] . . . is at the center of American Indian fiction" (*Other Destinies* 5). The same is true of much contemporary Indian poetry.

9. Chrystos, "Askenet" 241. Chrystos asks this question in a slightly different context.

10. Many of those interviewed by Bruchac in *Survival This Way* address these issues. Maurice Kenny (Mohawk) distinguishes between the sacred, which is not to be talked about, and the social, which may be (152). Elizabeth Cook-Lynn (Sioux) responds unambiguously when asked whether she deliberately avoids writing about certain aspects of Native culture: "I feel it's an invasion . . . of the traditions"; yet tradition seems paradoxically to have offered

her a basis for writing about the male-only Elk Society: not being knowledge-able about the society, she "felt all right imagining it because I'm a woman anyway and a woman isn't supposed to know anything about that . . . The fact is I'm only a poet. I'm not an historian, I'm not a linguist" (69). Similarly Gerald Vizenor, while unwilling to answer in specific terms questions about stories told by his uncle, maintains that there is "no limit" to the possible ways of alluding to traditional material (302, 309). Lance Henson (Cheyenne) and Har-old Littlebird (Laguna/Santo Domingo) address such issues in terms of the audience's needs or capabilities. Littlebird, who describes his book as "a real prayer" that is "all for anybody . . . not just Pueblo people," acknowledges that he has omitted cultural material that he considers "too touchy" but also that he tries to incorporate the English language with "a traditional sound," in order to "help other people who are non-Indian to be more aware of Indian music" (160, 163, 166). Henson, who is deeply involved in traditional Chey-enne culture, responds to questions about the accessibility of Indian poetry by suggesting that the interested reader might respond to the evocative quality of his poetry and further might learn to respond knowledgeably (109, 115).

11. Compare Greg Sarris: "In creating narratives for others about our histo-ries and religions, in what ways are we not only compromising those histories and religions but at the same time compromising our identities . . . as well as our resistance to the colonizer and dominant culture?" (68).

12. Hunter 49, 53, 46, 55, 43. In her interview with Bruchac, Rose affirms that her "community is urban Indian and is *pan* tribal" (*Survival* 254). To Coltelli she states that pantribalism is not opposed to tribal identity (129).

13. I have in mind poems like Chrystos's "White Girl Don't," "Table Man-ners," "I Was Minding My Own Business," and "In the Ritzy" (*Not Vanishing* 74, 73; *Dream On* 56, 51); and Rose's "The Mormons Next Door" and "Dear Grandfather Webb from England" (*Going to War* 42, 46). In "Askenet" Chrys-tos comments that she has often been characterized as "an 'angry' poet"; she finds this "very frustrating, because less than half of *Not Vanishing* [her only published collection at the time] is about anger." Instead, she emphasizes her use of writing "to box up pain & make it bearable" (239). Similarly at a reading in Boston in December 1996 she remarked that, rather than anger, her poems often more fundamentally express grief.

14. When Rose and Chrystos use first-person singular pronouns, we may assume that they speak, at least in part, autobiographically. Rose says that "everything I have ever written is fundamentally autobiographical, no matter what the topic or style," and that "poetry is both ultimate fact and ultimate fiction" ("Neon Scars" 253). And Chrystos says, "fiction writers can pretend that they write fantasy, with no reference to their own experiences, but poets of my genre . . . are writing from our very lives" ("Askenet" 238).

15. In a note to "The Endangered Roots" Rose says that she uses "the feel-ing" of the "twisted-twin" reference, which traditionally denotes one who was supposed to be born twins but was united just before birth, as a "persona."

16. Rose comments about the fact that she has no Indian name and about what a name confers (Hunter 54–55).

17. "I Like to Think" and "I Am Not Your Princess," like Rose's "Margaret Neumann" and "For the Complacent College Students" (*Going to War* 65–69 and 61–62), effectively demonstrate the active construction of meaning and identity in relationship, grounded in concrete experience and historicity, that Linda Alcoff defines as positionality.

18. The possibility of multiple centers is deeply suggestive of tribal people's conceptions of the world. Mircea Eliade maintains that the "multiplicity of centers and . . . [the] reiteration of the image of the world on smaller and smaller scales constitute one of the specific characteristics of traditional societies" (43). Among his examples is the repetition of "cosmic symbolism . . . in the structure of the sanctuary or the ceremonial house among the Algonquins and the Sioux" (46). Similarly Black Elk, as reported by Neihardt, tells us that "the Power of the World always works in circles"; he describes the world of his people as a world of circles, from "the circle of the four quarters" to the "teepees [which] . . . were round like the nests of birds, and . . . always set in a circle" (194–95). More recently, traditional Cheyenne poet Lance Henson has said, "Everybody's home should be the center of the world. It is there that children are raised and there that the important things in life occur" (Bruchac, *Survival* 108).

19. *The Halfbreed Chronicles,* in which "If I Am" was first published, marks an important transition in Rose's understanding of the meaning of mixed origins and the term *halfbreed,* an understanding that contributes to the power of many of the *Going to War* poems and her surer sense of relationship to variously characterized communities. See her interviews with Bruchac, Hunter, and Coltelli.

20. Sources for Hopi origin myths include Albert Yava, who tells us that Hopi tradition accommodates multiple versions of history: "Different villages and clans have their own special details, and different explanations" (11). See also G. M. Mullett, especially 1–6; and Hamilton A. Tyler, especially 95–97.

21. Young Bear characterized himself as "traditional-minded" in Wiley. With reference to his protectiveness of Mesquakie and other Native cultures, see his interview with Bruchac (*Survival* 347–48).

22. " 'I would be out of place in the tundra or desert, hunting moose for its meat and hide, tracking roadrunners for their feathers' is in reference to the Algonquin-speaking tribes of Canada and Northeastern Mexico" (*Invisible Musician* 98).

23. For Dickinson's poem, see *Complete Poems* 662.

24. Robert Dale Parker notes the difficulties posed by Young Bear's poetry for "non-Mesquakie readers versed in European and American poetic tradition" and probably "for those Mesquakie readers not so versed" (90).

25. Ashcroft, Griffiths, and Tiffin 58–59; as Owens also notes, though they focus on writing of peoples formerly colonized by Britain, they do not discuss American Indian literatures.

26. The themes of communication and a shared past converge appropri-

ately, in view of William Jones's observation that the Mesquakie language is "in some respects the most archaic of the Algonquian tongues" (*Ethnography* 1). Besides conveying a sense of ancient memory, the reference to Lake Agassiz might also function dialogically, by ironically recalling nineteenth-century Harvard naturalist Louis Agassiz's belief in the "biologically determined characteristics" of Native Americans (Krupat, *Ethnocriticism* 233).

27. Such passages lend credibility to David L. Moore's observation that Young Bear's poems "reveal a conflicted relationality between [his] . . . ironic persona and his land, his culture, his Mesquakie people, and his American nation" (378) and that his "persona . . . negotiate[s] the lack of a static cultural identity" ("Myth, History and Identity" 378, 283).

28. For example, Moore reads the poem as alluding in part to "a lost love who has apparently returned to her drunken husband" ("Myth, History and Identity" 379); this seems somewhat unlikely to me, yet the poem does require that all possibilities be considered.

29. On Mesquakie conservatism see Jones, *Ethnography of the Fox Indians* 1; Wiley quotes Young Bear as saying, "My role in the Mesquakie Tribal Settlement as a poet is very low key . . . There is no place for a contemporary Mesquakie poet. There is no word for 'poet' in our vocabulary."

Chapter 4

1. For further discussion of the meanings of place, see Beck and Walters, especially 67–81.

2. For a survey of the history of relations between American Indians and non-Natives, and of Federal Indian policy, see Olson and Wilson. On religious rights, discrimination, and recent legislation, see *NARF [Native American Rights Fund] Legal Review* 18, no. 2 (Summer 1993), a special issue on freedom of religion.

3. Unless otherwise noted, page numbers refer to *Woven Stone*, which includes Ortiz's first three collections of poetry, *Going for the Rain* (1976), *A Good Journey* (1977), and *Fight Back: For the Sake of the People, For the Sake of the Land* (1981).

4. Bakhtin's theory is limited here in part because he assumes an opposition between the authoritative and social and the individual and thereby largely overlooks the places where the individual and the social may not be at odds. (See Clark and Holquist 269–74, for a discussion of the political context of Bakhtin's aesthetics, which may be relevant here, too.) Bakhtin may obliquely offer an opening to communal dialogism when he allows that "when someone else's ideological discourse is internally persuasive for us and acknowledged by us, entirely different possibilities open up," though as he continues, the "fit" with Ortiz's practice becomes less and less promising: "consciousness awakens to independent ideological life precisely in a world of alien discourses surrounding it" ("Discourse in the Novel" 345). Ortiz's

story of how he learned to speak, in contrast, emphasizes integration into communal discourse (*Woven Stone* 6–7).

5. To similar effects, in "Mama's and Daddy's Words" (329–30) Ortiz gives the poem over to his parents, who speak of land and people in both the Acoma language and English.

6. For history, see Enge. For Alaska place names, see Orth.

7. Quoted in Bruchac, ed., *Raven Tells Stories* 48–49.

8. All quotations from Davis's poems are from *Soulcatcher.*

9. The titles of numerous poems not discussed here also demonstrate Barnes's interest in place and transience; representative are "Postcard from Poison Spider Creek, Wyoming," "Rest Stop at Horse Thief Spring," "Yuma: The Greyhound Depot," "Trying to Hide Out on Rich Mountain," "On Location at Tongue River," "Snowbound at the Bar 2, below Winding Stair," and "Postcard to Brian Bedard from Somewhere on the Illinois, near Tahlequah, Oklahoma," all in either *A Season of Loss* or *The Sawdust War.*

10. His imagination's absorption of his home ground can be seen, with different effects, in poems like "Wolf Watch: Winding Stair Mountain, 1923" (*Sawdust* 36–43; see chap. 6); and "An ex-Deputy Sheriff Remembers the Eastern Oklahoma Murderers" (*American Book of the Dead* 14–17).

11. In the work of the most strongly land-based poets, among them Ortiz and Davis, we may find the clearest sense of relationship to particular places, each with its own geographical features and borders and, often, its own vulnerability to invasion or appropriation. But this statement demands qualification. After all, Ortiz's concerns about land extend from Acoma to the whole Southwest and beyond. Others who write from a strong sense of belonging to particular places also complicate the generalization. Elizabeth Woody, for example, examines difficult issues of identity and relationship to place that arise on the reservation itself as well as elsewhere, in "Voice of the Land: Giving the Good Word." And Ray Young Bear implies his relationship to place indirectly, by evoking some aspects of his Mesquakie culture and "veiling" others.

12. In contrast, this is not so, on the same scale, for either the Tlingits or the Acoma Pueblo people, who, though they have experienced loss of land and of control over resources, have not, as communities, had to move to wholly unfamiliar places. Whiteman's Oneida ancestors were forced to sell their lands and move to Wisconsin from New York after the Revolutionary War, despite the fact that they had supported the colonists against Britain; Erdrich's Turtle Mountain Chippewa, the westernmost group of Anishinaabe in the United States, are in North Dakota as a result of the successive moves that began with their involvement in the French fur trade; and Harjo's Creeks were forced to move to Oklahoma from Alabama in the 1830s.

13. In one of the stories in Barnouw's collection a turtle is the father of the Ojibwa trickster (73–74), and Jones includes numerous stories of the cantankerous and enterprising Snapping Turtle, in *Ojibwa Texts.* Both of these texts, however, are composed of materials from Ojibwa communities far from Erdrich's Turtle Mountain.

Chapter 5

1. Hogan, *Seeing through the Sun* 56. All other quotations from Hogan's poetry will be parenthetically identified, with *Seeing through the Sun* shortened to *Seeing*, and *The Book of Medicines*, to *Medicines*.

2. Miller 5.

3. "Decolonizing Criticism" 11–12.

4. While it suggests the kind of dialogism that Moore discovers in the Tohono O'odhams' relation to landscape, this passage (which draws on the work of plant geneticist Barbara McClintock) also might imply an affinity with Greg Sarris's conception of knowledge as a process and a function of dialogue (see Sarris's chapters 1, 2, and 6, for example).

5. "Pagans Rewriting the Bible" 22–23.

6. "Decolonizing Criticism" 18. Also see 8–12, 15–18.

7. Coltelli 71; Coltelli quotes Hogan's "Autobiographical Sketch" (*Sun Tracks* 5 [1978]) 78.

8. Wiley 3B; Moore and Wilson 206.

9. Bruchac, *Survival* 348.

10. I am indebted to Brian Wogenson, whose conversation has helped me develop these ideas.

11. Malinowski and Abrams 186–87. One sign of Hayes's continuing importance for contemporary Native Americans is Paula Gunn Allen's "The Warrior" (*Shadow Country* 13–14).

12. As Robert Dale Parker observes, "in many ways, Young Bear's . . . poetry . . . [is] about trying *to be* . . . wherever Mesquakie culture is" (91).

13. Compare the ending of "My Grandmother's Words (and Mine) on the Last Spring Blizzard":

> (Despite a winter of doubt,
> I owe my existence to the ally
> who now rests on the ground outside
> with *His* brilliant white blanket
> covering the green grass-shoots
> of another year.)
> (*Invisible Musician* 68)

14. "Shadows of Clouds" (*Invisible Musician* 92) might support this reading.

15. I am grateful to Joan Dalla for illuminating these points, and for the many insights she contributed to my understanding of Young Bear's poems. The poem that precedes "Always Is He Criticized," "Fred Bloodclot Red's Composition: For Use on the Third Night of Footsteps" (80), implies that knowing one's vulnerability necessitates ongoing involvement in ritual.

16. See the first two chapters of *Black Eagle Child* for origin stories of stars and starhunters; see 149–51 and 163–64 for stories of world creation. Also see Jones, "Episodes . . ."

17. See *Winter of the Salamander* 24–26, 101, 130, and 169.

18. The *Philippine* coins could allude to the death of William Jones, Young Bear's problematical predecessor. If so, the reference probably implies concern about ethical telling.

19. Bruchac, *Survival* 96; Harjo, *Spiral of Memory:* "The Circular Dream," interview with Laura Coltelli, 62–63.

20. Benedikt xix, xx. Ray Young Bear's poetry, too, has been described as surrealistic. I would suggest that in Young Bear the "surreal" tends to reside in unexpected juxtapositions of images (which, as Ruppert notes, are often grounded in the oral tradition) or of discourses, whereas in Harjo the "surreal" is within the image itself.

21. *Spiral of Memory:* "Horses, Poetry, and Music," with Carol H. Grimes, 90; "Ancestral Voices," with Bill Moyers, 39; "Horses, Poetry, and Music" 95. Cherokee writer Ralph Salisbury's remarks on the Native sources of Indian writers' "surrealist" practices are instructive (30–31).

22. *Spiral of Memory:* "A Laughter of Absolute Sanity," with Angels Carabí, 137; "Ancestral Voices" 43; "A Laughter of Absolute Sanity" 134, 138, 139.

23. The titles of Harjo's books will be shortened as follows: *She Had Some Horses,* to *Horses; In Mad Love and War,* to *Mad Love; The Woman Who Fell from the Sky,* to *Woman.*

24. *Spiral of Memory:* "The Circular Dream" 61; "A Laughter of Absolute Sanity" 130–31 and 138–39.

25. *Spiral of Memory:* "The Spectrum of Other Languages," with Bill Aull, James McGowan, Bruce Morgan, Fay Rouseff-Baker, and Cai Fitzgerald, 108–9, 106.

26. For a summary of "Star Husband" stories and variants, see Reichard. Another partial parallel is with Momaday's story of the Kiowa twins' mother, who became the wife of the Sun and was killed by him as she attempted to return to the earth (*The Way to Rainy Mountain* 22–24).

27. "The word 'feminism' doesn't carry over to the tribal world, but a concept mirroring similar meanings would. Let's see, what would it then be called—empowerment, some kind of empowerment" (*Spiral of Memory* 65).

28. See Fenton, Arthur C. Parker, and Cornplanter for versions of the Iroquois story.

29. Especially illuminating are Andrew Wiget's and Kristine Holmes's discussions of Noni Daylight; Holmes's essay prompted me to consider Noni's possible relationship to Lila.

30. In "Family Album" Harjo, whose great grandfather was "half or nearly half African-American," remarks on the "irony" of "the racism directed toward African-Americans and African blood by a tribe whose members originally accepted Africans and often welcomed them as relatives . . . The acceptance of African-American slavery came with the embrace of European-American cultural values. It was then we also began to hate ourselves for our darkness. It's all connected; this attitude towards ownership of land has everything to do with how human beings are treated, with the attitude toward all living things" (24). See also *Spiral of Memory* 105.

31. *Spiral of Memory:* "In Love and War and Music," with Marilyn Kallet, 119; "The Spectrum of Other Languages" 101, 107.

32. Nancy Lang draws attention to the "multi-voiced, spiritual discourse" of the poem's double rainbow, which recalls stories of the Navajo hero twins "bending down to the earth in rainbow curves" (47).

33. See Swanton, *Religious Beliefs . . .* 479, 513.

34. *Spiral of Memory:* "In Love and War and Music" 108; see also 116 in the same interview. In these passages Harjo specifically acknowledges the importance to her of the essay "Uses of the Erotic: The Erotic as Power," in which Lorde defines the erotic as "a resource within each of us that lies in a deeply female and spiritual plane . . . a source of power and information . . . which rises from our deepest and nonrational knowledge" (53), "a well of replenishing and provocative force" (54), and as the bridge between the political and the spiritual. Lorde's conception is in many respects congruent with Harjo's sensibility and her evocations of mythic and spiritual power. Poems like "Deer Dancer" and "The Woman Who Fell from the Sky" seem especially clearly to reflect this affinity. For other references to Lorde, see Harjo's preface to *In Mad Love and War* and *The Spiral of Memory* 31, 62, 63. See also "Anchorage" (*Horses* 14–15) and "Reconciliation" (*Woman,* n.p.).

Chapter 6

1. Blaeser uses *minimalism* in her discussion of oral style; she describes Vizenor as having "emulated the oral tradition" (*Gerald Vizenor* 32, 199). Her use of *emulated* is especially helpful, for it implies that one may write in an oral tradition without necessarily replicating an oral style. Blaeser's book has been profoundly helpful to my understanding of oral tradition.

Native storytelling traditions tend to use relatively little imagery (or description), while lyric poetry and song often rely upon imagery to evoke what is not said. Examples of contemporary oral storytelling may be found in Tedlock, Attla, Nyman and Leer, and Cruikshank. Examples of traditional lyric poetry and song may be found in Astrov and Nellie Barnes.

2. Quoted in Blaeser, *Gerald Vizenor* 76.

3. All quotations from *Going for the Rain, A Good Journey,* and *Fight Back* are taken from *Woven Stone.*

4. Another notable instance of multiple voices engaged in the storytelling process is "And there is always one more story . . ." (*Woven Stone* 177–81), in which a child's participation signals continuity and perhaps, too, the possibility of change within continuity:

One time, / (or like Rainy said, "You're sposed to say, 'Onesa ponsa / time,' Daddy").

5. Language is an issue, too, in "They Come Around, The Wolves—and Coyote and Crow, Too" (*Woven Stone* 160–61), which begins with a lesson in

propriety: "You must talk with them . . . and call them Uncle or Brother / but never Cousin or In-law."

6. *Simon Ortiz* 41. Wiget refers specifically to "I Tell You Now," the final poem of *A Good Journey,* but the observation seems applicable to the often urgent story poems of *Fight Back,* too.

7. I have not found this story elsewhere. Boas and Parsons's "Santiago" story has many similar elements but also some important differences; for example, the boy is not poor, and the horse is not sick (68–71).

8. Owens, " 'The Song Is Very Short' " 59. The story also implies Owens's next observation: "Ultimately, of course, that same territory is space to be emptied and reoccupied by the colonial power."

9. Ortiz's "Poems from the Veterans' Hospital" (*Woven Stone* 270–80) and *From Sand Creek* also emphasize the visual and evocative, in contrast to the unambiguous narrative clarity of most of his poems discussed here.

10. *Gerald Vizenor* 110–11, 65–66; Blaeser quotes Vizenor's quotation of Native poet and educator Ted Mahto on "visual thinking."

Chapter 7

1. As Blaeser observes regarding Vizenor's writings about history, these poems "force recognition of the already embattled visions all readers bring to the text[s]" (*Gerald Vizenor* 85).

2. James H. O'Donnell III, "Pocahontas," in Bataille, ed., 206–7; Kenneth R. Shepherd, "Pocahontas," in Malinowski and Abrams, eds., 334–38; Champagne, ed., 1133–34. Kidwell discusses alternative motivations for the "rescue" of Smith (150–52). She comments as well on the cultural contexts and possible motives of Sacagawea (152–53).

3. See Clark and Edmonds; "Sacagawea," in *Biographical Dictionary of Indians of the Americas,* vol 2; Kathleen Donovan, "Sacagawea," in Bataille, ed., 219–22; Anderson; and "Sacagawea," in *Handbook of American Indians,* pt. 2.

4. See especially Clark and Edmonds, and Anderson.

5. "Paula Gunn Allen's 'The One Who Skins Cats' " 34, 37.

6. Betty Louise Bell (in "Pocahontas") writes especially persuasively about this issue, focusing on appropriations of Pocahontas by writers of romance and on the way that this Indian woman has been used to justify the whole English colonial enterprise.

7. The first title is from the second edition published in Cambridge, Massachusetts, in 1682, by Samuel Green. The second title is from the 1773 edition, printed in Boston by John Boyle. I quote from the 1930 "Lancaster Edition," based on the 1682 Cambridge edition.

8. Vaughn lists narratives first published into the 1890s, and even some publications of new accounts, as well as re-publications, into the 1940s. Continuing popular interest in captivity narratives is evident in Drimmer's anthology and movies like *Little Big Man* and *Dances with Wolves,* to cite just a few examples (see Stedman for others). For another poetic re-imagining of the

meanings of captivity, see Mary Oliver's "Lost Children" (12–15). Among recent studies of captivity narratives are Kolodny, *Land Before Her* 17–89; and Slotkin especially 94–145.

9. *Remove* is the term Rowlandson uses to designate chapters, each of which recounts one leg on her journey with the Indians.

10. I've consulted photocopies of the first London and the second American editions (the earliest extant), both published in 1682, as well as two other editions taken from the latter.

11. See, for example, Kolodny, *Land Before Her* 68–81.

12. Slotkin's assertions about Rowlandson's "insights" probably overstate matters; still, like Howe and Breitwieser, he reads her text as undermining the Puritan community's expectations (see 111–12). I mention him here especially because he is the one of these critics whose book could have been available to Erdrich before she wrote "Captivity."

13. See, for example, Howe 97 and 124.

14. For information on Jogues's life and death, see Talbot; see also Jogues's *Narrative of a Captivity Among the Mohawk Indians* and the other documents published in the same volume: the "Memoir" by John Gilmary Shea, letters from Jogues to various people, and letters from others announcing his death.

Regarding the "adoption" of Jogues, Shea refers to his having been "incorporated" into the Wolf "tribe" (Jogues 10); Talbot says that, when he visited the Mohawks as an ambassador, he was welcomed into the Wolf clan's "special protection and their adoption" (389). Describing his first captivity, Jogues himself refers to "a good old woman, who from her age and her care of me, as well as from her compassion for my sufferings, called me her nephew, as I called her aunt" (48). Kenny states that this elder woman "did not legally, in ceremony, adopt Isaac Jogues, but simply took him into his protective house" (68). Obviously, *adoption* is a term rife with the contending intentions of heteroglossia.

15. The name, Kenny tells us, means "Wolf-robe" (69); it is also the name of a younger Mohawk poet and artist, one of the people Kenny acknowledges in the dedication of *Between Two Rivers*.

16. Discussing Kenny's first "Peacemaker" poem, Bruchac illuminates "that dominant Iroquois image of the great pine (under whose four white roots the weapons of war were buried and at whose top an eagle always perches, vigilant, watching for any disturbance of the peace)." See "New Voices" 158.

17. I quote these two lines from the poem as it appears in the selections from *Blackrobe* included in *Between Two Rivers* (109), because I think Kenny has corrected the lines printed in the original: "whose faces margin the woods / on which I can discern paint."

The descriptive words Kenny attributes to Jogues at the beginning of this poem ("some marvelous bird . . . in plummage") may ironically echo Talbot's description of "Kiotsaeton and the Mohawk leaders, sharp featured and barbaric in their head-dress of brilliant plumage" (386–87).

18. The Indian who advised Jogues not to wear his habit when he visited

the Mohawks as an ambassador, explained that " 'nothing [is] more repulsive at first, than this doctrine, that seems to exterminate all that men hold dearest,' " and the habit " 'preach[ed the doctrine] as strongly as your lips' " (Jogues 9).

19. In a note Kenny says, "there is definite thought that Jogues was sent as a pawn by the French government . . . to keep a keen eye out for beaver pelts and other valued furs. Jogues may well have been duped in the veils of his religious ardor and zeal" (68).

20. Kenny's lines are even closer to words Talbot attributes to Jean de Brébeuf, Jogues's mentor at the Huron mission: " 'I hardly dare speak of the danger there is of ruining oneself among the impurities of these savages, in the case of one whose heart is not sufficiently full of God to resist firmly this poison' " (69). Recognizing such a source increases our sense of Kenny's complex dialogism.

21. See Kolodny, *Lay of the Land* and *Land Before Her.*

22. Compare Talbot 108–9, 158–59, 243–48, and 257–58, on Jogues's dreams and visions. Talbot doesn't understand any of these as implying a new acceptance of the Indians as "brothers and sisters"; the incident recorded on pages 257–58 might be most amenable to such an interpretation. Comparing Kenny's comments to Talbot's, more significantly, may highlight Kenny's dialogic response to a documentary source and his ability to engage creatively with a figure such as Jogues.

Chapter 8

1. Woody discusses the importance of Wyam and of its loss in "Wyam: Echo of Falling Water" (*Seven Hands* 63–68).

2. What does it mean to assume that Native poetry reflects oral tradition, for Indian writers who have come of age away from tribal cultures? Janice Gould, of mixed descent and an urban upbringing, implies such a question in the preface to *Earthquake Weather:*

> Mama taught us kids that we were Konkow [Maidu] Indians . . . She could not provide us, however, with a cultural heritage, which had been unraveling in our family for at least two generations as a consequence of intermarriage and the colonial legacy. Understanding our cultural heritage was something we had to do for ourselves: studying the hidden (and overt) "otherness" of our own lives, and tracing our family's being through ethnographic accounts, linguistic data, local histories, folklore, and whatever had not passed out of our relatives' memories. (xii)

Jana Sequoya identifies problems involved in incorporating sacred, community-creating oral materials into written texts for a wider audience. Sequoya, who is of mixed Chickasaw heritage, cites "the general pressures on the representative Native American writer to make a claim for authority vis-à-vis traditional tribal 'ways,' a claim that itself defies traditional modes of self-representation." Such pressures may make "the author's place . . . a site of transgression rather than of continuity," for incorporating elements of oral tradition may constitute "misuse in relation to the sacred cultures of particular tribal communities" ("Telling the *différance*" 98; "How(!) Is an Indian?" 467, 456). Young Bear's protective strategies respond to such concerns. (Sequoya focuses on Momaday's and Silko's uses of privileged materials in their fiction; in "Special Problems" Paula Gunn Allen raises similar questions regarding Silko's work, though, as Sequoya notes, Allen's critique must be read in light of her own uses of traditional material.)

3. In her note on this poem Woody explains *blood quantum* and illuminates the poem's third section: "This poem refers to the Declaration of Sovereignty issued by the Confederated Tribes of Warm Springs, Oregon, in 1992. It restates that tribal government is the senior government in our area, and that we exist as a sovereign entity with the right to conduct our business as such, by our ancient law and languages" (128). In "Voice of the Land: Giving the Good Word" Woody elaborates on some of the emotional, familial, and political implications of this sovereignty.

4. Jana Sequoya's essays illuminate such matters.

Abate, Frank R., ed. *American Places Dictionary.* Vol. 3: *Midwest.* Detroit: Omnigraphics, 1994.

Alcoff, Linda. "Cultural Feminism versus Post-Structuralism: The Identity Crisis in Feminist Theory." *Signs* 13.3 (1988): 405–36.

Alexie, Sherman. *The Summer of Black Widows.* New York: Hanging Loose Press, 1996.

Allen, Paula Gunn. "Bringing Home the Fact: Tradition and Continuity in the Imagination." Swann and Krupat 563–79.

———. *Shadow Country.* Los Angeles: American Indian Studies Center, 1982.

———. *Skins and Bones: Poems, 1979–87.* Albuquerque: West End Press, 1988.

———. "Special Problems in Teaching Leslie Marmon Silko's *Ceremony.*" *American Indian Quarterly* 14.4 (1990): 379–86.

Anderson, Irving W. "Probing the Riddle of the Bird Woman." *Montana: The Magazine of Western History* 23.4 (1973): 3–17.

Anzaldúa, Gloria. *Borderlands / La Frontera.* San Francisco: Aunt Lute Books, 1987.

Ashcroft, Bill, Gareth Griffiths, and Helen Tiffin. *The Empire Writes Back: Theory and Practice in Post-Colonial Literatures.* New York: Routledge, 1989.

Astrov, Margot, ed. *The Winged Serpent: American Indian Prose and Poetry.* 1946. Boston: Beacon Press, 1992.

Attla, Catherine. *Sitsiy Yugh Noholnik Ts'in': As My Grandfather Told It.* Fairbanks: Alaska Native Language Center and Yukon-Koyukuk School District, 1983.

Babcock-Abrahams, Barbara. "'A Tolerated Margin of Mess': The Trickster and His Tales Reconsidered." *Journal of the Folklore Institute* 11 (1975): 147–86. Rptd. in *Critical Essays on Native American Literature,* ed. Andrew Wiget. Philadelphia: Hall, 1985. 153–85.

Bakhtin, M. M. "Discourse in Life and Discourse in Art (Concerning Sociological Poetics)." In *Contemporary Literary Criticism: Literary and Cultural Studies,* ed. Robert Con Davis and Ronald Schleifer. New York: Longman, 1989. 391–410. (Originally published under the name of V. N. Voloshinov.)

———. "Discourse in the Novel." *The Dialogic Imagination.* Trans. Michael Holquist and Caryl Emerson. Austin: University of Texas Press, 1981. 259–422.

———. "The Problem of Speech Genres." *Speech Genres and Other Late Essays.* Trans. Vern W. McGee. Austin: University of Texas Press, 1986. 60–102.

Barnes, Jim. "A MELUS Interview: Jim Barnes," with Gretchen Bataille. *MELUS* 10.4 (1983): 57–65.

———. *A Season of Loss.* West Lafayette: Purdue University Press, 1989.

———. "On Native Ground." Swann and Krupat 85–97.

———. *The Sawdust War.* Urbana: University of Illinois Press, 1992.

———. *The American Book of the Dead.* Urbana: University of Illinois Press, 1982.

Barnes, Nellie. "American Indian Verse: Characteristics of Style." *Bulletin of the University of Kansas, Humanistic Studies* 2 (1921): 1–64.

Barnouw, Victor. *Wisconsin Chippewa Myths and Their Relation to Chippewa Life.* Madison: University of Wisconsin Press, 1977.

Bataille, Gretchen, ed. *Native American Women: A Biographical Dictionary.* New York: Garland, 1993.

Beck, Peggy, Anna L. Walters, and Nia Francisco. *The Sacred: Ways of Knowledge, Sources of Life.* Tsaile, Ariz.: Navajo Community College Press, 1990.

Belin, Esther G. "In the Cycle of the Whirl." Ortiz, *Speaking for the Generations* 50–71.

Bell, Betty Louise. "Almost the Whole Truth: Gerald Vizenor's Shadow-Working and Native American Autobiography." *a/b: Auto/Biography Studies* 7.2 (Fall 1992): 180–95.

———. "Pocahontas: 'Little Mischief' and the 'Dirty Men.' " *SAIL* 6.1 (Spring 1994): 63–70.

Bender, Thomas. *Community and Social Change in America.* Baltimore: Johns Hopkins University Press, 1978.

Benedikt, Michael, ed. *The Poetry of Surrealism: An Anthology.* Boston: Little, Brown, 1974.

Biographical Dictionary of Indians of the Americas. Vol. 2. 2nd ed. Newport Beach, Calif.: American Indian Publishers, 1991.

Bird, Gloria. "Breaking the Silence: Writing as Witness." Ortiz, *Speaking for the Generations* 26–48.

Blaeser, Kimberly M. *Gerald Vizenor: Writing in the Oral Tradition.* Norman: University of Oklahoma Press, 1996.

———. "Native Literature: Seeking a Critical Center." *Looking at the Words of Our People: First Nations Analysis of Literature.* Ed. Jeannette Armstrong. Penticton, B.C.: Theytus Books, 1993. 51–62.

———. "Pagans Rewriting the Bible: Heterodoxy and the Representation of Spirituality in Native American Literature." *Ariel: A Review of International English Literature* 25.1 (January 1994): 12–31.

———. *Trailing You.* Greenfield Center, N.Y.: Greenfield Review Press, 1994.

Boas, Franz. *Keresan Texts.* Pt. 1. New York: American Ethnological Society, 1928.

Boas, Franz, and Elsie C. Parsons. "Spanish Tales from Laguna and Zuni, N. Mex." *Journal of American Folk-Lore* 33 (January–March 1920): 47–72.

Breitwieser, Mitchell Robert. *American Puritanism and the Defense of Mourning: Religion, Grief, and Ethnology in Mary White Rowlandson's Captivity Narrative.* Madison: University of Wisconsin Press, 1990.

Bright, William. "The Natural History of Old Man Coyote." *Recovering the Word: Essays on Native American Literature.* Ed. Brian Swann and Arnold Krupat. Berkeley: University of California Press, 1987. 339–87.

Bruchac, Joseph. "New Voices from the Longhouse: Some Contemporary Iroquois Writers and Their Relationship to the Tradition of the Ho-de-no-sau-nee." In Schöler, *Coyote Was Here.* 147–60.

————. *Survival This Way: Interviews with American Indian Poets.* Tucson: University of Arizona Press, 1987.

————, ed. *Raven Tells Stories: An Anthology of Alaskan Native Writing.* Greenfield Center, N.Y.: Greenfield Review Press, 1991.

Champagne, Duane, ed. *The Native North American Almanac.* Detroit: Gale Research Press, 1994.

Chona, Maria. *The Autobiography of a Papago Woman.* Ed. Ruth Underhill. Menasha, Wis.: American Anthropological Association, 1936. Rptd. as *Papago Woman.* New York: Holt, Rinehart, and Winston, 1979.

Chrystos. "Askenet, Meaning 'Raw' in My Language." *Inversions: Writing by Dykes, Queers, and Lesbians.* Ed. Betsy Warland. Vancouver: Press Gang, 1991. 237–47.

————. *Dream On.* Vancouver: Press Gang, 1991.

————. *Not Vanishing.* Vancouver: Press Gang, 1988.

Clark, Ella E., and Margot Edmonds. *Sacagawea of the Lewis and Clark Expedition.* Berkeley: University of California Press, 1979.

Clark, Katerina, and Michael Holquist. *Mikhail Bakhtin.* Cambridge: Harvard University Press, 1984.

Clifford, James. "Identity in Mashpee." *The Predicament of Culture.* Cambridge: Harvard University Press, 1988. 277–346.

Coltelli, Laura. *Winged Words: American Indian Writers Speak.* Lincoln: University of Nebraska Press, 1990.

Cornplanter, Jesse J. *Legends of the Longhouse.* Philadelphia: Lippincott, 1938.

Cruikshank, Julie, in collaboration with Angela Sidney, Kitty Smith, and Annie Ned. *Life Lived Like a Story: Life Stories of Three Yukon Native Elders.* Lincoln: University of Nebraska Press, 1990.

Davis, Robert. *Soulcatcher.* Sitka, Alaska: Raven's Bones, 1986.

Deloria, Vine, Jr. "Out of Chaos." Dooling and Jordan-Smith 259–68.

DeShazer, Mary K. *A Poetics of Resistance: Women Writing in El Salvador, South Africa, and the United States.* Ann Arbor: University of Michigan Press, 1994.

Dickinson, Emily. *Complete Poems.* Ed. Thomas Johnson. Boston: Little, Brown, 1960.

Dooling, D. M., and Paul Jordan-Smith, eds. *I Become Part of It: Sacred Dimensions in Native American Life.* San Francisco: HarperCollins, 1989.

Drimmer, Frederick, ed. *Scalps and Tomahawks: Narratives of Indian Captivity.* New York: Coward McCann, 1961.

Eliade, Mircea. *The Sacred and the Profane: The Nature of Religion.* New York: Harcourt, Brace, Jovanovich, 1959.

Enge, Marilee. "The Cross and the Totem." *Alaska* 59 (August 1993): 42–46.

Erdrich, Louise. "A Writer's Sense of Place." *A Place of Sense: Essays in Search of the Midwest.* Ed. Michael Martone. Iowa City: University of Iowa Press, 1988. 34–44.

————. *Jacklight.* New York: Holt, Rinehart, Winston, 1984.

Fenton, William N. "This Island, The World on the Turtle's Back." *Journal of American Folklore* 75 (1962): 283–300.

Gill, Sam. "The Trees Stood Deep Rooted." In Dooling and Jordan-Smith 21–31.

Gould, Janice. *Earthquake Weather.* Tucson: University of Arizona Press, 1996.

Green, Rayna, ed. *That's What She Said: Contemporary Poetry and Fiction by Native American Women.* Bloomington: Indiana University Press, 1984.

Harjo, Joy. "Family Album." *Progressive* 56.3 (March 1992): 22–25.

———. *In Mad Love and War.* Hanover, N.H.: Wesleyan University Press, 1990.

———. "Oklahoma: The Prairie of Words." Hobson 43–45.

———. "Ordinary Spirit." Swann and Krupat 263–70.

———. *She Had Some Horses.* New York: Thunder's Mouth, 1983.

———. *The Spiral of Memory: Interviews.* Ed. Laura Coltelli. Ann Arbor: University of Michigan Press, 1996.

———. *The Woman Who Fell from the Sky.* New York: Norton, 1994.

———. *What Moon Drove Me to This?* New York: I. Reed Books, 1979.

Henson, Lance. *Selected Poems, 1970–1983.* Greenfield, N.Y.: Greenfield Review Press, 1985.

Hicks, Emily D. *Border Writing: The Multidimensional Text.* Minneapolis: University of Minnesota Press, 1991.

Hitchcock, Peter. *Dialogics of the Oppressed.* Minneapolis: University of Minnesota Press, 1993.

Hobson, Geary, ed. *The Remembered Earth: An Anthology of Contemporary Native American Literature.* Albuquerque: Red Earth Press, 1979. Albuquerque: University of New Mexico Press, 1981.

Hodge, Frederick Webb, ed. *Handbook of American Indians North of Mexico.* Part 2. Washington, D.C.: U.S. Government Printing Office, 1912. Grosse Pointe, Mich.: Scholarly Press, 1968.

Hogan, Linda. *Dwellings: A Spiritual History of the Living World.* New York: Norton, 1995.

———. *Savings.* Minneapolis: Coffee House, 1988.

———. *Seeing through the Sun.* Amherst: University of Massachusetts Press, 1985.

———. *The Book of Medicines.* Minneapolis: Coffee House, 1993.

———. "The Two Lives." Swann and Krupat 231–49.

Holmes, Kristine. " 'This Woman Can Cross Any Line': Feminist Tricksters in the Works of Nora Naranjo-Morse and Joy Harjo." *SAIL* 7.1 (Spring 1995): 45–63.

Howe, Susan. *The Birth-mark: Unsettling the Wilderness in American Literary History.* Hanover, N.H.: Wesleyan University Press / University Press of New England, 1993.

Hunter, Carol. "An Interview with Wendy Rose." Schöler, *Coyote Was Here* 40–56.

Jogues, Isaac. *Narrative of a Captivity among the Mohawk Indians, and A Description of New Netherland in 1642–3,* with *A Memoir of the Holy Missionary* by John Gilmary Shea. New York: Press of the Historical Society, 1856. Rpt. New York: Garland, 1977. (Vol. 67 in the Garland Library of Narratives of North American Indian Captivities.)

Jones, William. "Episodes in the Culture-Hero Myth of the Sauks and Foxes." *Journal of American Folklore* 14.55 (October–December 1901): 225–39.

———. *Ethnography of the Fox Indians.* Ed. Margaret Welpley Fisher. Bureau of American Ethnology Bulletin no. 125. Washington, D.C.: U.S. Government Printing Office, 1939.

———. *Fox Texts.* Vol. 1. Publications of the American Ethnological Society. Ed. Franz Boas. Leyden: E. J. Brill, 1907.

———. *Ojibwa Texts.* Pt. 2. Ed. Truman Michelson. New York: G. E. Stechert, 1919.

Kenny, Maurice. *Between Two Rivers: Selected Poems, 1956–1984.* Fredonia, N.Y.: White Pine, 1987.

———. *Blackrobe: Isaac Jogues.* Saranac, N.Y.: North Country Community College Press, 1982.

———. "Tinselled Bucks: A Historical Study in Indian Homosexuality." *Living the Spirit: A Gay American Indian Anthology.* Ed. Will Roscoe. New York: St. Martin's Press, 1988. 15–31.

Kidwell, Clara Sue. "What Would Pocahontas Think Now? Women and Cultural Persistence." *Callaloo* 17.1 (Winter 1994): 149–59.

Kolodny, Annette. *The Land Before Her: Fantasy and Experience of the American Frontiers, 1630–1860.* Chapel Hill: University of North Carolina Press, 1984.

———. *The Lay of the Land: Metaphor as Experience and History in American Life and Letters.* Chapel Hill: University of North Carolina Press, 1975.

Kroeber, Karl. "The Wolf Comes: Indian Poetry and Linguistic Criticism." *Smoothing the Ground: Essays on Native American Oral Literature.* Ed. Brian Swann. Berkeley: University of California Press, 1983. 98–111.

Krupat, Arnold. *Ethnocriticism: Ethnography, History, Literature.* Berkeley: University of California Press, 1992.

———. *For Those Who Come After: A Study in Native American Autobiography.* Berkeley: University of California Press, 1985.

———. *The Voice in the Margin: Native American Literature and the Canon.* Berkeley: University of California Press, 1993.

LaDuke, Winona. "Like Tributaries to a River." *Sierra* (December 1996): 38–45.

LaFlesche, Francis. *A Dictionary of the Osage Language.* Bureau of American Ethnology Bulletin no. 109. Washington, D.C.: U.S. Government Printing Office, 1932.

Lang, Nancy. " 'Twin Gods Bending Over': Joy Harjo and Poetic Memory." *MELUS* 18.3 (Fall 1993): 41–49.

Lorde, Audre. "Uses of the Erotic: The Erotic as Power." *Sister Outsider: Essays and Speeches.* Trumansberg, N.Y.: Crossing Press, 1984. 53–59.

McCaffrey, Larry, and Tom Marshall. "Head Water: An Interview with Gerald Vizenor." *Chicago Review* 39.3–4 (1993): 50–54.

Malinowski, Sharon, and George H. J. Abrams, eds. *Notable Native Americans.* New York: Gale Research, 1995.

Miller, Carol. "The Story Is Brimming Around: An Interview with Linda Hogan." *SAIL* 2.4 (1990): 1–9.

Momaday, N. Scott. *House Made of Dawn.* New York: Harper and Row, 1968.

———. "The Man Made of Words." Hobson 162–73.

———. *The Names.* New York: Harper and Row, 1976.

———. "The Native Voice." *The Columbia Literary History of the United States,* ed. Emory Elliott. New York: Cambridge University Press, 1988. 5–15.

———. *The Way to Rainy Mountain.* Albuquerque: University of New Mexico Press, 1969.

Moore, David L. "Decolonizing Criticism: Reading Dialectics and Dialogics in Native American Literatures." *SAIL* 6.4 (Winter 1994): 7–35.

———. "Myth, History, and Identity in Silko and Young Bear." *New Voices in Native American Literary Criticism.* Ed. Arnold Krupat. Washington, D.C.: Smithsonian Institution Press, 1993. 370–95.

Moore, David, and Michael Wilson. "Staying Afloat in a Chaotic World: A Conversation with Ray Young Bear." *Callaloo* 17.1 (1994). 205–12.

Mullet, G. M. *Spider Woman Stories: Legends of the Hopi Indians.* Tucson: University of Arizona Press, 1979.

Murray, David. *Forked Tongues: Speech, Writing and Representation in North American Indian Texts.* Bloomington: Indiana University Press, 1991.

NARF [Native American Rights Fund] Legal Review. Second special edition on Freedom of Religion. "A Time for Justice." Ed. Ray Ramirez. 18.2 (Summer 1993).

Neihardt, John. *Black Elk Speaks.* 1939. Rpt. Lincoln: University of Nebraska Press, 1979.

Niatum, Duane, ed. *Harper's Anthology of Twentieth Century Native American Poetry.* San Francisco: Harper, 1988.

Nyman, Elizabeth, and Jeff Leer. *Gágiwdul.àt: Brought Forth to Reconfirm. The Legacy of a Taku River Tlingit Clan.* Whitehorse, Canada: Yukon Native Language Centre; and Fairbanks: Alaska Native Language Center, 1993.

Oliver, Mary. *American Primitive.* Boston: Little, Brown, 1983.

Olson, James, and Raymond Wilson. *Native Americans in the Twentieth Century.* Urbana: University of Illinois Press, 1987.

Ong, Walter J. *Orality and Literacy: The Technologizing of the Word.* London: Methuen, 1982.

Orth, Donald J. *Dictionary of Alaska Place Names.* U.S. Geological Professional Paper no. 567. Washington, D.C.: U.S. Government Printing Office, 1971.

Ortiz, Simon J. *After and Before the Lightning.* Tucson: University of Arizona Press, 1994.

———. "Always the Stories: A Brief History and Thoughts on My Writing." Schöler, *Coyote Was Here* 57–69.

———. *From Sand Creek.* New York: Thunder's Mouth, 1981.

———. "Song/Poetry and Language—Expression and Perception." *Sun Tracks* 3.2 (Spring 1977): 9–12.

———. "The Language We Know." Swann and Krupat 185–94.

———. "Towards a National Indian Literature: Cultural Authenticity in Nationalism." *MELUS* 8.2 (1981): 7–12.

———. *Woven Stone.* Tucson: University of Arizona Press, 1990.

———, ed. *Speaking for the Generations: Native Writers on Writing.* Tucson: University of Arizona Press, 1998.

Owens, Louis. *Other Destinies: Understanding the American Indian Novel.* Norman: University of Oklahoma Press, 1992.

———. " 'The Song Is Very Short': Native American Literature and Literary Theory." *Weber Studies* 12.3 (Fall 1995): 51–62.

Oxford English Dictionary. 2d ed. Oxford: Oxford University Press, 1989.

Parker, Arthur C. *Seneca Myths and Folk Tales.* 1923. Rpt. University of Nebraska Press, 1989.

Parker, Robert Dale. "To Be There, No Authority to Anything: Ontological Desire and Cultural and Poetic Authority in the Poetry of Ray A. Young Bear." *Arizona Quarterly* 50.4 (Winter 1994): 89–115.

Pratt, Mary Louise. *Imperial Eyes: Travel Writing and Transculturation.* New York: Routledge, 1992.

Rainwater, Catherine. "Reading between Worlds: Narrativity in the Fiction of Louise Erdrich." *American Literature* 62.3 (September 1990): 405–22.

Ramsey, Jarold W. *Reading the Fire: Essays in the Traditional Indian Literatures of the Far West.* Lincoln: University of Nebraska Press, 1983.

Reichard, Gladys A. "Literary Types and Dissemination of Myths." *Journal of American Folklore* 34 (1921): 269–307.

Revard, Carter. *Ponca War Dancers.* Norman, Okla.: Point Riders Press, 1980.

Rivera, Tomás. "Chicano Literature: The Establishment of Community." *A Decade of Chicano Literature (1970–1979): Critical Essays and Bibliography.* Ed. Luis Leal et al. Santa Barbara, Calif.: Editorial La Causa, 1982. 9–17.

Rosaldo, Renato. "Politics, Patriarchs, and Laughter." *Cultural Critique* 6 (1987): 65–86.

Rose, Wendy. *Going to War with All My Relations.* Flagstaff, Ariz.: Northland-Entrada, 1993.

———. *Lost Copper.* Banning, Calif.: Malki Museum Press, 1980.

———. "Neon Scars." Swann and Krupat 253–61.

———. *The Halfbreed Chronicles.* Los Angeles: West End Press, 1985.

———. "You . . . Who Have Removed Us: At What Cost?" *Messengers of the Wind: Native American Women Tell Their Life Stories.* Ed. Jane Katz. New York: Ballantine Books, 1995. 205–13.

Rowlandson, Mary. *The Narrative of the Captivity of Mrs. Mary Rowlandson.* Lancaster edition. Boston: Houghton Mifflin, 1930.

Ruoff, A. LaVonne Brown. *American Indian Literatures.* New York: Modern Language Association, 1990.

Ruppert, James. "The Uses of Oral Tradition in Six Contemporary Native American Poets." *American Indian Culture and Research Journal* 4.4 (1980): 87–110.

Saldívar, José David. "The Limits of Cultural Studies." *American Literary History* 2 (1990): 251–66.

Salisbury, Ralph. "Between Lightning and Thunder." Swann and Krupat 15–35.

Sarris, Gregg. *Keeping Slug Woman Alive: A Holistic Approach to American Indian Texts.* Berkeley: University of California Press, 1993.

Schöler, Bo. "A Heart Made out of Crickets: An Interview with Linda Hogan." *Journal of Ethnic Studies* 16.1 (1988): 107–17.

——, ed. *Coyote Was Here: Essays on Contemporary Native American Literature and Mobilization*. Aarhus, Denmark: Seklos, 1984.

Sekaquaptewa, Emory. "One More Smile for a Hopi Clown." Dooling and Jordan Smith 150–57.

Sequoya, Jana. "How(!) Is an Indian? A Contest of Stories." *New Voices in Native American Literary Criticism*. Ed. Arnold Krupat. Washington, D.C.: Smithsonian Institution Press, 1993. 453–73.

Sequoya-Magdeleno, Jana. "Telling the *différance:* Representations of Identity in the Discourse of Indianness." *The Ethnic Canon: Histories, Institutions, and Interventions*. Ed. David Palumbo-Liu. Minneapolis: University of Minnesota Press, 1995. 88–116.

Silko, Leslie Marmon. "Landscape, History, and the Pueblo Imagination: From a High Arid Plateau in New Mexico." *On Nature: Nature, Landscape, and Natural History*. Ed. Daniel Halpern. San Francisco: North Point Press, 1987. 83–94.

Slotkin, Richard. *Regeneration through Violence: The Mythology of the American Frontier, 1600–1860*. Middletown, Conn.: Wesleyan University Press, 1973.

Smith, Patricia Clark. "Coyote Ortiz: Canis latrans latrans in the Poetry of Simon Ortiz." *Studies in American Indian Literature*. Ed. Paula Gunn Allen. New York: Modern Language Association, 1983. 192–210.

Stedman, Raymond William. *Shadows of the Indian: Stereotypes in American Culture*. Norman: University of Oklahoma Press, 1982.

Swann, Brian. "Introduction: Only the Beginning." Niatum xiii–xxxii.

Swann, Brian, and Arnold Krupat, eds. *I Tell You Now: Autobiographical Essays by Native American Writers*. Lincoln: University of Nebraska Press, 1987.

Swanton, John R. "Religious Beliefs and Medical Practices of the Creek Indians." *Forty-second Annual Report of the Bureau of American Ethnology, 1924–25*. Washington, D.C.: U.S. Government Printing Office, 1928. 473–672.

Talbot, Francis. *Saint Among Savages: The Life of Isaac Jogues*. New York: Harper and Brothers, 1935.

TallMountain, Mary. *The Light on the Tent Wall: A Bridging*. Los Angeles: University of California, American Indian Studies Center, 1990.

——. "Paula Gunn Allen's 'The One Who Skins Cats.'" *SAIL* 7.3 (Fall 1983): 69–75. Rptd. in *SAIL* 5.2 (Summer 1993): 34–38.

Tedlock, Dennis, trans. *Finding the Center: Narrative Poetry of the Zuni Indians*. Lincoln: University of Nebraska Press, 1972.

Tremblay, Gail. *Indian Singing in Twentieth Century America*. Corvallis, Oreg.: Calyx, 1990.

TuSmith, Bonnie. *All My Relatives: Community in Contemporary Ethnic American Literature*. Ann Arbor: University of Michigan Press, 1993.

Tyler, Hamilton A. *Pueblo Gods and Myths*. Norman: University of Oklahoma Press, 1964.

Vaughn, Alden T. *Narratives of North American Indian Captivity: A Selective Bibliography*. New York: Garland, 1983.

Vizenor, Gerald *Earthdivers: Tribal Narratives of Mixed Descent*. Minneapolis: University of Minnesota Press, 1981.

———. *Landfill Meditation: Crossblood Stories*. Hanover, N.H.: Wesleyan University Press, 1991.

———. *Manifest Manners*. Hanover, N.H.: Wesleyan University Press, 1994.

———. *The People Named the Chippewa: Narrative Histories*. Minneapolis: University of Minnesota Press, 1984.

———. "Trickster Discourse: Comic Holotropes and Language Games." *Narrative Chance: Postmodern Discourse on Native American Indian Literatures*. Ed. G. Vizenor. Albuquerque: University of New Mexico Press, 1989. 187–208.

———. *Wordarrows: Indians and Whites in the New Fur Trade*. Minneapolis: University of Minnesota Press, 1978.

Walters, Anna Lee. *Talking Indian: Reflections on Survival and Writing*. Ithaca, N.Y.: Firebrand Books, 1992.

Welch, James. *Riding the Earthboy 40*. Rev. ed. New York: Harper and Row, 1976.

Whiteman, Roberta Hill. *Star Quilt*. Minneapolis: Holy Cow! Press, 1984.

Wiget, Andrew. "Nightriding with Noni Daylight: The Many Horse Songs of Joy Harjo." *Native American Literatures*. Ed. Laura Coltelli. Pisa: SEU, 1989. 185–96.

———. *Simon Ortiz*. Boise State University Western Writers Series no. 74. Boise: Boise State University Press, 1986.

Wiley, Debora. "Indian Mythology Has a New Vehicle in Iowa Poet's Verse." *Des Moines Sunday Register,* 2 September 1990, 1B, 3B.

Williams, Walter. *The Spirit and the Flesh: Sexual Diversity in American Indian Culture*. Boston: Beacon Press, 1986.

Wong, Hertha D. *Sending My Heart Back across the Years: Tradition and Innovation in Native American Autobiography*. New York: Oxford University Press, 1992.

Woodard, Charles L. *Ancestral Voice: Conversations with N. Scott Momaday*. Lincoln: University of Nebraska Press, 1989.

Woody, Elizabeth. *Luminaries of the Humble*. Tucson: University of Arizona Press, 1994.

———. *Seven Hands Seven Hearts*. Portland, Oreg.: Eighth Mountain Press, 1994.

———. "Voice of the Land: Giving the Good Word." Ortiz, *Speaking for the Generations* 148–73.

Yava, Albert. "Way Back in the Distant Past." *The South Corner of Time*. Ed. Larry Evers. Tucson: University of Arizona Press, 1980. 8–13.

Young Bear, Ray A. *Black Eagle Child: The Facepaint Narratives*. Iowa City: University of Iowa Press, 1992.

———. *The Invisible Musician*. Duluth, Minn.: Holy Cow! Press, 1990.

———. *Winter of the Salamander: The Keeper of Importance*. New York: Harper, 1980.

Zolbrod, Paul. *Reading the Voice: Native American Oral Poetry on the Page*. Salt Lake City: University of Utah Press, 1995.

Zumthor, Paul. *Oral Poetry: An Introduction*. Trans. Kathryn Murphy-Judy. Minneapolis: University of Minnesota Press, 1990.

SUGGESTIONS FOR FURTHER READING

Listed below is a selection of poetry not included in this study. A few of these books are by poets I've discussed in the preceding chapters, but most are by writers whose work I have not discussed at all. This should not be taken as anything like a complete list of contemporary Indian poets, but rather as an indication of their diversity and growing numbers, and as a place where those who wish to continue studying this rich literature might begin.

Sherman Alexie (Spokane/Coeur d'Alene). *The Business of Fancydancing.* Brooklyn, N.Y.: Hanging Loose Press, 1992.

Paula Gunn Allen (Laguna). *Life Is a Fatal Disease: Selected Poems 1964–1994.* Albuquerque: West End Press, 1997.

———. *Shadow Country.* Los Angeles: American Indian Studies Center, 1982.

Jim Barnes (Choctaw). *La Plata Cantata.* West Lafayette, Ind.: Purdue University Press, 1989.

Fred Bigjim (Inupiat). *Sinrock.* Portland, Oreg.: Press-22, 1983.

Gloria Bird (Spokane). *Full Moon on the Reservation.* Greenfield Center, N.Y.: Greenfield Review Press, 1993.

———. *The River of History.* Portland, Oreg.: Trask House Books, 1997.

Peter Blue Cloud (Mohawk). *Clans of Many Nations: Selected Poems 1969–94.* Fredonia, N.Y.: White Pine Press, 1995.

Joseph Bruchac (Abenaki). *Near the Mountains.* Fredonia, N.Y.: White Pine Press, 1987.

Barney Bush (Shawnee/Cayuga). *Inherit the Blood.* New York: Thunder's Mouth, 1985.

Gladys Cardiff (Eastern Cherokee). *To Frighten a Storm.* Port Townsend, Washington: Copper Canyon, 1976.

Elizabeth Cook-Lynn (Sioux). *Seek the House of Relatives.* Marvin, S.D.: Blue Cloud Quarterly Press, 1983.

Chrystos (Menominee). *Fire Power.* Vancouver, B.C.: Press Gang, 1995.

Nora Marks Dauenhauer (Tlingit). *The Droning Shaman.* Haines, Alaska: Black Current Press, 1988.

Jimmie Durham (Cherokee). *Columbus Day.* Albuquerque: West End Press, 1993.

Anita Endrezze (Yaqui). *At the Helm of Twilight.* Seattle: Broken Moon Press, 1992.

Louise Erdrich (Chippewa). *Baptism of Desire.* New York: Harper and Row, 1989.

Nia Francisco (Navajo). *Blue Horses for Navajo Women.* Greenfield Center, N.Y.: Greenfield Review Press, 1988.

Diane Glancy (Cherokee). *Claiming Breath.* Lincoln: University of Nebraska Press, 1992.

———. *Lone Dog's Winter Count.* Albuquerque: West End Press, 1991.

————. *One Age in a Dream*. Minneapolis: Milkweed Editions, 1986.

Janice Gould (Maidu). *Beneath My Heart*. Ithaca, N.Y.: Firebrand Books, 1990.

————. *Earthquake Weather*. Tucson: University of Arizona Press, 1996.

Lance Henson (Cheyenne). *Strong Heart Song: Lines from a Revolutionary Text*. Albuquerque: West End Press, 1997.

Karoniaktatie (Mohawk). *Landscape*. Marvin, S.D.: Blue Cloud Quarterly Press, 1984.

Maurice Kenny (Mohawk). *Tekonwatonti/Molly Brant*. Fredonia, N.Y.: White Pine Press, 1992.

Harold L. Littlebird (Laguna/Santo Domingo). *On Mountains' Breath*. Santa Fe: Tooth of Time Books, 1982.

Adrian C. Louis (Paiute). *Fire Water World*. Albuquerque: West End Press, 1989.

Victoria Lena Manyarrows (Eastern Cherokee). *Songs from the Native Lands*. San Francisco: Nopal Press, 1995.

Deborah Miranda (Ohlone/Costanoan/Esselen). *Indian Cartography*. Greenfield Center, N.Y.: Greenfield Review Press, 1999.

N. Scott Momaday (Kiowa). *In the Presence of the Sun*. New York: St. Martin's Press, 1992.

Nora Naranjo-Morse (Pueblo). *Mud Woman: Poems from the Clay*. Tucson: University of Arizona Press, 1992.

Duane Niatum (Klallam). *Drawings of the Song Animals: New and Selected Poems*. Duluth: Holy Cow! Press, 1991.

Louis Littlecoon Oliver (Creek). *Chasers of the Sun: Creek Indian Thoughts*. Greenfield Center, N.Y.: Greenfield Review Press, 1990.

Simon J. Ortiz (Acoma). *From Sand Creek*. New York: Thunder's Mouth, 1981.

Carter Revard (Osage). *An Eagle Nation*. Tucson: University of Arizona Press, 1993.

Wendy Rose (Hopi/Miwok). *The Halfbreed Chronicles*. Los Angeles: West End, 1985.

Ralph Salisbury (Cherokee). *Going to the Water: Poems of a Cherokee Heritage*. Eugene, Oregon: Pacific House Books, 1983.

Luci Tapahonso (Navajo). *Blue Horses Rush In*. Tucson: University of Arizona Press, 1997.

————. *Sáanii Dahataał: The Women Are Singing*. Tucson: University of Arizona Press, 1993.

Gail Tremblay (Onondaga/Micmac). *Indian Singing*. Revised Edition. Corvallis, Oreg.: Calyx Books, 1998.

Gerald Vizenor (Anishinaabe). *Matsushima: Pine Islands*. Minneapolis: Nodin, 1984.

————. *Seventeen Chirps: Haiku in English*. Minneapolis: Nodin, 1964.

Roberta Hill Whiteman (Oneida). *Philadelphia Flowers*. Duluth: Holy Cow! Press, 1996.

Ofelia Zepeda (Tohono O'odham). *Ocean Power: Poems from the Desert*. Tucson: University of Arizona Press, 1995.

INDEX

Alexie, Sherman, 122; "Capital Punishment," 214; "Defending Walt Whitman," 211–12; "Drum as Love, Fear, and Prayer," 215; "The First and Last Ghost Dance of Lester Falls Apart," 4–5, 10; "That Place Where Ghosts of Salmon Jump," 209

Allen, Paula Gunn, 36–37, 188; "The One Who Skins Cats," 183–87; "Pocahontas to Her English Husband, John Rolfe," 183–87

Anzaldúa, Gloria, 5–6, 7, 8, 16

audience, 47–49, 53–83 passim, 222nn. 2, 4; and ethical telling, 51–52, 57; related to identity, 50–51. See also communal orientation; community; disclosure, dilemmas of; language; oral tradition

authoritative discourse, 10–11

Bakhtin, M. M.: and border conditions, 10–11; and Native American contexts and culture, 10–11, 59, 91, 214, 221n. 16, 225n. 4; theory of language of, 9–11, 214, 218nn. 7–8, 219nn. 16, 22, 221n. 16, 222n. 2; and traditional Native language theories, 43, 45. See also dialogism; hybridization

Barnes, Jim, 105–7; "After the Great Plains," 112; "Another Country," 112–13; "Autobiography, Chapter X: Circus in the Blood," 110–11; "Autobiography, Chapter XVII: Floating the Big Piney," 112; "Call It Going with the Sun," 108–9; "Castle Keep," 113; "Contemporary Native American Poetry," 115–16; "An ex-Deputy Sheriff Remembers . . . ," 226n. 10;

"Fourche Maline Bottoms," 111–12; "Ghost Fog," 115; "The Long Lone Nevada Night Highway," 109–10; "Near Crater Lake," 107, 115; "On Native Ground," 105, 106–7; "Right Place, Wrong Time," 116; "A Season of Loss," 108; "Wolf Watch: Winding Stair Mountain, 1923," 179–80, 226n. 10

Belin, Esther G., "In the Cycle of the Whirl," 2, 5, 7

Bell, Betty Louise, 220n. 4, 230n. 6

Bird, Gloria, "Breaking the Silence," 2, 3, 5, 11

Black Elk, 224n. 18

Blaeser, Kimberly M., 9, 11, 114, 129, 179, 183, 217n. 6, 220nn. 3, 5, 229n. 1, 230n. 1; "Certificate of Live Birth . . . ," 205–6

Blue Cloud, Peter, "Ochre Iron," 120–21

border crossing, 20–27, 79, 161–62, 170

border theory, 5–9; contrasted in Chicano/a and Native contexts, 5, 7, 8; as treated by Native American critics, 8–9

borders and borderlands, 2, 4–5, 7, 10, 15, 20, 50, 138, 207; and ambivalence, 6; and audience, 15–16, 46, 49; and creativity, 7; and danger, 6, 29; geographical, 5–6; internalized, 7; and oppression, 6; and political struggle, 8

Breitwieser, Mitchell, 193

Bruchac, Joseph, 204, 221n. 13, 231n. 16

Brumble, H. David, 220n. 5

Cardiff, Gladys, "Where Fire Burns," 40